# Vicissitudes
# of the I

## An Introduction
## to the Philosophy of Mind

**Hollibert E. Phillips**

*Whitman College*
*Walla Walla, Washington*

PRENTICE HALL
Upper Saddle River, New Jersey 07458

*Library of Congress Cataloging-in-Publication Data*

PHILLIPS, HOLLIBERT E.
   Vicissitudes of the I : an introduction to the philosophy of mind
/ Hollibert E. Phillips.
      p.   cm.
   Includes bibliographical references and index.
   ISBN   0–13–108721–5
   1. Philosophy of mind.   I. Title.
BD418.3.P43   1995                                     94–4967
128′ .2—dc20                                           CIP

Acquisitions editor: Ted Bolen
Editorial/production supervision: Merrill Peterson
Copy editor: Rene D. Lynch
Cover designer: Bruce Kenselaar
Production coordinator: Peter Havens
Editorial assistant: Nicole Gray

© 1995 by Prentice-Hall, Inc.
A Pearson Education Company
Upper Saddle River, NJ 07458

Printed in the United States of America

10  9  8  7  6  5  4  3  2  1

ISBN 0-13-108721-5

Prentice-Hall International (UK) Limited,London
Prentice-Hall of Australia Pty. Limited, Sydney
Prentice-Hall Canada Inc., Toronto
Prentice-Hall Hispanoamericana, S.A., Mexico
Prentice-Hall of India Private Limited, New Delhi
Prentice-Hall of Japan, Inc., Tokyo
Pearson Education Asia Pte. Ltd., Singapore
Editora Prentice-Hall do Brasil, Ltda., Rio de Janeiro

# Contents

## ___ 6 _____

### *DO* I: *REALLY?, 138*

*to*
*my parents*
*Hutchinson and Jane*
*and*
*to*
*Marx Wartofsky*
*my teacher and exemplar*

# Preface

## THE PLACE OF THIS WORK IN THE CORPUS
## OF RELEVANT WORKS

We would like first to say a word on the title. The term "vicissitudes" may be a new one for some readers of this book, but it is far less threatening than it looks or sounds. In one of its meanings, it characterizes the ups and downs, the changes in fortune of objects, institutions, and so on. As it appears in our title, it tersely and aptly captures the changing story of what mind is conceived to be. That complex story is what the present book is about.

My main goals in writing this work included (1) *evenness of accessibility* to the newcomer to philosophy, (2) *comprehensiveness and adequacy* of theoretical coverage, (3) *topical currency,* and (4) a *lively, clear, and engaging prose style* likely to hold the interest of the student throughout.

With respect to these desired goals, the story of comparable texts is one of mixed success. *The Nature of Mind* by David Rosenthal, for example, is an excellent anthology, by far the best to date, in my opinion. But as in most anthologies written by their contributors for different target audiences and with different objectives in mind, unevenness of accessibility to the newcomer to philosophy and in particular to the philosophy of mind is a predictably bruising experience. Shaffer's *Philosophy of Mind* is a very informative book and for this reason alone a good supplementary text, but I find it lacking, especially with respect to features 3 and 4 above. Another single-author work, Keith Campbell's *Body and Mind,* is a particularly useful student's companion, but it often drops the topics it tackles much too soon. Numerous other single-author works pick out a specific area in the philosophy of mind as their focus, but in so doing they are of limited value as basic texts for introductory purposes.

The present work is distinctive in its attempt to incorporate all four features. A partial example of how feature 2 works is found in Chapter Two, entitled "Hume and the Lost *I*," where an independent section on identity has been included to serve as a preparation for the discussion of personal identity. This deliberate preparatory approach seems to give students an appreciably greater grasp of the issues of personal identity than is possible without it. It is a feature virtually missing from practically all of the introductory texts. Finally, with features 2 and 3 especially in mind, suggestions for further reading appearing at the ends of chapters refer the student to specific pages or chapters of relevant works. In this way, the scope of the covered material is expanded to meet the mutual interests of teacher and student.

## THE TARGET AUDIENCE

The book is written primarily with undergraduates and the general reader in mind, though advanced readers should find it useful. Because of the range of material it covers and the manner of approach adopted, it can be employed in a variety of courses other than Philosophy of Mind. It is suitable, for example, for such courses as Introduction to Philosophy, Problems in Philosophy, Theories of Mind, Philosophy of Psychology, and Introduction to Analytic Philosophy, as well as courses which serve to introduce one to issues in the field of mind and cognitive science.

## ON STRATEGY

The adoption of a unifying focus, the *I*, assists the reader to understand the material. This feature is almost always absent from introductory texts, though it obviously has great pedagogical value. But beyond the first two chapters where the Cartesian *I* is expressly addressed, the theme is intended to function in this work much like the sound of a distant drum, and less like a constant and obtrusive rumble. It is intimated throughout by chapter titles as well as by section headings. A very important objective is that the reader become a fellow explorer rather than a mere hiker. To aid in this role, the book makes no attempt to turn the reader into a consumer of settled information. Instead, where appropriate, as in the first two chapters, the reader has the opportunity to reflect upon and critically examine seminal portions of classic texts. Descartes, for example, is *not* summarily dismissed after token mention, as though he does not now much matter. The reader has the chance to explore his thinking, and the supplementary reading has been selected with this in mind. Throughout, the book addresses theories as scrutinizingly as possible. It raises stubborn questions and issues. Sometimes it embeds them in thought-experiments—cases, I have called them—in such a way as to enlist the reader's reflective opinion.


## OVERVIEW OF THE BOOK

Perhaps the most remarkable thing about humans is not that they think but that they *are aware* that they can think, and they are aware of *themselves*. I, H. E. P., can and do think that I think. And you can say the same with respect to yourself. In so doing, whatever it is that thinks is capable of distancing itself from the object of its thought, from itself, and of taking account of this object as something that possesses the capacity for thought. It can, as subject, reflect upon itself as object and in so doing know from the inside what cannot be known from the outside. This line of reasoning warrants the view that, in terms of *knowledge* of itself as object, the thinking subject is uniquely placed, hence advantaged, and thus it has what is sometimes referred to as *privileged epistemic access* to certain of its own states.

But what is the identity of this peculiar subject? Intuitively, such a subject must be something which can do things like consciously attend to itself. In his *Discourse on Method* Descartes says: "But immediately afterwards I noticed that whilst I thus wished to think all things false, it was absolutely essential that the 'I' who thought this should be somewhat, . . . that I was a substance the whole essence or nature of which is to think, and that for its existence there is no need of any place, nor does it depend on any material thing; so that this 'me,' that is to say, the soul by which I am what I am, is entirely distinct from body . . . "[1] The term "I" and the expressions "the self" and "the mind" are sometimes used in an attempt to identify or to refer to this subject, this Cartesian "somewhat." But while language at times offers clues to the identity of some things, linguistic form or usage alone by no means provides any obvious guarantee that there is anything which corresponds to what seems to be picked out by a given bit of language. In fact, there may be nothing in reality named by a given linguistic expression. Hence the term "subject" cannot without argument claim immunity from this possibility. Our intuitions notwithstanding, what seems to be a conscious thing may not even be a thing at all. The issues of *what* there is and the *nature* of what there is are not settled solely by reference to the way we talk. Nor are they settled by unexamined intuition.

Thus we may properly ask the following sorts of question: Does the term "I" refer to some *peculiar* thing? Does it refer, say, to a self or a mind? Indeed, is the referent a thing at all, let alone a peculiar thing? (We refer, for example, to human voices as though they were things, and we assign characteristics to them, but voices are not things at all.) And assuming that the referent of the

[1] René Descartes, *The Philosophical Works of Descartes*, trans. Elizabeth S. Haldane and G. R. T. Ross (Cambridge: Cambridge University Press, 1931), I, 101.

term "I" is a thing, peculiar or not, can its character be known and described? If so, how exactly? And in that case, what is the relationship between it and the body with which it is most closely associated?

But now suppose that there really is no Cartesian "somewhat" or anything even remotely like it to which the "I" refers. What am I then? What exactly is my self? What, in short, is the nature of mind? Or might it be, as some contend, that the term "I"—like the terms "gremlin" or "dragon"—is not a referring one at all, and that in thinking that it is a referring term we have merely succumbed to a bewitchment of language?

Quite apart from the fact that there is heightened interest today in matters of mind—thanks in no small measure to intense research activity in the areas of cognitive science—for many, the questions we have posed are not merely puzzling metaphysical questions. They are personally very troubling because they affect us intimately. For such persons, these questions raise issues of deep, ongoing concern, issues of personal religious faith, of human freedom or the absence of it, of ethics, and so on. As the titles and sequence of chapters suggest, the present work discusses the questions in a historically systematic and, we hope, a novel and useful way.

A primary objective in Chapters One and Two is to engage the reader with the primary sources as much as possible. This is reflected in the "Suggestions for Further Reading" appearing at the end of each chapter, some of which are divided between the classical texts and secondary commentary. From the outset, the reader is involved as a fellow inquirer who discovers from seminal works the ideas that have come to set much of the direction of subsequent discourse in the philosophy of mind. This accounts for the fact that sizable portions of crucial passages from Descartes, Locke, Hume, and Reid enter into the text of the first two chapters.[2] The guiding principle is that there is never an adequate substitute for direct acquaintance with the classic or original texts. Without some critical acquaintance with the primary sources to support our own ideas, much of what we gather is just so much philosophic gossip. In this book, claims, issues, arguments, and counterarguments are subjected to systematic, critical scrutiny. The objective is twofold: a substantial understanding of the primary material addressed and a critical awareness of the significance and complexity of the issues and questions involved.

Chapter Two devotes considerable attention to the concept of identity because it underlies crucial questions in the philosophy of mind, especially the question of personal identity. Thus the section entitled "The Notion of Identity," while an independently instructive unit, is essential to a thorough grasp of the issues involved in determining personal identity. Again, through case studies the reader is actively engaged as a fellow inquirer.

Chapter Three completes the *historico/theoretical ascent,* so far as theories

---

[2]In cases where English was the language in which the work was originally written, all passages reproduced in this work preserve the original English spelling.

of mind go, and brings us face to face with issues and questions of strong contemporary interest, debate, and research activity. Research in the fields of cognitive science has greatly sharpened these issues and questions. Artificial intelligence and connectionism are discussed in the same chapter. This has the advantage of giving perspective to many of the current debates having to do with notions such as artificial intelligence and information processing. Functionalism receives extended and informative treatment.

Chapters Four and Five take account of the broad theoretical ascent of the preceding chapters. These chapters single out specific notions or considerations which have proven pivotal and particularly troublesome in the ongoing debate over the nature of mind. They are the considerations which now seem to identify or demarcate the principal battle lines. The concepts "consciousness," "intentionality," "belief," "desire," indeed, the entire repertoire of folk psychology, are among the most seriously contested issues. Of these, consciousness, the subject of Chapter Four, stands out as the issue which at the moment receives greatest attention. This is so because it is that phenomenon which above all else we have come to regard as setting off objects capable of cognition from those that are not. Consciousness constitutes the focus of the current debate. In this light, the related issues of folk psychology, considered in Chapter Five, are extensions of this fundamental issue.

Chapter Six is a glance over the shoulder and an attempt to figure out the question—to borrow the title of one of Thomas Nagel's works—"What Does It All Mean?"[3] This chapter looks again at the notion of personal identity and in an ethical context considers the related issues of personal freedom and responsibility. It discusses qualia, qualitative mental states, again. Their distinctive character confronts the reductionist with questions which simply will not go away. If AI or connectionism or some suitable modification of either is the correct way of conceiving of the mental and derivatively of persons, then the next tenant in the apartment may well be an "anthrobot." But that eventuality will give rise to brave new questions.

There is one final word. Except for the first two chapters, where the Cartesian *I* as self is explicitly addressed, as a unifying theme in this work the issue of the *I* and its nature is left largely implicit in the discussion as we proceed from one distinctive theoretical position to the next. As the chapter titles indicate, the *I* is an ongoing affair with as much variety as there are theories of mind. On the central question of how to understand the *I,* each theory has its peculiar entailments.

[3] Thomas Nagel, *What Does It All Mean?* (New York: Oxford University Press, 1987).

## ACKNOWLEDGMENTS

I am grateful to Whitman College for granting me a year's sabbatical, during which time I completed most of the work for this book. Several colleagues, students, and friends encouraged me and made valuable comments on the manuscript. I owe them my gratitude. I especially want to thank my colleagues Ron Condon and Joseph Maier at Whitman, and John Stuhr of the University of Oregon, for their willingness to read and comment on the entire manuscript. Casie Buckner, an undergraduate, also read the entire manuscript and offered useful suggestions. Her reading helped determine the entries in the glossary. Special thanks, too, to Philip Phillips of MIT—more recently of the University of Illinois. Wes Woods solved all my computing problems. I wish, in addition, to express sincere appreciation to Prentice Hall's reviewers for their assistance in shaping the project: Curtis Brown, Trinity University; Mary Ann Carroll, Appalachian State University; Irwin Goldstein, Davidson College; John L. King, University of North Carolina/Greensboro; David G. Stern, University of California/Berkeley; and John J. Stuhr, University of Oregon. My editor Ted Bolen, Nicole Gray, and Larry Armstrong were always extremely gracious and helpful. Very special thanks should also go to Rene Lynch, my copy editor. My wife, Carmella, was a constant source of encouragement and to her I am especially indebted.

References from *The Philosophical Works of Descartes*, by René Descartes, translated by Elizabeth S. Haldane and G. R. T. Ross (Cambridge: Cambridge University Press, 1931), are used with the permission of Cambridge University Press. References from David Hume's *Treatise of Human Nature*, ed. L. A. Selby-Bigge (Oxford: At the Clarendon Press, 1949), are used with the permission of Oxford University Press.

# 1

## The Cartesian I and Other Dualisms

> I know that I exist, and I inquire what I am, I whom I know
> to exist
>
> —*René Descartes*[1]

### INTRODUCTION

Let us begin by doing a modest bit of supposing. Suppose that, as part of a narrative, you say to someone: "At that, she took her hat and her leave." For privacy's sake we refer to the someone to whom you were speaking by the expression *P*. You would be amused, if not embarrassed, were *P* to have thought that the person in question had taken *two* things with her—her hat, one thing, and her leave, another thing. If it came to that, you probably would explain that all you meant to say was that she, whoever she was, had left and had taken her hat. You might add, for the sake of excessive clarification, that her hat is the kind of thing she might have omitted to take with her. But she left, and there was nothing further (namely, her leave) that through absentmindedness she might have neglected to take along. Her leave did not refer to a kind of thing at all. We say, at times, what we do not literally mean.[2]

---

[1]René Descartes, *The Philosophical Works of Descartes,* trans. Elizabeth S. Haldane and G. R. T. Ross (Cambridge: Cambridge University Press, 1931), I, 152.

[2]This does not imply, of course, that issues concerning what does or does not exist can be simply resolved by avoiding nonliteral forms of speech.

1

Let us try another bit of supposing. This time you are asked the question: "Where is your mind?" You think a bit and you reply: "In my head, of course." "Where exactly in your head?" comes the query. "Well, in my brain," you reply. "Any special place in your brain?" Your interlocutor presses. "I'm not sure where, but somewhere in there," you oblige. The reaction is quick. Your interlocutor reasons: "If it is *in* your brain it just is *not* your brain, but something *different* from it. Indeed, it will have to *be* something, maybe spatial, to sustain the relation of being *in*. You have a mind to be sure, and so do I, but what and where it is looks puzzling to me." After a brief pause: "It might well be your brain, though, but then again your brain is just another piece of meat. Living, of course. But then if it is the brain, it has weight and is three-dimensional. That doesn't sound right. I'm stumped." "Well," you speculate, "it might be something like horsepower in an engine. My car for example." A pause, and then your interlocutor argues: "That won't work. Horsepower is not a thing at all, so it cannot *do* anything. All this talk about horsepower is misleading. It is just another compact way of saying what kind of push or thrust a car or such things are capable of, given certain mechanical specifications. So if my mind is like horsepower, not only does it not do anything, it is not even an it. I repeat, horsepower does not refer to a kind of thing at all. But what is my mind then? In fact, do I *have* a mind? How can I know that I have just one? I'm stumped. Help!" In reply you say: "I have never thought that deeply about mind so I don't really know. All I know is that my mind is in my head." "But that's where we started," protests your interlocutor. "Where do we go from here?" Well, that, in a nutshell, is some of what this book is about; it picks up the pieces of the conversation.

The difficulty of identifying mind is real. The problem of mind, in particular its nature and its relation to body, commonly referred to as the mind/body problem, is of very long standing. It continues today to occupy the attention of very capable thinkers holding diverse views. Some think the problem is such that its solution is beyond the reach of humans.[3] Others think the solution is so simple that the presumed difficulty of the problem is the result of mismanaged talk. For one thing, they say, we talk of mind as though it were a peculiar kind of nonmaterial or spiritual thing so that mind and body are two very distinct kinds of thing—hence a *dualism of substance*. For another, we persist in mind-talk that makes mental processes or properties seem mysterious, hence not amenable to empirical research. All this is mistaken, such people think. Getting rid of prescientific mind-talk is one way to cure ourselves of some of our mistakes. These mistakes, they contend, are basically three in kind: (1) mistakes having to do with what sorts of things exist—*ontological mistakes;* (2) mistakes about the nature of what does exist—*metaphysical mistakes;* and (3) mistakes about knowledge or the truth of the claims we make—*epistemological*

[3]See Colin McGinn, *The Problem of Consciousness* (Oxford, England: Basil Blackwell, Inc., 1991), pp. 1–22.

*mistakes.* And there are others who think that we can some day unravel the secret of the problem by experimenting with models of mind. We will be able some day to make minds. It's just a matter of time.

There is one other preliminary. When you did your supposing at the outset, you called to the attention of *P* that the referents of "leave" and "hat" are not in the same ontological category. To think that they are is to commit what Gilbert Ryle termed a category mistake.[4] Indeed Ryle thinks that Descartes commits precisely this mistake by supposing that a mind, like a body, is a kind of thing. Hats are actual things that exist, and a leave of the kind in question is not. A hat exists as a physical object that you can encounter in space; the leave in question is not in any sense a spatial entity. Though you engaged in some reasoning, your observation regarding "her leave" (that it is not the kind of thing one could possibly have neglected to take along) you would consider eminently obvious. You just had to do some mental seeing and the truth of what you were saying would be in full view. This sort of seeing comes quite close to what later on we will be talking about when we speak of *intuition*. This term comes from the Latin, *intueor*, meaning "I gaze on." What is known by simply gazing on it might include color with respect to vision (physical seeing), for example. Its truth is there for the seeing. Truth or knowledge arrived at by means of this mental seeing or intuition is direct, that is, noninferential. The following qualify as examples of this sort: "All fathers are male"; "If I am thinking, I am alive."

Much controversy surrounds this way of documenting our knowledge assertions, which does not always yield the same results for everyone. What one person might consider intuitively obvious another may have grave doubts about. To compound matters, whereas with ordinary physical seeing a norm can be established against which vision can be tested or compared and, if necessary, corrected, no such possibility exists for intuitive seeing. With respect to intuitive seeing, there is nothing analogous to optometry. Indeed, the notion of a science of intuition seems a contradiction. Education and enculturation do cultivate our abilities to see things, but cultivation which is the upshot of these is something rather different from the natural and untouched seeing of intuition. So anchoring a philosophy or a system of knowledge on a claim held intuitively can be risky.

We make some statements or claims for whose warrant we must appeal to the truth of other statements. We get at their truth indirectly, not at once by direct mental seeing, as with intuition. For such statements, we need full-blown arguments to *demonstrate* their truth. To accomplish this objective, we need well-founded premises—statements whose truth is not in dispute—and validly structured arguments. This way of supporting our claims appeals to rational people, to people who insist that we earn the right to their credibility. We should note

[4]For a discussion of this sort of mistake, see Gilbert Ryle, *The Concept of Mind* (London: Hutchinson & Co., 1960), chap. 1. See also the glossary following Chapter Six in this book.

that if the truth of any premise is in dispute, the argument may be valid but not sound. So if, as is usually the case, truth is the issue, validity alone will not suffice: The statements whose warrant we appeal to must themselves be true. Note the following: "All *A*'s are *B*'s," "All *B*'s are *C*'s," therefore "All *A*'s are *C*'s." This is a valid argument in virtue of the fact that it is impossible for the premises to be true and the conclusion false. We say that such an argument is formally valid. But we do not know that the argument is sound until we can determine whether it is true that all *A*'s are indeed *B*'s, and also that all *B*'s are indeed *C*'s. Making such determinations is not always easy. Indeed, some may say that it is rarely ever easy since most statements which are not tautologies are, in principle, always subject to doubt. Such people might say that the best we can do is treat such statements *as* true without *knowing* them to be true. This view clearly has skeptical consequences. So both *intuition* and *demonstration* can be problematic.

Descartes, with whose philosophy of mind we commence our inquiry, made great use of both ways of establishing claims. But we do not always know which strategy, intuition, or demonstration he is employing to ground certain of his claims. At those times we must speculate and look critically at the consequences of his having engaged in the one or the other. This is true with respect to Descartes's *cogito* argument—*cogito* in Latin meaning "I think." The term "argument" can be misleading here if indeed intuition was the strategy. At any rate, whatever his strategy, his fundamental claim is that he knows with absolute certainty that he thinks, and in virtue of this alone he knows that he exists as mind—he uses the term "I"—a real thing, a thinking *substance*.[5] Its sole nature is to think. Body, on the other hand, is corporeal, wholly different in substance. This view is a substance dualism—since two substances are contrasted. This form of dualism is often contrasted with what is called "property" dualism, according to which mental phenomena, though arising from a physical source, the brain, involve qualities or properties which are not themselves physical or are physically reducible. To say that a property is not physically reducible is to say that it cannot be described in terms of a physical vocabulary.

And now, commencing with Descartes, let us undertake to consider as closely and as critically as possible the most significant views regarding the na-

---

[5]The term "substance" is a technical one in philosophy and differs in employment from philosopher to philosopher. Descartes defines it as follows: "[A] thing which so exists that it needs no other thing in order to exist." See Principle LI, *Principles of Philosophy*, I, 239–40, in *The Philosophical Works of Descartes*, translated by Elizabeth S. Haldane and G. R. T. Ross (Cambridge, England: Cambridge University Press, 1931). To explore this definition fully would go well beyond the scope of the present work. He says in his *Replies to Objection*: "The mind and body are really distinct. . . .

[W]e clearly conceive mind, that it is a substance which thinks, without body, that is to say, without an extended substance; . . . and, on the other hand, we as clearly conceive body without mind. . . . Hence, at least by the omnipotence of God, the mind can exist without the body, and the body without the mind. Now, substances which can exist independently of each other, are distinct." (Proposition IV, p. 187, in Richard H. Popkin, ed., *The Philosophy of the 16th and 17th Centuries* (New York: Free Press, 1966).

ture of mind and the very complex notions and issues closely associated with those views.

## CARTESIAN DUALISM

### The I Discovered and Exposed

Descartes was not the first to develop a metaphysics which distinguished sharply between the material and the immaterial, between nonmaterial mind or soul, on the one hand, and material body, on the other. This distinction is to be found as early as Pythagoras and after him—and perhaps owing to him—in Plato, for both of whom the life of contemplation was qualitatively superior to the life of bodily activity. And much like Descartes after him, St. Augustine, Bishop of Hippo, reasoned: "If I am mistaken, I exist. A nonexistent being cannot be mistaken; therefore I must exist."[6] That *I* was, for Augustine, a substance distinct from body. He says, again like Descartes: "[W]hen the mind knows itself, it knows its substance: when it is sure of itself, it is sure of its substance. That it is sure of itself is what our argument has proved. . . . If it avoids tacking on to itself anything derived from its thoughts of such material things, so as to suppose itself similar in kind to them, then the account of itself which remains will be the account of what alone it is."[7] But it was Descartes who gave systematic statement to the distinction between the *I* as mind, self, or soul on the one hand and body on the other.

The distinction is made both in the *Discourse on Method* and in the *Meditations on First Philosophy*. In Part Four of the *Discourse on Method* he argues:

> But immediately afterwards I noticed that whilst I thus wished to think all things false, it was absolutely essential that the 'I' who thought this should be somewhat, and remarking that this truth *'I think, therefore I am'* was so certain and so assured that all the most extravagant suppositions brought forward by the sceptics were incapable of shaking it, I came to the conclusion that I could receive it without scruple as the first principle of the Philosophy for which I was seeking.
>
> And then, examining attentively that which I was, I saw that I could conceive that I had no body, and that there was no world nor place where I might be; but yet that I could not for all that conceive that I was not. On the contrary, I saw from the very fact that I thought of doubting the truth of other things, it very evidently and certainly followed that I was; on the other hand if I had only ceased from thinking, even if all the rest of what I had ever imagined had really existed, I should have no reason for thinking that I had existed. From that I knew that I was a substance the whole essence or nature of which is to think, and that for its existence there is no need of any place, nor does it depend on any material thing; so that

---

[6]Augustine, *Concerning the City of God*, trans. Henry Bettenson (London: Penguin Books, 1984), XI, sec. 26, p. 460.

[7]Augustine, *The Trinity*, Bk. X, sec. 16, as appears in *Augustine: Later Works*. Selected and translated by John Burnaby (Philadelphia: Westminster Press, 1955), pp. 86–87.

this 'me,' that is to say, the soul by which I am what I am, is entirely distinct from body, and is even more easy to know than is the latter; and even if body were not, the soul would not cease to be what it is.[8]

The form of his reasoning seems, at first glance, quite straightforward. That which doubts must be something, for doubting requires a doubter, hence more generally a thinker, doubting being an instance of thinking. *Cogito, ergo sum*: I think, therefore I am, that is, an *I* exists. Since I think, I am something; I exist as a thing. Indeed, I exist as a substance whose whole essence, says Descartes, is *thinking*.

The movement from premise to conclusion seems to be based on sheer reflection on what Descartes thinks is entailed by the premise, "I think." The reasoning is something like: "If I think, it follows that there must exist an *I* that thinks." A nonexistent *I* has no properties, hence cannot think. On this interpretation of the argument, Descartes appears to rest his conclusion on our intuitive grasp of what seems to be ontologically presupposed by our thinking, "I think." And on this account, the move from premise to the conclusion "I think" would be entirely intuitive. That is to say, the existence of some real thing is presupposed by our thinking "I think," and that real thing is an *I*. But this noninferential move leaves open the question as to whether the truth of an existential proposition can be settled in this way. This intuitive interpretation, however, is just one possibility, but a troublesome one, for it seems to *"beg the question"*[9] with respect to both the nature of the *I* and its independent existence as a thinking thing. That is to say, the intuitive interpretation seems to be taking for granted exactly what, on Descartes's own stringent methodological terms, needs to be shown.

Another possibility is that the movement from premise to conclusion is deductive or inferential rather than intuitive. In his *Rules for the Direction of the Mind* he observes: "[W]e shall here take note of all those mental operations by which we are able, wholly without fear of illusion, to arrive at the knowledge of things. Now I admit only two, viz. intuition and induction."[10] It is clear that in this passage Descartes intends deduction rather than induction as commonly understood, for just a little later in the same work, he makes this clearer.

> Hence now we are in a position to raise the question as to why we have, besides intuition, given supplementary method of knowing, viz. knowing by deduction, by which we understand all necessary inference from other facts that are known with certainty. . . . But the first principles themselves are given by intuition alone while, on the contrary, the remote conclusions are furnished only by deduction. These two methods are the most certain routes to knowledge, and the mind should admit no others.[11]

[8]Descartes, *The Philosophical Works*, I, 101.
[9]See the glossary for a definition of "begging the question."
[10]Descartes, *The Philosophical Works*, II, 7.
[11]Descartes, *The Philosophical Works*, II, 8.

The form, then, of the deductive move is roughly the following: "I think"; "Thinking is a property"; "Properties inhere in substances"; "Therefore, thinking inheres in a substance." That substance, in this case, is the thinking *I*. I am a substance whose essence it is to think.

We should note, however, that adopting this strategy would involve appealing to a general, non-self-evident proposition—the proposition that properties inhere in substances—one which while plausible is nonetheless doubtful. The truth of this proposition cannot be known by intuition. Indeed, it is precisely this kind of assertion which Descartes is at pains to exclude in his search for an unshakable grounding for his philosophy. This recourse could prove quite costly in light of Descartes's epistemic, and presumably nonnegotiable, principle: to accept as true only that which is certain without a doubt. It is a difficulty which Descartes, however belatedly, or inadequately, recognized. In his *Reply to Objections* he says:

> He who says, *"I think, hence I am or exist, "* does not deduce existence from thought by a syllogism, but by a simple act of mental vision, he recognizes it as if it were a thing which is known through itself *per se*. This is evident from the fact that if it were deduced syllogistically, the major permise, that *everything that thinks is or exists*, would have to be known previously; but it has been learned rather from the individual's experience—that unless he exists he cannot think. For our mind is so constituted by nature that general propositions are formed out of the knowledge of particulars.[12]

Descartes's disavowal notwithstanding, there is reason to suppose that even in the passage just quoted, something like what he is here formally disallowing is indeed at work in his drawing the conclusion that an *I* exists.

From what he has so far claimed, two distinct ontological categories emerge: the nonextended, immaterial *I*, "which, to exist, has no need of space nor of any material thing or body," and an extended, material substance. This distinction, too, will prove very problematic for it gives rise to the question of how two so totally dissimilar substances or entities can conceivably interact—indeed how perception of body by mind is possible. Whether by way of intuition—by which Descartes means "the undoubting conception of an unclouded and attentive mind, and springs from the light of reason alone,"[13]—or by deduction—by which he means "the necessary inference from other facts that are known with certainty,"[14]—the *I*, so far as Descartes is concerned, has been identified and characterized. It is a substance, "a thing which doubts, understands, [conceives], affirms, denies, wills, refuses, which also imagines and feels."[15] For Descartes, these claims regarding the existence of the *I* and its essence are all "clearly and distinctly" certain, that is, true beyond rational doubt.

[12]Descartes, *The Philosophical Works*, II, 38.

[13]Descartes, *The Philosophical Works*, II, 7.

[14]Descartes, *The Philosophical Works*, II, 8.

[15]Descartes, *The Philosophical Works*, I, 153.

### The I Challenged

His epistemic precautions notwithstanding, Descartes's reasoning or methodology, and with it his metaphysical conclusions, have proven vulnerable on many fronts, both in his own day and since then.

Recall that Descartes characterizes mind or ego as a "substance whose whole essence or nature was merely to think, and which, in order to exist, needed no place nor depended on no material thing," from which it follows, according to him, that mind is "entirely distinct from the body." Note also that both in the *Discourse on Method* and in the sixth Meditation Descartes likens the relationship between mind and body to be like that of a pilot or seaman to the ship he controls.

> Nature teaches me by these sensations of pain, hunger, thirst, etc., that I am not only lodged in my body as a pilot in a vessel, but that I am very closely united to it, and so to speak so intermingled with it that I seem to compose with it one whole. For if that were not the case, when my body is hurt, I, who am merely a thinking thing, should not feel pain, for I should perceive this wound by the understanding only, just as a sailor perceives by sight when something is damaged in his vessel; and when my body has need of drink or food, I should clearly understand the fact without being warned of it by confused feelings of hunger and thirst.[16]

Several questions arise. If mind and body are so different in kind that they have absolutely nothing in common, what exactly is the nature of the association between them and how is it possible? As Descartes contends, there evidently is some association, indeed an intimate one. Why, for example, may mind not just as well be in the vicinity of the body with which it is thought to be associated rather than being *in* that body? Why, moreover, be associated at all with a particular spatiotemporal thing, and why with just one? This question raises a closely related one, the question of how nonmaterial entities like minds, unlike material entities, are distinguished, the one from the other. Or, differently: In virtue of what considerations is any thing rendered or countable as a single mind?

Typically we individuate things with reference to some set of physically discernible characteristics and relations. Our conventions permit us to speak of apples as individual things even when they are yet part of something else, namely, a tree. So, too, we speak of a tree as an individual thing even though what we single out is firmly a part of something else. In short, in keeping with our conventions, a necessary condition for being set apart as a thing is that what is so regarded be in some sense countable. Our paradigms in this regard are all physical, or spatiotemporal. Now according to Descartes, mind is nonspatiotemporal. But this poses an ontological problem. How are minds individuated? By counting bodies with which they are presumably associated? What

---

[16]Descartes, *The Philosophical Works*, I, 192.

prevents our supposing that a single body may possess more than one mind? For possessing no other characteristic but thinking or thought, and having nothing in common with bodies, mind cannot be distinguished in the way bodies are. And if we fail at individuation, we also fail at identification. The moral is, "No individuation, no identification."

Assuming that the individuation puzzle is solved, a much more serious problem, not unknown to Descartes, remains. Descartes has no difficulty allowing that mind and body do interact. He says, recall:

> Nature teaches me by these sensations of pain, hunger, thirst, etc., that I am not only lodged in my body as a pilot in a vessel, but that I am very closely united to it, and so to speak so intermingled with it that I seem to compose with it one whole. For if that were not the case, when my body is hurt, I, who am merely a thinking thing, should not feel pain, for I should perceive this wound by the understanding only, just as a sailor perceives by sight when something is damaged in his vessel; and when my body has need of drink or food, I should clearly understand the fact without being warned of it by confused feelings of hunger and thirst. . . .[17]

But he also says:

> [T]here is a great difference between mind and body, inasmuch as body is by nature always divisible, and the mind, is entirely indivisible. For, as a matter of fact, when I consider the mind, that is to say, myself inasmuch as I am only a thinking thing, I cannot distinguish in myself any parts, but apprehend myself to be clearly one and entire; and although the whole mind seems to be united to the whole body, yet if a foot, or an arm, or some other part, is separated from my body, I am aware that nothing has been taken away from my mind. And the faculties of willing, feeling, conceiving, etc., cannot be properly speaking said to be its parts, for it is one and the same mind which employs itself in willing and in feeling and understanding. But it is quite otherwise with corporeal or extended objects, for there is not one of these imaginable by me which my mind cannot easily divide into parts, and which consequently I do not recognise as being divisible; this would be sufficient to teach me that the mind or soul of man is entirely different from the body, . . .[18]

Note also the following in his *The Passions of the Soul:*

> [T]he soul is really joined to the whole body, and . . . we cannot, properly speaking, say that it exists in any one of its parts to the exclusion of the others, because it is one and in some manner indivisible, owing to the disposition of its organs, which are so related to one another that when any one of them is removed, that renders the whole body defective; and because it is of a nature which has no relation to extension, nor dimensions, nor other properties of which the body is composed, . . .

[17]Descartes, *The Philosophical Works*, I, 192.
[18]Descartes, *The Philosophical Works*, I, 196.

[A]lthough the soul is joined to the whole body, there is yet in that a certain part in which it exercises its functions more particularly than in all the others; and it is usually believed that it is with it that the organs of sense are connected, . . . But in examining the matter with care, it seems as though I had clearly ascertained that the part of the body in which the soul exercises its functions immediately is in nowise the heart, nor the whole of the brain, but . . . a certain very small gland which is situated in the middle of its substance and so suspended above the duct whereby the animal spirits in its anterior cavities have communication with those in the posterior, that the slightest movements which take place in it may alter very greatly the course of these spirits; and reciprocally that the smallest changes which occur in the course of the spirits may do much to change the movements of this gland.[19]

By this ingenious compromise, Descartes hoped to preserve the distinction between immaterial mind and material, mechanical body and at the same time to provide a basis for their mutual interaction. But how can mind and body possibly interact given their exclusive natures? They possess nothing in common. Mind is immaterial, entirely free and unextended. Minds, unlike bodies, are thus not subject to the laws of motion. On Descartes's terms, mind and body could not be metaphysically more unlike. The possibility of mind/body interaction would therefore call into serious question the very distinction which Descartes makes between mind and body.

Causation between objects of the same ontological category is a commonplace occurrence in our experience. Physical objects causally interact. In fact, it is from our experience of this physical phenomenon that we derive the notion of a cause. I have no difficulty willing to go to the park or to the dining room and I physically go. There seems to be no mind/body glitches which get in the way of execution of that which I will. At least I am aware of none. But on Cartesian premises this interaction between mind and body should be entirely mysterious. Descartes, of course, is acutely aware of the difficulty his two-substance account poses and, as we have seen, attempts a reconciliation. But the strategy is clearly in trouble. Tongue in cheek, perhaps, Descartes calls the pineal gland to the rescue, supposing it to be ontologically somewhere between being pure body and pure mind. But this ploy will not do. Too much logical stress is brought to bear on the obscure pineal gland.

This does not necessarily doom causal interaction between mind and body. But the Cartesian solution seems ruled out, at least on logical grounds. Marjorie Grene concludes her 1991 *Aquinas Lecture* with the observation that "Descartes could save the unity of man in the face of his sharp dualism, only through the radical impairment of the concept of substance itself."[20] Since his concept of substance is such that no two substances can possibly interact, if mind and body do in fact interact it would follow that they really are not two

[19]Descartes, *The Philosophical Works*, I, 345–46.
[20]Marjorie Grene, *The Aquinas Lecture, 1991: Descartes Among the Scholastics* (Milwaukee, Wis.: Marquette University Press, 1991), p. 40.

substances. In Descartes's system mind and body do interact; therefore they are not two substances.

To resume our criticism, an issue is raised by the mind-altering properties of drugs like cocaine, morphine, and the like. In the sixth Meditation, Descartes contends that thinking is not a property of bodies, only of minds. But patients diagnosed as having mental disorders often show marked improvement after treatment with certain chemicals. Indeed, treatment of mental problems is more often than not directed at the patient's body, her central nervous system; that is, at her chemistry rather than at her psyche as something distinct from her neurochemistry. In fact, what is now known of the structure, workings, and capabilities of the brain and central nervous system lead us to suppose that Descartes might have *misidentified* the ego. Perhaps, after all, some bodies—physical systems—under certain conditions are capable of thought. Mind may not be, after all, a thing or substance but a capacity possessed by certain physical systems. If that is so, the Cartesian ego hypothesis is one we can get along just fine without. Entities should not be multiplied beyond necessity. This is a fundamental principle in the development of plausible scientific theories.

Descartes's *cogito* argument, by which the essence or nature of mind comes to be known with certainty, poses a further problem. Recall that Descartes, so far as that argument goes, makes no ontological distinction between the referents of "I," "mind," and "soul." They pick out the same thinking substance. But there are times when the term "I" need not be understood as referring to soul or mind or anything immaterial or unextended. For example, the term "I" in the sentence "I am seated here on this log" seems to refer to something that is material and extended. Or, at least, partly so. The terms "soul" or "mind" can without loss of meaning substitute for the term "I" in only some of its uses, but not in others. Descartes's *I* is not the sort of thing that is situated on a log. Hence it is the referent of this sense of "I"—the introspected *I*—which Descartes takes to be identical with soul or mind.

We wonder, however, why Descartes chooses just this sense of "I" as the ontological foundation of his first philosophy. Certainly, there is nothing about linguistic habit that would give this sense precedence over some other possibility. The *I* that thinks seems to be precisely the same *I* that sometimes sits and walks and seeks nourishment. Nothing in logic requires that this introspective sense of "I" be singled out to ground the *cogito* argument. What is more, a move like this seems to beg the question from the start, since what the term "I" must refer to is already presupposed. Has Descartes stacked the deck from the outset?

As David Hume observes so tellingly, introspection yields only thoughts, but no entities, certainly no mind that thinks. "For my part," he notes, "when I enter most intimately into what I call *myself*, I always stumble on some particular perception or other, of heat or cold, light or shade, love or hatred, pain or pleasure. I never can catch *myself* at any time without a perception, and never can observe any thing but the perception."[21] No thing, clear and distinct, is intuited by sheer reflection. Descartes's intuited *I* seems to be the product of a line of reasoning which assumes its existence. Or, if not, warrant for the existence of the *I* seems to be derived from an implied argument whose major premise is not certain. Recall our discussion of this skeptical feature in the introduction to the chapter. Either existence of the *I* is logically guaranteed by consciously saying "I think," so no further argument is necessary, or it is not so guaranteed. Failing this guarantee, however, we must resort to inference. But in that case, we are then stuck with finding a suitable, indubitable first premise. This premise would have to be general, hence, no doubt, empirical and perhaps impossible to come by.

In spite of some contemporary thinking, none of these challenges to Cartesian dualism taken singly or cumulatively can be considered decisive. This means that Cartesian dualism has not been shown once and for all to be false. For all we know, there may well be an ego in the sense held by Descartes. Indeed, many thoughtful people still support substance dualism. The following section considers their arguments. The challenges noted above do, however, place the view into extremely serious doubt, enough to make it appear overwhelmingly implausible. The entity at issue, the intuited, nonspatiotemporal substance which is mind or ego, except for tenuous claims from introspection, remains entirely inscrutable and beyond individuation.

### The I Protected

Among the most interesting arguments in favor of dualism, and in particular of Cartesian dualism, is one formulated in defense of the irreducibility of certain mental phenomena, at least of the subjective *I*. Indeed, this argument is sometimes offered as providing conclusive grounds for a dualism of substance. Supporters claim that no physical description of the world, however complete, can possibly do justice to the referents of token-reflexive terms such as "I," "myself," and the like, which are unanalyzable in physical terms. Defending this view in his essay "Personal Identity," Geoffrey Madell writes:

> No description of what is in fact my body and of its connection to some set of experiences could possibly entail or imply that what is thus described is mine. No description, no matter how elaborate, which does not feature a first-person ascription can possibly entail or imply the truth of a proposition which does feature such an ascription. . . . The point in fact goes back to McTaggart, who argued that knowledge of the self cannot be knowledge "by description," since it's one thing to know that some set of properties, specified in the description, is instantiated, while it is quite another to know that such a set of properties is mine. In brief, I can know some set of properties to be instantiated without knowing that they are mine, and I can refer to myself without knowing what, if any, properties

[21]David Hume, *A Treatise of Human Nature*, ed. L. A. Selby-Bigge (Oxford: Clarendon Press, 1949). I (IV), sec. vi, 252.

I have . . . . There can, then, be nothing by virtue of which some present experience is mine, since, no matter what the condition is, it cannot follow from the fact that this condition is satisfied that the experience is mine.[22]

In one sense, obviously not intended by Madell, the claim made in the first sentence of this passage is self-refuting: If the description succeeds in picking out *my* body as *my* body, then it *ipso facto* entails that the body so picked out is *mine*. That this is not the sense intended by Madell is seen from the second sentence in the passage, along with the supporting reference to McTaggart. No description of a body and its "connection to some set of experiences" can possibly "feature" first-person ascriptions such as "I," "my," "mine," and so on. So no description "however elaborate" can establish that such and such a body is mine. Indeed, this conclusion precisely denies the possibility of a description of a body as uniquely mine. From this we must take it that the expression "description of what is in fact my body," which we find in the first sentence of the passage above, is equivalent in force to something like "description of a body which as a matter of fact turns out to be my body." Bodies can be physically described, but the unique referent of the term "*my* body" cannot. Hence, Madell contends, "No description . . . which does not feature a first-person ascription can possibly entail or imply the truth of a proposition which does feature such an ascription." Noting that his view is totally incompatible with physicalism, Madell concludes by insisting that "the only view of the mind-body relationship which can accommodate this view is dualism."[23]

In response, several observations are in order. Self-ascriptions are made by users of some natural language. They are used derivatively, and perhaps dubiously, by entities such as certain human artifacts—robots, computers, and the like—or some trained pets. One view argues for the existence of a substantial or Cartesian *I* on the basis of an entity's ability to employ token-reflexive terms like "I," "my," and so on to make self-ascriptions. This view seems to regard this ability to employ a natural language as a sufficient condition for the possession of a nonphysical self.

But this view immediately gives rise to questions about origins: questions regarding the origin of language use, and, concomitantly, the origin of the presumed *I*. Has the *I* been elementally always part of what there is, perhaps in the Cartesian sense, or did the *I* emerge as a result of the capacity to employ language? And can any human artifact whatsoever capable of using self-ascribing language appropriately qualify as possessing a self? More exactly, which of the following is true?

1. Only entities capable of employing language self-ascriptively possess selves.
2. Only entities with selves are capable of employing language self-ascriptively.

---

[22]Geoffrey Madell, "Personal Identity and the Mind-Body Problem," in *The Case for Dualism*, eds. John R. Smythies and John Beloff (Charlottesville: University Press of Virginia, 1989), pp. 27–28.

[23]Geoffrey Madell, p. 40.

The second alternative seems to beg the question. It excludes on *a priori* grounds any human artifact, however structurally or functionally indistinguishable from humans, from the class of self-ascribers. In this way the first alternative seems to reduce to the second. Why, we wonder, is language so crucial, so fundamental, to making the metaphysical determination. And then to complicate things further, how does the irreducibility argument run with reference to fetuses and humans in vegetative conditions—all presumably languageless and thereby incapable as far as we know of making self-ascriptions.

But perhaps, though dualists like Madell roundly reject it as a possibility, the ineluctable *I* is not unanalyzable or irreducible after all, in the sense that no physical explanation of the mental is possible even in principle. Perhaps it can be accounted for, after a fashion, in terms of what Donald Davidson and others have termed the thesis of supervenience, according to which all mental phenomena without exception supervene upon the physical. Thus a change in an organism's mental states occurs if, and only if, there is a corresponding change in the organism's brain states. Of course, this is a materialist view, but it does seem to hold a high degree of plausibility. According to Searle, all such phenomena are caused by and realized in the physical.[24] More will be said on this topic in Chapter Four.

The Cartesian *I* has had other views expressed in its support. Because religion is so pervasive a phenomenon, it is not surprising that the religious view has an extremely large number of adherents. This view may be best understood as a set of contentions or claims based on deep-seated conviction rather than on well-formulated argument. With respect to early Islam, for example, Robert Bellah writes: "The act and word of God stand outside the natural world and break or threaten to break every natural structure."[25] Personal or mystic experiences, special revelations, or purported encounters with the Holy, the testimony of holy persons and teachers, supernatural events, and sacred records and traditions are appealed to in support of the real existence of something substantially, ergo irreducibly, different from the physical. Those who hold some version of the religious view—primarily substance dualists—claim, as a basic tenet, that reality is not entirely physical. There is that which transcends the physical, is not caused by nor reducible to it, and cannot be ascertained by methods appropriate to the physical sciences. For adherents of this view, the Cartesian *I* or soul is a prime example.

Difficulties with this view are many. For one thing, by their own admission its adherents acknowledge that its existential claims and its methods are not testable, at least not by ordinary scientific standards. What is probably even more serious is that by distancing its claims from the sphere of the testable the view leaves itself holding dubious epistemic credentials. For another, claims which constitute its corpus are wildly and widely divergent—dependent over-

[24]John Searle, *Intentionality* (Cambridge: Cambridge University Press, 1983), p. ix.
[25]Robert Bellah, *Beyond Belief* (Berkeley: University of California Press, 1991), p. 149.

much upon both geography and history for their content. In short, the view presents neither a coherent set of propositions or well-developed argument nor a reliable method of any sort. On the contrary, its own biography seems to be more one of serious retractions and gradual defeat than of successes. This report card greatly jeopardizes its credibility. The religious view does absolutely nothing to establish the existence of a substantial Cartesian ego or a dualism of substances. At most it constitutes a position which is itself in need of fundamental support.

Psi phenomena—paranormal cognition or extrasensory perception and paranormal action or psychokinesis—and purported out-of-body experiences, if genuine and irreducible, in some measure support the view that there is indeed a trans- or non-physical ego. But again claim and fact are very much apart. First-person explanations are untrustworthy, and the purported phenomena can neither be verified nor replicated with any semblance of experimental consistency. Such data as are agreed upon as being open to public scrutiny can be physically explained by some version of electromagnetic theory, for example. The record to date warrants the conclusion that this view, like the preceding, stands on extremely wobbly legs.

### Can the I Survive?

The case for Cartesian or substance dualism is not a reassuring one, at least not if we are looking for rigorous and telling arguments.[26] It is true that there is no such thing as a presuppositionless theory of knowledge—hence no claim to knowledge which is not itself subject to its own presuppositions. But it is hardly correct to say that our commonly accepted tests of epistemic adequacy unfairly favor a physicalist view of the world. While that view may indeed be presupposed, the issue is not at all one of fairness or unfairness but rather of what a reasonable believer is justified in believing, given a specific set of contingencies. It is an issue regarding criteria for making rational judgments, an issue of the adequacy of evidentiary support and of critical standards of assessment. If the existential claims in favor of the Cartesian *I* are rationally derived, then they cannot be accorded special epistemic status because of their purported uniqueness. They must submit to ordinary tests of rational admissibility. Granted, nothing that has so far been said has demonstrated that the very notion of a nonphysical substance is unintelligible or incoherent or impossible. The claim, however, is that asserting its existence is not *now* a matter of rational belief.

This is perhaps a good place to note that Descartes, at least for the most part, employs the terms "ego," "I," and "mind" interchangeably, to designate a thinking, nonspatiotemporal substance having nothing in common with

---

[26]For a defense of "an essentially Cartesian view of. . . the human mind," see Zeno Vendler's "Descartes' Res Cogitans" in his *Res Cogitans* (Ithaca, N.Y.: Cornell University Press, 1972), pp. 144, 161–62, 182–83, 205–7.

body—hence a dualism of substance. Other accounts, however, have regarded these notions as entirely explicable within a single-substance, usually physicalist, view of what there is. Ontological shifts—evident also in the treatment of other closely related concepts like "the self," "person," "personal identity," "agency," "consciousness," and the like—will be central in the issues discussed throughout the remainder of this book.

## OTHER FORMS OF DUALISM

### The I Goes Up in Smoke

From the Cartesian ontology of mind as unique substance but capable of interacting, though inexplicably, with body, we move to *mind as epiphenomenon*, to mind that clearly exists but is the causally impotent result of brain processes. The term "epiphenomenalism," as this view is called, derives from the Greek prefix *epi-* meaning "above," as in Ptolemaic *epi-*cycles, and "phenomena" meaning "appearances." Epiphenomenalism is neither an obscure nor an entirely new view. We find bold outlines of it in Thomas Hobbes's thoroughgoing materialism. More recently, Thomas Huxley claimed: "The soul stands to the body as the bell of a clock to the works, and consciousness answers to the sound which the bell gives out when it is struck. . . . [I]n men, as in brutes, there is no proof that any state of consciousness is the cause of change in the motion of the matter of the organism."[27] And of George Santayana, John Lachs remarks: "In the long history of human thought, no philosopher can match Santayana in affirming the impotence of mind. . . . We have ample evidence, he thinks, not only of the existence of mind, but also of its radical distinction from the body."[28] Indeed, Santayana's writing on the relationship between mind and body is quite extensive. In one essay, "Body and Mind," Santayana writes:

> The internal relations of ideas, . . . are dialectical; their realm is eternal and absolutely irrelevant to the march of events. If we must speak, therefore, of causal relations between mind and body, we should say that matter is the pervasive cause of the distribution of mind, and mind the pervasive cause of the discovery and value of matter. To ask for an efficient cause, to trace back a force or investigate origins, is to have already turned one's face in the direction of matter and mechanical laws: no success in that undertaking can fail to be a triumph for materialism.[29]

On the face of it, epiphenomenalism seems an implausible theory of mind. How could it ever be contended with any degree of seriousness that mind is

---

[27]Thomas H. Huxley, "Animal Automatism," in his *Methods and Results: Essays* (New York: D. Appleton and Company, 1896), pp. 237–46.

[28]John Lachs, *George Santayana* (Boston: Twayne Publishers, 1988), p. 89.

[29]Logan P. Smith, *Little Essays Drawn from the Writings of George Santayana* (Freeport, N.Y.: Books for Libraries Press, 1967), p. 18.

causally impotent? After all, I know that, by being uniquely privy to my own thoughts and their relation to certain things I do, my physical presence at this time in this room is the result of a number of intentions I carried out and decisions I made. I did not with unbridgeable detachment observe my body regularly making its way to this place and removing books and so on from shelves and at different stages, to my surprise, creating intelligible sentences at the console of a computer. No. I thought, antecedently, to do just those things which I intentionally did. Thought or mental activity causally preceded the complex set of bodily movements I engaged in. In short, certain of my movements were intended. They were agent-caused. This account seems intuitively obvious.

But we often get carried away by the obvious. We need to remind ourselves that the obvious and the plausible are sometimes, if not always, the function of our expectations. And these expectations, in turn, are themselves functions of time and habituation of one kind or other. It is also true that one time's implausibles are another's commonplaces, or nearly so. So a charge of implausibility is not necessarily fatal to a position.

According to the epiphenomenalist, mind is a product of the activity of the brain, a sort of efflux. The causal relationship between brain and mind is, by rough analogy, something like the relationship between a fire and the smoke produced by it. The fire is the cause of the existence of the smoke, but the smoke has no causal effect on the fire. Causation is in one direction only. In like manner, the physical brain is the precondition and cause of the mental, but the mental is itself the cause of nothing. It observes, but it has no effects. Mental relations are purely internal, entirely innocuous so far as the causal web of the material world is concerned.

The presupposition which, more than anything else, seems to inform this view of mind is captured in the dictum, "Whatever there is is physical." Among other things, the Cartesian *I* ran afoul of this dictum and partly on that account was deemed nonexistent. What then, in keeping with the physicalist dictum, is the metaphysical status of intentions, will, desire, belief, consciousness, and the like? The answer proposed by the epiphenomenalist, with a view no doubt to avoiding multiplying substances and causal agents beyond necessity, regards mind as a reality but without physical properties, which is to say that it is physically irreducible. A peculiar form of dualism results: one substance— thereby avoiding the bedeviling problems of interactionism—but possessing two sets of properties. One set is causally efficacious, the other causally impotent.

But this peculiar feature, the causal impotence of the mental, brings the theory into sharp conflict with physical science. Either the mental is physical and like everything else physical can effect changes in other things physical, or it is nonphysical and we are again in all likelihood faced with full-blown Cartesian dualism. The middle ground which this theory occupies is fraught with many logical perils.

Perhaps the most insightful critic of the epiphenomenalist view, though himself by clear implication an epiphenomenalist, is John Lachs. (In support of epiphenomenalism he remarks, no doubt unguardedly: "Computers can now reproduce all the higher cognitive functions of the mind and thereby attest that the hypothesis of mental causation is superfluous even when it comes to accounting for characteristically mental or conscious activities.")[30] In his essay, "Epiphenomenalism and the Notion of Cause," Lachs writes:

> How are the mental acts that constitute a mind "created"? What meaning can be attached to the word "cause" in the sentence "Each mental act has as its total cause one of several brain processes"? Epiphenomenalists are conspicuously silent on these issues. The reason for the silence, however, is not hard to find. Epiphenomenalism is incompatible with each of the three major theories of the nature of causation. [I]f anyone wishes to maintain that the relation of the mind to the body is epiphenomenal, he cannot also claim that it is an instance of the relation of causal *entailment* or that the generation of mental acts is the result of causal *activity*. [O]n the *regularity* view of causation, epiphenomenalism cannot even be stated as a distinct and recognizable theory.[31]

The causal difficulty seems intractable. For once causation is admitted in the relationship between body and mind—in this case, nonreciprocal causal activity from neural processes to mental phenomena, then a rather strange conundrum emerges: Lo and behold, the universe contains effectless effects, effects which cannot themselves be causes! This state of affairs is scarcely intelligible, for it violates a fundamental principle that cause and effect belong to the same ontic realm, hence effects are *ipso facto* themselves potential causes. The epiphenomenalist seems to claim that one ontological category is capable of causing to exist another and different category. The one is totally distinct metaphysically but is in intimate relation with the other in virtue of its being its cause. Either we give up or greatly modify the standard logic with respect to how causes work, or we seek a vastly different account of the emergence of mind.

Explaining the central claim of the epiphenomenalist's position is no easy matter. While the notion "causation" figures in the statement of that claim, it turns out from what has been said so far that its employment seems entirely vacuous: No standard sense of the term "cause" fits. In short, we do not have a theory of mind—indeed, no theory at all—for (1) it is not clear what the central claim amounts to and, more serious, (2) by countenancing two distinct metaphysical types—causally impotent mental phenomena and also physical phenomena which alone can function as causes—the view insulates itself against scientific assessment.

So much for the bad news. The good news is that supposing we concede that the basis of life on the planet is entirely physical, then it should follow that any phenomenon whatsover, consciousness included, can be explained in physicalist terms. It would do no good to deny the existence of consciousness. But admitting to its existence should not constitute a systematic embarrassment to

[30]Lachs, *George Santayana*, p. 88.
[31]John Lachs, "Epiphenomenalism and the Notion of Cause," *The Journal of Philosophy*, 60 (1963), 141–42.

physicalism. On this view the epiphenomenalist's hunch may be right, but it is a hunch awaiting clearer conception. So it may well be that the causal account provided for my being here in this room is flawed in a fundamental way. It may well be that I cannot rely on introspective awareness to explain the events leading to my being here and doing the things I clearly am doing. Perhaps internal gazing, like external seeing, is not always a reliable guide to knowing. What is more, perhaps unlike external seeing whose reports can be corrected by further seeing, internal seeing—which, in figurative terms, is what introspection is—is incapable of self-correction. But this is not the place to go any further into the subject of consciousness. This will be done in Chapter Four.

### The I In Hiding

It has been proposed that the bearer or subject of conscious states is not something whose sole or essential quality is thinking—the Cartesian *I*, for example. Nor, alternatively, is it anything obviously or reducibly physical. It is ontologically distinct from either thought or extension. This view seems to have derived its inspiration from and bears close resemblance to a central feature of Spinoza's metaphysics—and to this intriguing view we turn in order to set the stage.

In Proposition X of the *Ethics*, Spinoza contends: *"Each particular attribute of the one substance must be conceived through itself."* His proof: "An attribute is that which the intellect perceives of substance, as constituting its essence, and, therefore, must be conceived through itself." And then this clarifying note follows:

> It is thus evident that, though two attributes are, in fact, conceived as distinct— that is, one without the help of the other—yet we cannot, therefore, conclude that they constitute two entities, or two different substances. For it is the nature of substance that each of its attributes is conceived through itself, inasmuch as all the attributes it has have always existed simultaneously in it, and none could be produced by any other; but each expresses the reality or being of substance. It is, then, far from an absurdity to ascribe several attributes to one substance: for nothing in nature is more clear than that each and every entity must be conceived under some attribute. . . .[32]

Spinoza's answer to the question, "What is there?" is "substance and its attributes.[33] There is, for him, just one substance, which he defines as: "That which *is* in itself and *is conceived* through itself." [Italics mine]. Now had Descartes drawn out the logical entailments of his characterization of substance as "that which so exists that it needs no other to exist," he could hardly have allowed for multiple substances. Instead of two distinct substances, one material and the other immaterial, he would, like Spinoza, have allowed for just one substance and its attributes.[34] The internal logic of both characterizations

---

[32] See Spinoza's *Ethics*, Proposition X, and the proof and note immediately following.

[33] See Spinoza's *Ethics*, Propositions VII, VIII, and X. See especially *Note II* of Proposition VIII, and the *Proof* and *Note* following Proposition X.

[34] See the preceding footnote.

should have yielded much the same ontological consequence—one substance, with attributes. Instead, Descartes emerges with two substances, mind and body with thought and extension being respectively their essential defining qualities. Spinoza, adhering strictly to the logic of his definition of substance, emerges with one substance possessing two attributes, thought and extension. Spinoza as a consequence, unlike Descartes, has no mind/body interaction problem. This is so expressly because by definition substance is not only ontologically *in* itself, that is, ontologically all-encompassing, but so far as it can be known, is conceived only *through* itself. Nothing can possibly exist outside the bounds of substance, and to conceive of substance we cannot appeal to any reality not already secured within the metaphysical framework of substance itself. Any individual entity whatsoever, human or other, rock or raccoon, because of being of necessity a mode of substance, must be conceived of in terms of the attributes of thought and extension. Let us call Spinoza's view *the double-aspect view*.

It should be noted, however, that Spinoza's intention is not altogether clear from the texts. Does he intend that the attributes thought and extension be understood as features essentially defining or constitutive of substance— as his discussion at times seems to suggest? Or, for the same reason, are they to be understood as assignments reflective of our essential human limitation in contemplating substance? At any rate, an open and two-fold question remains unanswered: What exactly is an attribute and what is the nature of its attachment to that of which it is an attribute?

Influenced in some measure, perhaps, by Spinoza's metaphysics, some philosophers, notably Peter Strawson, have developed a view which structurally bears some resemblance to Spinoza's monism, consisting of one substance defined by thought and extension. Call his *the person theory*. In this view the concept of a person, the analogue of substance, is ontologically central and primitive in the following way. By person, Strawson intends a type of entity such that *both* predicates ascribing states of consciousness, *P*-predicates, and predicates making material or physical ascriptions, *M*-predicates, apply equally.[35] We say things like "I weigh less today"; "I sat there with my arms folded"; "The girl sitting there believes in Santa Claus"; "I know your name"; "I am perplexed"; and so on. But what is said of the subject in these examples differs widely. Take the sentence, "The girl sitting there believes in Santa Claus." Now what we see sitting is a body and to this body we seem to ascribe a particular belief, not by virtue of her sitting in that place but because of some proposition to which, all things being equal, she is willing to give assent. But we could not possibly, according to Strawson, be making the belief ascription to a body. This would be to ascribe consciousness to bodies, and bodies qua bodies are not appropriate subjects of

[35]Peter F. Strawson, *Individuals* (London: Methuen & Co., Ltd., 1959), pp. 101–3. Spinoza's monism also inspires Thomas Nagel's subscribing to a "dual-aspect theory." See his footnote commenting on Searle's identifying him as a property dualist, in *The New York Review of Books*, XL, no. 5 (March 4, 1993), 40.

conscious states. The subject of belief is one and the same as that to which physical ascriptions are made. Hence the subject of belief is the person who is the girl. And were she to confess to believing in Santa Claus and say, "I believe in Santa Claus," the subject of the self-attribution would not, following Strawson, be the Cartesian ego, but the *person* she is. And this person is not reducible to thought or to extension. Strawson contends:

> For it becomes impossible to see how we could come by the idea of different, distinguishable, identifiable subjects of experiences— different consciousnesses— *if this idea is thought of as logically primitive*, as a logical ingredient in the compound-idea of a person, the latter being composed of two subjects. For there could never be any question of assigning an experience, as such, to any subject other than oneself; and therefore never any question of assigning it to oneself either, never any question of ascribing it to a subject at all. So the concept of the pure individual consciousness—the pure ego— is a concept that cannot exist; or, at least, cannot exist as a primary concept in terms of which the concept of a person can be analyzed.[36]

For Strawson, it is precisely because both types of predicate, as specified above, do apply equally to the *very same things* that the concept of a person is deemed primitive. The entity in question is not some Cartesian, hence immaterial, ego; nor is it a corporeal thing. Also, it is not an amalgam of matter and consciousness, but both kinds of ascriptions have equal and undiminished application to it. The notion of being a person is basic and unanalyzable, that is, not reducible to nor explicable in terms of any notion prior to it or more basic. So the *I* or person is, on this view, the subject of two different kinds of predicate.

But as elegant a view as this may appear, we may contend that it places the subject or object—the person, that is—in ontological limbo. Thus nothing descriptive can be said of it except that both *M*- and *P*-predicates apply equally to it. Clearly, on Strawson's account, the *person* sitting here before this computer, unlike the computer itself, is not in any sense just a body, that is, not a material thing. Certain sorts of bodied talk apply to it, but so, too, does mental talk. The two kinds of talk are about *it.* But it is not an amalgam of the two kinds of thing. To complicate the matter further, speaking of persons as *having* bodies and as *possessing* minds would be rather unusual for then there would be three sorts of thing involved. This, of course, is not the way Strawson would have it. So let's grant him that. But even with that concession, it still looks as though Strawson's metaphysics must yet allow many kinds of thing, among them: (1) persons, (2) concrete, weighty objects which look like *mere* bodies but are not—organisms in conscious states, for example, and (3) objects like rocks and pieces of wood and so on to which only *M*-predicates apply.

The category of person, on Strawson's view, is particularly bothersome, for beyond the claim that two kinds of attribution apply equally, no further identifi-

[36]Strawson, *Individuals*, p. 102.

cation seems possible. Indeed, one cannot tell how these attributes attach to their subject. Is the attachment in our conception, as it presumably is with Spinoza's account of the relation thought and extension bear to substance? Or is the attachment constitutive in the sense that in some way or other these attributes are exhaustively what a person is? What exactly is it to be an attribute? Strawson's person is strikingly reminiscent of John Locke's inscrutable "I-know-not-what"—his characterization of substance—and is burdened with similar difficulties. We must take Strawson's concept of a person as a basic presumption whose warrant is derived from features of our linguistic behavior, that in speaking about ourselves we employ two kinds of talk in the peculiar ways that we do. Thus on Strawson's account, what exactly is the person? No one can tell. The *I* of self-reference has gone, as it were, into empirically unassailable metaphysical hiding.

We could argue that Strawson's person is bought at too high a price, the price of multiplying entities, or kinds of entity, beyond necessity. Perhaps some sufficiently complex type of material thing is capable of two distinct kinds of predication, thought and extension. Perhaps human beings are nothing more than complex organizations of mere matter. We do speak the way we ordinarily do and ascribe the two types of predicate to what seems to be one and the same thing, which in turn seems to have an inscrutable nature all its own. We do feel quite justified in making the sort of ascriptions that we make. This may be credited to nothing more than to the vagaries of linguistic usage. The way we talk cannot be relied upon to determine what there is. The universality of a manner of speech may constitute nothing but a clear hint at the existence of an *implicit* ontological presumption. Whether that presumption is warranted is a matter to determine by careful inquiry. That we do employ two seemingly distinct kinds of predicate to talk about ourselves may show only that we are especially complex organizations of entirely physical stuff.

### Assessing the I

*In sum,* perhaps the main objection which may be raised against any form of dualism is that its central assertion resists expression as a scientific hypothesis. Cartesian dualism argues for mind as immaterial thing. But this view raises the interactionist issue: How could an immaterial thing possibly interact with material things? More fundamentally, there is a perceptual question: How could immaterial minds possibly perceive material bodies? Epiphenomenalism argues for mind as nonthing, as impotent effect—effect without the capacity to bring about further effects—as the upshot of suitably complex material causes. But is the notion of an immaterial thing, like the notion of an impotent effect (an effect which cannot itself causally affect anything whatever), an intelligible one? If intelligibility is a problem for any view, testability is *ipso facto* ruled out. But here again, intelligibility is not only, or even primarily, a function of linguistic practice but of ontological commitments as well. Intelligibility is, like rationality, a complex mental phenomenon, determined by a complex of factors.

There is no good reason to suppose that it would even have occured to Descartes that his conclusion affirming the existence of an immaterial mind whose essence it is to think was so much mumbo jumbo. Even today, many think that the notion of being an immaterial thing is a perfectly intelligible one.

Also, in defense of a monist interpretation of epiphenomenalism, the unacceptability of the notion of an impotent effect may indicate more a refusal to refine a useful and a familiar paradigm—whatever is caused can itself be a cause—than a failure of ontology. Indeed, supposing physicalism is a grounding for all viable claims. Then some epiphenomenalist account which acknowledges the mental but avoids any kind of substance dualism seems a reasonable recourse. In that case we do seem to give up something which most of us have come to regard as a clear given, the intuitive assurance that we do engage in deliberation and as a result do specific things. Mind on this account becomes functionally idle. But then what emerges is not a refined form of epiphenomenalism at all but a view termed the identity theory, where the mental is reduced to the physical. This possibility will be discussed in the following chapter.

Double-aspect and person "theories" fare hardly any better. In each case the subject of conscious states cannot be investigated. And it is not clear what exactly is picked out by the terms "attributes" or "aspects." As a consequence, how these concepts attach to their peculiar objects remains uncertain. The underlying issue here is not so much one of intelligibility but one of designation. What exactly do these terms designate, and how are they distinguished or known?

At this stage, two related observations are in order. Dualists of any stripe may counter the charge that their positions are incapable of scientific investigations with a *tu quoque* response. *With respect to testability,* all views are in virtually the same shape when it comes to knowing. The mind/body problem cannot even in principle be expressed as a testable hypothesis. To do so is already to reduce one term in the problem, whatever term it is that stands for the subject of conscious states, and this move can only be justified on pragmatic grounds. Ontological commitments seem always to frame the way in which a problem is conceived and addressed. Strictly then, there are no philosophical theories of mind, once testability is regarded as a necessary condition for theory status.

The other related observation is that it is partly in deference to this countercharge—though not necessarily in agreement with it—that the term "theory" has so far been rather sparingly employed in this work, or enclosed in quotation marks. Less felicitous terms like "view" and "position" have been used in places where the term "theory" comes quite naturally to mind. But perhaps more important, this strategy has been adopted partly to leave open the real issue. This is whether the term "theory" can properly apply to claims which—like Freudian psychoanalysis or Adlerian psychology—are in principle untestable. Are some views of mind properly theories and others not? What exactly constitutes the line of demarcation? More narrowly, on grounds of testability, can dualism of any sort constitute a theory?

## IN BRIEF

In this chapter we discussed the Cartesian view of the nature of mind and body and the relationship between them. The view holds that mind and body are two distinct substances. Mind on this view has thinking or thought as its sole distinguishing attribute. Body, on the other hand, is distinguished by being extended but nonthinking. The immaterial, indivisible mind and the material, divisible body are metaphysically distinct in virtue of the fact that they have absolutely nothing in common. We noted that this mutual independence poses serious difficulties for Descartes. For instance, it is difficult on this view to see how perception of material bodies by an immaterial mind is possible. The absolute independence of the two sorts of thing seems to make mutual interaction impossible.

We discussed strengths and weaknesses of substance dualism and proceeded to some alternative forms of dualism—epiphenomenalism and dual-aspect theories. These forms, while avoiding some of the difficulties of Cartesian dualism, encounter serious difficulties of their own. Epiphenomenalism, for example, faces the problem of accounting for the phenomenon of impotent effects—effects which cannot in turn be causes. Its account of mind as the causally impotent product of brain processes requires that it show how on any of the three standard theories of causation[37] this result is possible. Finally, we noted that while dualism in any form perhaps cannot be shown to be false, its plausibility remains in very serious doubt.

## SUGGESTIONS FOR FURTHER READING

### Classical Texts

DESCARTES, RENÉ, *The Philosophical Works of Descartes*, trans. Elizabeth S. Haldane and G. R. T. Ross. Cambridge, England: Cambridge University Press, 1931. A basic and one of the most complete translations of Descartes's philosophical works. See especially *The Passions of the Soul* in Vol. I, pages 329–429. Vol. II consists of "Objections" to the "Meditations" and Descartes's "Replies" to them.

DESCARTES, RENÉ, *Discourse on Method* and *Meditations on First Philosophy*, trans. Donald A. Cress. Indianapolis, Ind.: Hackett Publishing Company, 1980. See especially the first, second, and sixth meditations.

Another eminently good selection that should be consulted is the two-volume *The Philosophical Writings of Descartes*, trans. John Cottingham, Robert Stoothoff, and Dugald Murdoch. Cambridge, England: Cambridge University Press, 1984.

SPINOZA, BARUCH, *Ethics*, in *The Philosophy of the 16th and 17th Centuries*, ed. Richard H. Popkin. New York: Free Press, 1966. See in particular Propositions VII-X, pp. 249–52.

[37]See in the glossary under Agent view of causation, Entailment view of causation, and Regularity view of causation.

## Commentary

SHAFFER, JEROME A., *Philosophy of Mind.* Englewood Cliffs, N.J.: Prentice Hall, Inc. 1986. In particular, see Chapters One and Four.

TAYLOR, RICHARD, *Metaphysics* (4th ed.). Englewood Cliffs, N.J.: Prentice Hall, Inc. 1992. See especially Chapters Two and Three.

# 2

## Hume and the Lost I

An oak that grows from a small plant to a large tree is still the
same oak, tho' there be not one particle of matter or figure of
its parts the same.

—*David Hume*[1]

### NO I CONTACT

Descartes cannot doubt the fact that he doubts. As a consequence he determines that it is indubitably true, whatever else may be the case, that he is a
doubting, a thinking, thing, a substance whose whole essence it is to think.
Moreover, that thinking thing is wholly distinct from body. David Hume, an
eighteenth-century philosopher, also thinks, but he confesses to not being able,
to find any but particular, that is, individual and distinct, perceptions, however
much he introspects. "For my part, when I enter most intimately into what I
call *myself*, I always stumble on some particular perception or other. . . ."[2] Not
only does he not encounter a Cartesian ego—a thing or self whose function it
is to think—but, he concludes, there is no such entity to be discovered. No self
as thing exists. Call Hume's *the bundle theory of mind*. Hume's criticism of the
Cartesian view, the *I* as substance view of mind, is especially demonstrative of
his radical empiricism. His argument runs as follows:

---

[1]Dave Hume, *A Treatise of Human Nature*, ed. L. A. Selby-Bigge (Oxford: Clarendon Press,
1949), I (IV), vi, 257.

[2]Hume, *A Treatise of Human Nature*, p. 252.

There are some philosophers, who imagine we are every moment intimately conscious of what we call our Self; that we feel its existence and its continuance in existence; and are certain, beyond the evidence of a demonstration, both of its perfect identity and simplicity. The strongest sensation, the most violent passion, say they, instead of distracting us from this view, only fix it the more intensely, and make us consider their influence on *self* either by their pain or pleasure. To attempt a farther proof of this were to weaken its evidence; since no proof can be deriv'd from any fact, of which we are so intimately conscious; nor is there any thing, of which we can be certain, if we doubt of this.

Unluckily all these positive assertions are contrary to that very experience, which is pleaded for them, nor have we any idea of *self*, after the manner it is here explain'd. For from what impression cou'd this idea be deriv'd? This question 'tis impossible to answer without a manifest contradiction and absurdity; and yet 'tis a question, which must necessarily be answer'd, if we wou'd have the idea of self pass for clear and intelligible. It must be some one impression, that gives rise to every real idea. But self or person is not any one impression, but that to which our several impressions and ideas are suppos'd to have a reference. If any impression gives rise to the idea of self, that impression must continue invariably the same, thro' the whole course of our lives; since self is suppos'd to exist after that manner. But there is no impression constant and invariable. Pain and pleasure, grief and joy, passions and sensation succeed each other, and never all exist at the same time. It cannot, therefore, be from any of these impressions, or from any other, that the idea of self is deriv'd; and consequently there is no such idea.... For my part, when I enter most intimately into what I call *myself*, I always stumble on some particular perception or other, of heat or cold, light or shade, love or hatred, pain or pleasure. I never can catch *myself* at any time without a perception, and never can observe any thing but the perception. When my perceptions are remov'd for any time, as by sound sleep; so long am I insensible of *myself*, and may truly be said not to exist. And were all my perceptions remov'd by death, and cou'd I neither think, nor feel, nor see, nor love, nor hate after the dissolution of body, I shou'd be entirely annihilated, nor do I conceive what is farther requisite to make me a perfect non-entity.[3]

Let us work our way through Hume's view and, for the moment, suppose that Hume is right. Am I, then—my self, my mind—constituted of nothing but perceptions? Am I, as Hume contends, nothing but "a bundle or collection of different perceptions"? Here, for instance, are some of the things I seem reasonably sure about. I grew up on a small island quite distant from where I now live. I went to primary and secondary school there. Between that time and now I did many things too numerous to mention here. And now, seated before a computer doing several things which I set myself, I find myself reminiscing about some of those dreadful elementary school days, about some of the fears and hopes I had then. I remember my determination to realize a good deal of the hopes—the fears having been sufficiently realized without my assistance. In fact, as I think of it, that determination accounted in no small measure for my being here in this kind of place. Some of the things I recall simply seem to

[3]Hume, *A Treatise of Human Nature*, pp.251–52.

bound back into consciousness. They appear as vivid to me now as though they occurred only yesterday.

I must admit that, like Hume, I have no *impression* of an *I* or self which did all these things. No amount of inward gazing discloses any enduring *I*, certainly nothing which has remained constant and invariable such that I can with certainty identify it as my very self. But without doubt I, H. E. P., and no other did those things. I started then and there, and here I am now. As a consequence my memory leads me to believe quite firmly that the *I*, the self, of today is inextricably connected to the *I* or person of those school days. Indeed, in some essential way, it is continuous with—though not invariably the same as—that person. What therefore is it that has these recollections? Nothing but "a bundle or collection of different perceptions," says Hume, "which succeed each other with an inconceivable rapidity, and are in a perpetual flux and movement."[4] But how can that possibly be? It is certain that the recollections are not detachedly here and unpossessed—I have them. At least, on Hume's terms, perceptions qua perceptions are distinct episodes or events or existences. No persisting something-or-other binds them into a unitary collection. Perceptions remain separate, distinct, and fleeting. Indeed, according to Hume, they "exist no where,"[5] for "all our perceptions are not susceptible of a local union, either with what is extended or unextended."[6] They inhere neither in some immaterial substance nor in something material. They inhere in nothing whatsoever for they cannot be spatially located.

If certain perceptions are supposed to be of *my* mind and not *yours,* how are these diverse perceptions distinguished? Why do I regard a given set as mine, and you think that another set is yours? After all, since perceptions exist in no particular region of space, I cannot assume that mine are where I am and yours where you are. More radically, can we even determine that a particular perception belongs to anybody? These are some of the perplexing questions to which Hume's view on mind gives rise.

Shifting imagery, but certainly not making the determination of mind any easier, Hume characterizes the mind as "a kind of theatre," but he hastens to qualify what he intends by this misleading imagery. "There is properly no *simplicity* in it at one time, nor *identity* in different; whatever natural propension we may have to imagine that simplicity and identity. The comparison of the theatre must not mislead us. They are the successive perceptions only, that constitute the mind; nor have we the most distant notion of the place, where these scenes are represented, or of the materials, of which it is compos'd."[7]

More questions arise. If perceptions, and perceptions only, constitute mind, then do they merely exist; do they occur willy-nilly? What is the ontological status of the *I* as it appears in the following passages from Hume: "[W]hen

[4]Hume, *A Treatise of Human Nature*, p. 252.
[5]Hume, *A Treatise of Human Nature*, p. 236.
[6]Hume, *A Treatise of Human Nature*, p. 250.
[7]Hume, *A Treatise of Human Nature*, p. 253.

I enter most intimately into what I call *myself,* I always stumble. . . . ";"I never can catch *myself* at any time without a perception, . . . "? Are preceptions entering perceptions and discovering nothing but perceptions? What reasons can they possibly have for doing any entering of any sort? And with their incredibly brief life span and lack of unity, how can they accomplish a continuous act like that of entering? What, in short, is it about Hume, or anyone, for that matter, that has the capability of self-introspection?

The attempt to account for mind in terms of perceptions alone, without dependence on anything material—a live material body, say—encounters seemingly insuperable difficulties. This is especially true when, adopting Hume's terms, we try to figure out how minds are individuated. As mere bundles of perceptions—bundles which nevertheless are not in any way united to form a unified whole—how do they manage to function as though they were in fact unified systems?

To compound things, there is also the issue of memory. How, given Hume's view of mind, is memory of anything whatever possible? To remember anything is to remember it as a whole. Do perceptions remember singly or as a complex system?

A perception is always had by something capable of perceiving. The notion that there are perceptions but that nothing whatsoever is having them is incomprehensible. Perceptions as distinct atomic entities would have no propensity, indeed no capacity, themselves to have perceptions, or to exhibit memory, or to think—if that is the right word—of themselves in units *temporally* larger than themselves. And what is one to make of the notion of perceptions perceiving or, for that matter, thinking of themselves? On Hume's account, the notion of perception itself becomes highly problematic. For one thing, the perceiving perception and the perception perceived seem to have to be cotemporal or coterminous to complete the perceptual episode. Because perceptions are nonenduring, that is, momentary, how is memory possible, on Hume's account? The perceptual basis for memory seems irremediably insecure. Hume seems to have had two distinct senses of the notion, an active one and a passive one. Sometimes he refers to the act of perceiving, at other times to what is perceived. In either sense, we are faced with an insurmountable temporal and spatial problem. Indeed, the notion of perceptions taking note of perceptions seems at bottom quite incoherent. Some physical conception of mind is a necessary condition for both memory and perception.

Recall from the passage above that Hume could find no impression from which an *I* could be derived. He concluded, therefore, that there was no *I* to be found. But if impressions are themselves "deriv'd," what is it that is responsible for doing the deriving; what is it that is capable of having impressions? Where or what is the genesis, where the logical terminus of perceptions? How did this perceptual apparatus get off the ground?

Hume's notion of causality also poses a peculiar problem. It involves the connection we would normally make between certain episodes of cognition,

on the one hand, and actions which we ordinarily would consider to be motivated by them on the other. For Hume every idea worth taking seriously must
be traceable to some impression. Causes are not traceable to impressions. Hume
acknowledges that causality is the sort of notion we cannot ordinarily do without. What then is its origin? It is, he explains, a notion which we, constituted
as we are, have contributed to experience in order to make sense of our experiences. He does not deny the existence of causes—demonstration does not
solve the problem of whether there are or are not. But he does question why
we suppose that the idea refers to something "out there," something of which
we can have an impression. He therefore offers a cautious definition of a cause.
He says: "*A cause* is an object precedent and contiguous to another, and so
united with it, that the idea of the one determines the mind to form the idea
of the other, and the impression of the one to form a more lively idea of the
other."[8] This account holds for all causation, physical as well as mental.

The causal problem posed here is with respect to mental causation, and
the specific worry to which we call attention is epistemological in nature. As we
have seen in discussing epiphenomenalism, and as will become more evident
later in this book, the notion of mental causation is extremely problematic. For
the present, let us understand it to express the commonly held belief that
thought is at times causally responsible for action. For example, my belief that
a certain bank is about to fail causes me to close my account there and with-
draw my savings. If Hume's analysis of causation is correct, then we do not *know*
that there are mental causes, that our deliberating or inferring results in any
action. We may notice only that as a matter of fact certain sorts of actions as a
rule follow upon certain sorts of mental activities, with the upshot that we make
causal assignments. "We need," Hume says, "only reflect on what has been
prov'd at large, that we are never sensible of any connexion betwixt causes and
effects, and that 'tis only by our experiences of their constant conjunction, we
can arrive at any knowledge of this relation."[9]

But we do not bear the same relation to our thoughts as we do to objects
like hammers or woolen sweaters. In the case of hammers, we note what follows from their contacts with nails; in the case of sweaters, with what characteristically follows from wearing them. Our thoughts are inextricably and intimately internal; hammers and sweaters, however, are external entitites. Indeed,
some deliberation-cum-action episodes bear striking resemblance to internal
states such as love and hate, states Hume considers *bona fide* impressions. If we
allow that there is mental causation, we are directly aware of our internal
deliberating—and of our consequent and corresponding doing of this or that.
This is more like having an impression than observing mental episodes
followed by specified doings and then, on the basis of perceived regularities,
making causal assignments. Hume's account of causation fits ill with certain

---

[8]Hume, *A Treatise of Human Nature*, p. 170.
[9]Hume, *A Treatise of Human Nature*, p. 247.

first-person causal reports such as: "I struck *X*, thinking *X* was the culprit," or "I closed my account on the grounds that I felt sure that the bank was on the verge of failure."

Hume's account of causation, however, has the dubious merit of escaping the Cartesian problem of accounting for the causal interaction between mind and matter. Hume permits mental causes to have physical effects and vice versa. He says: "Now as all objects which are not contrary, are susceptible of a constant conjunction, and as no real objects are contrary; I have inferr'd from these principles, that to consider the matter *a priori*, any thing may produce any thing, and that we shall never discover a reason, why any object may or may not be the cause of any other, however great, or however little the resemblance be betwixt them."[10]

The criticisms noted so far do not support the existence of an invariant *I* as the bearer of experiences, as the agent of perceptions. What should be clear, nonetheless, is that Hume's account of mind raises extremely difficult problems, some, if not all, of which he was aware and, doubtlessly, was bothered by. In the appendix to the *Treatise* he writes:

> I had entertain'd some hopes, that however deficient our theory of the intellectual world might be, it wou'd be free from those contradictions, and absurdities, which seem to attend every explication, that human reason can give of the material world. But upon a more strict review of the section concerning *personal identity*, I find myself involv'd in such a labyrinth, that, I must confess, I neither know how to correct my former opinions, nor how to render them consistent.[11]

But Hume was not explicit with regard to what he considered the "contradictions, and absurdities," nowhere in the texts—in the *Treatise* or elsewhere. And perhaps explicit mention is unnecessary, for his system stands or falls on the logic of the principles of the empiricism which Hume himself lays down. The absurdities and misadventures he laments are of his own logical unmaking.

As Hume displays them, perceptions, bereft of self, of person, or of body, seem a sorry bunch. They have no ancestors, only numerical antecedents; no masters, only solitary contemporaries; no principle of unity to connect them. In mind so constituted, "there is properly no *simplicity* . . . at any one time, nor *identity* in different; whatever natural propension we may have to imagine that simplicity and identity."[12] This position raises critical issues with respect to personal identity. But in order to be in a position to do justice to these issues, we need first to address the very fundamental concept of identity. A reasonably clear understanding of this notion is inescapable, if for no other reason than that in its absence, issues whose focus is personal identity—or any mind/brain

---

[10]Hume, *A Treatise of Human Nature*, p. 247.
[11]Hume, *A Treatise of Human Nature*, p. 633.
[12]Hume, *A Treatise of Human Nature*, p. 253.

identity theory, for that matter—cannot be fully understood, much less addressed. Because of its inherent philosophic interest, the concept of identity has been the subject of considerable attention.


## THE NOTION OF IDENTITY

In this section we tackle the notion of identity. Experience has made it clear that the better the understanding of what constitutes *identity*, of the various ways in which identity is conceived, and of the many issues central to establishing identity, the better our appreciation of the rather tricky problems having to do with *personal identity*. Hence a very helpful, indeed, essential way of getting at the notion of personal identity is to do so via an understanding of the concept of identity itself as a preparatory exercise.

Etymologically, the term "identity" and its grammatical derivatives call attention to a relation, that of sameness. This sameness may be asserted in reference to the relation which some one thing or object bears to itself over time. We use the terms "thing" and "object" here broadly to refer to whatever may be picked out as an individual physical object. On the other hand, identity may be asserted in reference to the relation which some one thing bears to some thing other than itself, that is, identity between two separate and distinct entities. We sometimes say, for example, that this coin is the same as that one over there, this book the same as that one, and so on. But we also say things like, "The little boy in this picture *is* the tall man in that uniform."

Identity is a relation between objects, things, or "thing-states"—where the term "thing-state" refers to a state picked out or individuated at a given time. Identity is not a property of a thing or things (unless, somewhat contentiously, we consider *relations* to be properties). To say that something $X$ is identical with something $Y$ is to say, more or less equivalently, though just as misleadingly, that the thing picked out by the term that designates $X$ is the same as the thing picked out by the term that designates $Y$. The term "skunk," for example, picks out the same animal as the term "polecat." The designating terms differ, but what is designated by them is one and the same thing. We can express the relation quite tersely by saying that $X$ is $Y$. And there are times when we express an identity relationship by saying that, in some sense to be specified, some thing or object persists over time as one and the same thing. Frequently, of course, the job of performing the identity relation is carried out by expressions such as "is identical with," "is the same as," or by simply interposing "is" between the terms designating the objects in the identity relation.

Identities may be represented in the following ways: (1) $(a = a)$—to indicate that, for any thing whatever, that thing is identical with itself and (2) $(a = b)$—to indicate that $a$ and $b$, picked out under different aspects, are one and the same thing. The first identity relation, that given in (1), straightforwardly expresses a strictly logical identity: The term on the left of the equality sign—

which we will read as "is identical with"—is also the only term appearing on the right of the sign. Hence, insofar as form alone is the consideration, this identity relation poses no inherently perplexing problem. Ordinarily, therefore, statements of this form are said to be trivially true.

The identity relation ($a = b$), however, is tricky and has been the subject of considerable discussion and lively debate. The reason is not difficult to see. It says, for instance, that something picked out by one designator "$a$" is identical with something picked out by another designator "$b$." Note that what is involved here is not identity of meaning of terms standing for the objects in the identity relation but identity of what the terms refer to; not identity of meaning but identity of reference. The expression "the Evening Star is identical with the Morning Star" expresses an empirical truth, a truth ascertainable by reference to experimentation of some kind or other. But the expressions "Evening Star" and "Morning Star" do not have the same meaning. They do not have the same *sense*, though they have the same *reference*—the planet Venus. The identity has to do solely with the fact that those terms pick out one and the same object, which appears at two distinctly different times in the sky, the one in the evening and the other in the morning. The term "strict" is correctly used to designate the kind of identity represented by this familiar example, precisely because two semantically different expressions do, as a matter of fact, pick out one and the same object. Since the objects referred to by the two expressions are in fact indistinguishably one and the same, it follows that what is true of the one is also true of the other. We can express this relation simply and in a formally precise way. The relation may read something like this: For anything $x$ and for anything $y$, if $x$ is identical with $y$, then any property $x$ has $y$ also has, and equivalently any property $y$ has, $x$ also has. Which is to say, negatively expressed, that $x$ has no property which $y$ does not have, and vice versa. We can express this identity formally as follows: $(x)(y)[(x = y) \supset (F)(Fx \equiv Fy)]$. This way of understanding the identity relation is often referred to as *Leibniz's Law* or the principle of *the indiscernibility of identicals*.[13]

The symbolic form ($a = b$) may also represent instances where the identity relation between referents is anything but clear cut. For example, take the sentence "The little stream that ran by my house ten years ago is the same little stream that runs by it today." Ordinarily, a speaker who needs to utter this expression, say, to an audience unfamiliar with the geography of her old habitat, will scarcely, in the circumstances, assert anything as pointless as a trivial identity statement. The statement is meant to be informative, to say something about a specific stream. But while there seems to be some tacit understanding as to what is meant by "the same stream," what is identical with what, the identity in question is anything but straightforward. On the face of it, a stream seems a very different object from an apple on a table. True, both are physical entities but, all things being equal, an apple seems to be the same apple it was an

---

[13]Not to be confused with *the identity of indiscernibles*. See glossary.

hour ago in a way in which a flowing stream over the same stretch of time is not the same stream. But a flowing stream—even for a moment—poses an altogether different problem with respect to its persistence over time. Nothing about it remains obviously the same. It makes sense to say that the same apple I put in the refrigerator yesterday is the one I ate at lunch today. But we produce a quite different account of "same" when we say that the same stream we took a dip in yesterday is the same one we dipped in today.

But differences can be misleading. Only careful analysis will determine whether there is a substantive difference and if so what that difference consists in. The central issue in each instance, is that of identity or persistence of an object over time. Is a stream any different from an apple or, for that matter, from any other physical object, regardless of kind? What identity talk of the form "*a* = *b*" typically claims, whether with respect to apples, streams, or other physical objects, is that something persists over time as one and the same thing. But this form alone does not yield much specific substantive information. The identity issues raised by numerous instances like these are extremely important and merit close scrutiny.

How is identity of the form (*a* = *b*) to be generalized to fit any and all instances, and how, as a closely related question, does the characterization work *in practice* for any and all instances? These are difficult questions. To highlight the complexity of the problem, let us consider the following puzzling cases, which raise the issue of identity in different though not exhaustive ways.

*Case 2.1:   Chisholm's U.S.S. South Dakota with a Jewelled Twist.*     In an interesting update of the traditional problem of the ship of Theseus,[14] Roderick Chisholm poses the problem as follows. Imagine a ship—call it the "U.S.S. South Dakota"—made entirely of wood. One day one plank is removed and replaced by one made of aluminum. The change is so slight that there is no question as to the survival of the U.S.S. South Dakota. Plank by plank is removed and is replaced in this very gradual way until the ship which originally started its career with all wooden parts is now constituted entirely of aluminum. But, as if to complicate things, it just so happens that someone retrieves all the discarded planks and reassembles them in precisely the same arrangement in which they originally were as parts of the U.S.S. South Dakota, making a ship of them. There are now two numerically distinct ships, the one wooden and the other aluminum. They have no single part in common. Indeed, the ship which now bears the name "U.S.S. South Dakota" is made entirely of aluminum. Is it misidentified, that is, misnamed?

And now, the jeweled twist. Suppose that, instead of the U.S.S. South Dakota, the original wooden ship—call it the "Jewelled South"—is privately owned by a partnership consisting of two persons. Suppose, further, that one

---

[14]For the traditional story see Thomas Hobbes, "Of Identity and Difference," *Concerning Body,* chap. XI, sec. 7, in *The Metaphysical System of Hobbes* pp. 85–87, ed. Mary Whiton Calkins (La Salle, Ill.: Open Court Publishing Company, 1963).

partner is a "tightwad" and that, while the ship is new, as occasion permits, he converts part of his profits into jewelry and, unbeknown to his partner, embeds it very discreetly into certain of the wooden planks—where it remains undetected. Suppose, lastly, that for some reason or other, he is away for a considerable length of time and, knowing nothing of the transformation of the ship of which he is part owner, returns at long last to find in port two ships. One of these—looking as proud as ever—he recognizes as the one of which he thinks he is part owner; the other, made of aluminum, he has no knowledge of whatever.

Is the "Jewelled South" the ship with the as-yet-undetected jewels still embedded in its planks, the ship which on first glance the absentee partner immediately recognizes? Or is the "Jewelled South" the aluminum ship *without* the jewels, which the newly arrived partner *never* set foot on and does not *know*? Put bluntly, which of the two ships *is* the "Jewelled South"? What precisely determines continuity of identity? Is identity a purely intrinsic notion?

*Case 2.2: The Christmas Blocks.* A youngster is given a set of building blocks as a Christmas gift. With it she can construct a wide variety of objects. At one and the same sitting, and using the same pieces, she puts together first a house (call it house-occurrence number one), then a barn, after that a woodshed, and finally a house (call it house-occurrence number two). As it turns out, house-occurrence number two is, piece for piece and place by place, an exact replica of house-occurrence number one. There is no physical, that is, structural difference between the two occurrences. What exactly is the identity relation between them? Are they one and the same house?

*Case 2.3: The Dry River.* The river Rio floods its banks every year in the rainy season. But when that season is over, what was a rampaging torrent completely disappears, leaving a dry riverbed for several months. Then the rains come, and the process is repeated over and over again. Since at times there is no water at all— and one cannot conceivably point to or identify a nonexistent river—there is at those times no river Rio. This circumstance notwithstanding, is there, in fact, just one and only one river which happens to be called Rio and which, year after year pulls off a disappearing stunt and shows up again, or are there several distinctly different rivers?

All three cases involve identity with respect to physical objects. But the issues raised by these cannot be satisfactorily grappled with in the absence of some understanding of what it is for something to be a physical object. So let us attempt that understanding.

To be picked out as a physical object is at the very least to have passed some test of individuation. Such and such can be individuated if and only if the such and such in question is in some way realizable as one spatiotemporally continuous entity, separable or separate from its environs, however constituted.

To say that anything is spatiotemporal is already to have ascribed physicality to it. In short, to be realizable as one physical object is one and the same as being realizable as one single thing. Since almost every physical object is to some extent reducible, we must allow for simpler as well as more complex physical objects, that is, complexes of similar physical objects. The trunk of a tree, while part of the tree, is a single physical object. An apple is a physical object, but so also is the Columbia River, for each can be and often is considered one single thing. We may object that the "one-thing-ness" of the Columbia is very different from that of an apple, indeed so different that to treat them similarly as two individual members of the same class is to commit a category error. An apple can be exhibited in its entirety in one clearly defined place at a precise moment of time and displayed again and again as the same apple. But of a river whose constituents are in constant and irrevocable flow, none of these things seems to be true. This challenge attempts to get at the general question of how to determine identity and under what circumstances a physical object like a river may be said to persist.

Let us consider identity with respect to something like a river. Suppose from a position of unobstructed view with regard to the Columbia River we announce, while pointing in the appropriate direction, "That is the Columbia." The most that our pointing can accomplish is to call attention to a particular region of a constantly flowing *surface,* which in some sense nonetheless belongs to the river. But the river is not identical with its surface or any portion of its surface. In fact, the region pointed out, like all other regions of the river, is on its way out, downstream. On reaching the ocean it is no longer associated with the river. The river, thought of as enduring, cannot therefore be identified with any of its regions—surface or subsurface—or with its specific water contents at any given time. Indeed, the river cannot be pointed to at all, if for no other reason than that it survives whichever of its parts may at any time be singled out by pointing. The river has no enduring parts; its constituents are in constant flow. What then is the thing, the physical object which is the river? Quine offers a proposal which has considerable merit.

> A thing—whether a river or a human body or a stone—is *at any one moment* [italics mine] a sum of simultaneous momentary states of spatially scattered atoms or other small physical constituents. Now just as the thing at a moment is a sum of these spatially small parts, so we may think of the thing *over a period* [italics mine] as a sum of the temporally small parts which are its successive momentary states. Combining these conceptions, we see a thing as extended in time and in space alike; the thing becomes a sum of momentary states of particles, or briefly particle-moments, scattered over a stretch of time as well as space. All this applies as well to the river or human body as to the stone. There is only a difference of detail in the two cases: in the case of the stone the constituent particle-moments pair off fairly completely from one date to another as momentary states of the same particles, whereas in the case of the river or human body there is more heterogeneity in this respect. . . . And each thing is identical with itself; we *can* step

into the same river twice. What we cannot do is step into the same temporal part of the river twice, where the part is temporally shorter than a stepping-while.[15]

Largely consistent with Quine's analysis is Chisholm's characterization of familiar physical things—rivers, picket lines, trees, and so on—as "logical constructions upon," or as "accidents of," what he calls "evolving systems of composita."[16] Chisholm uses the term "compositum" to stand for "anything that has a part."[17] To say, for example, that a thing is its several parts is to say that it is composed of those parts. The thing in question is a compositum, but individual parts may be added or subtracted and correspondingly new composita emerge. From time to time, or from moment to moment, depending on the frame of reference, the identifiable thing whose parts are so disposed evolves. It goes from being one compositum answering to one definite description to another compositum, and so on for every change. But it is not permanently or more closely identified with any one compositum. One necessary condition, however, is that the most recent compositum be continuous with its predecessor. In light of this evolution, this exchange, an emergent compositum may have no part in common with its more distant ancestors.

With regard to this last point, while continuity of composita in this way is a necessary condition for the persistence of a thing's identity, this condition is not sufficient. It must be supplemented by a further but also necessary condition. This further condition may be expressed by saying that emergent composita will have to be recognized as composita of the same sort of thing. Hirsch considers this further condition in terms of what are called "sortals."[18] A sortal term identifies a thing—a tree, for example—as persisting over time as one and the same thing throughout its changing career. So if the kind of thing were a river, the emergent composita will have to be recognized as composita of a river and not of, say, a lake only—where a lake happens to occur somewhere within the course of the river in question—or of a sea or ocean.

Consider the following scenarios. (1) A straight ornamental pin is made into a needle simply by flattening its head and having an eye put where the head was. (2) A small gold vase is fashioned into a bracelet, then is subsequently converted into something else, a leopard-like figurine. From pin to needle, and from vase to leopard, the composita are spatiotemporally and qualitatively con-

[15]W. V. O. Quine, Methods of Logic (3rd. ed.) (New York: Holt, Rinehart & Winston, 1972), pp. 211–223.

[16]Roderick Chisholm, "The Loose and Popular and the Strict and Philosophical Senses of Identity," in *Perception and Personal Identity*, eds. Norman S. Care and Robert H. Grimm (Cleveland, Ohio: Case Western Reserve University, 1969), pp. 99–100.

[17]Norman S. Care and Robert M. Grimm, eds., *Perception and Personal Identity*, p. 90. See also pp. 89–100 for a full discussion of composita and the ways in which they differ from conjunctiva.

[18]For a discussion of sortals see Eli Hirsch, *The Concept of Identity* (New York: Oxford University Press, 1982, pp. 37–71.

tinuous but they are not throughout, in either of the two scenarios, composita of one sort of thing. At different stages something very different emerges. In the absence of this condition, that emergent composita be of the same sort of thing, a condition necessary for individuating things by type, spatiotemporal and qualitative continuity run amuck. There is the absurd consequence that nothing ever ceases to be.

This account, embracing spatiotemporal and qualitative continuity as well as distinctness of sort of thing individuated, is easily seen to be true of rivers, but it is no less true of any and all physical objects. Hence to step twice into the same car, or stream, or house is to step into two distinct composita, into the equivalent of what Quine, with reference to rivers, terms "river-stages." You cannot bite twice into the same "apple-stage"—or into the same apple-compositum—though one may indeed bite twice into the same apple.

Appearances aside, no physical object is immune to constant change, for motion, hence change, is a permanent feature of the microstructure of all physical objects. All physical objects are at the microlevel fluid. One consideration which emerges from the foregoing discussion is that it is not a necessary condition for anything to possess any property permanently in order to be that specific thing. There is, in reality, simply no such thing.

Let us turn to the three cases we sketched out above. Case 2.3, the Dry River case, seems straightforward. During the rainy season, recall, a river exists. That season over, for several months no water at all is to be found anywhere along the entire course of its bed. Rivers, qua rivers, always contain water along their course, and rivers do not go into hiding—appealing to pregnant clouds will scarcely make a convincing case for a river in hiding. It can thus be concluded on good grounds that during those waterless months, and in regard to the relevant riverbed, river Rio in fact does not exist. It has no being, since for a physical object to exist it must *be somewhere* and, identifiably itself, *be some what*. Hence the year-to-year use of the name Rio notwithstanding, no one and the same river Rio persists from year to year. At best, there are, during those river times, only "river episodes" commonly called by the same name Rio. That these "river episodes" are regarded as being of one and the same river, is entirely a matter of habit. The river of any given year is not the river of the past years returned, nor the river of the years to come arrived much too early.

This future river has to have an identity different from its predecessor. This conclusion is reminiscent of a view held by both the very influential seventeenth-century English philosopher John Locke and the eighteenth-century Scottish philosopher Reid. In his *An Essay Concerning Human Understanding* Locke contends: "That therefore that had one beginning is the same thing, and that which had a different beginning in time and place from that, is not the same but divers."[19] And Reid, similarly, says: "That which hath ceased to exist cannot be the same with that which afterwards begins to exist;

---

[19]John Locke, *An Essay Concerning Human Understanding*, ed. Peter Nidditch (Oxford: Clarendon Press, 1975), II, xxvii, sec. i, 328.

for this would be to suppose a being to exist after it ceased to exist, and to have had existance before it was produced, which are manifest contradictions. Continued uninterrupted existence is therefore necessarily implied in identity."[20] To reason that river continuity is preserved via water molecules, however few, which always make their way back to the region they once occupied seems an extremely farfetched way of accounting for identity over time. Indeed, by this argument, no physical object ever ceases to exist since it is conceivable that microparticles traceable to any given thing persist somewhere or other. On that basis, that thing's reconstitution cannot logically be ruled out. This seems a case of begging the question. The reasoning is: "In reality, nothing ever ceases to exist, so everything that ever was still is." The question is not similarly begged if the expression "cease to be" is taken to mean, unequivocally, that that to which it refers has no being whatever. To suppose, on the other hand, that "cease to be" might mean "having no being; but not quite" would indulge the absurdity just pointed out.

The issue of identity involved in Case 2.2, The Christmas Blocks, is much like that raised in the illustration above where a ring and a pin alternate with each other. In each instance there were two numerically distinct acts of creation with spatiotemporally distinct results. In neither case would it make sense to hold that through the intervening episodes some *thing*—whether house or ring—persisted. For example, it would make little sense to contend that house-occurrence$_1$, HO$_1$, survived the creation of the intervening objects to become one and the same with house-occurrence$_2$, HO$_2$. The second house-occurrence, like the second ring-occurrence, resulted merely from doing *again* in the same way what was done before. Hence HO$_1$ is in this sense *the same as,* but *not one and the same as* HO$_2$. In all instances such as these, we have what may be called an "identity of replication," but not one of persistence over time. While the building blocks and the precious metal remained intact, no ghostly or transcendent house or ring persisted, awaiting its reincarnation.

And now for the issue involving Case 2.1, that of establishing the identity of the Jewelled South. This case presents an identity problem interesting in its own right and quite unlike the ones encountered in the cases so far discussed. Recall that originally there was a single ship whose career over a given period of time was such that where originally there were wooden planks there are now aluminum replacements. All the discarded wooden originals were, plank for plank, reassembled to form what turned out to be a ship physically indistinguishable from the original wooden ship. So now there are two ships at anchor in port, one whose planking is entirely of aluminum while the other is of wood.

Let us bear in mind that to refer at any time to "the ship" is not to pick out some transcendent entity, something over and above the totality of ship-parts suitably prepared and assembled in keeping with some predetermined form. The entity, the physical object, which results from this activity is what on-

[20]Thomas Reid, *Essays on the Intellectual Powers of Man*, ed. James Walker (Boston: Phillips, Sampson and Company, 1855), essay III, chap. 3, p. 342.

tologically is "the ship." The ship is not some ghostly thing embodied. Following Quine, we may regard it, in terms applicable to any physical object whatever, as constituted of "stages." A ship has "ship-stages," a river has "river-stages," and so on. For any ship $S$, the stages are spatiotemporal stages of $S$; for any river $R$, the stages are spatiotemporal stages of $R$. Both $S$ and $R$ are specific instances of two distinct sorts of thing, each with a recognizably different career. Hence, as we observed earlier, it is possible to enter the same ship or river twice, but not the same ship- or river-stage. The ship, or the river, as long as it lasts, is not a fixed entity but an ongoing series of nonpermanent stages.

If this view is correct, then the continuity, hence the identity, of any ship $S$ or any river $R$ is preserved not by virtue of the persistence of any given set of micro- or macroconstituents, or of some ghostly inhabitant, but solely because the specific spatiotemporal stages are continuous. The thing individuated persists, but not as the embodiment of all of its original parts. In Chisholm's idiom, "Between the time of the first encounter and that of the second, some part in all probability, will have been added, or taken away, with the result that we encounter *different composita,* though we may wish to say that in so doing we encounter *one and the same physical thing.* "[21] It is in terms of continued identity in this sense that any actual physical object is thought of as always being identical with itself at different times. Indeed, with respect to purely physical objects, this view seems undefeatable.

But something is oddly amiss. Consistent with our reasoning, the aluminum ship is unmistakably the Jewelled South. It alone answers to the flow of continuity we recognized as commencing with the wooden Jewelled South. It represents a new compositum continuous with its antecedents. Our identification is determined not on the basis of metaphysical considerations but on the strength of the fact that the ongoing composita were of one and the same recognizable entity named and continuously known throughout its career as the Jewelled South. The name in this instance serves as an identity marker; it singles out a particular ongoing career. Hobbes seems to have got it right when he observes: "[I]f the name be given for such form as is the beginning of motion, then, as long as that motion remains, it will be the same *individual* thing; as that man will be always the same, whose actions and thoughts proceed from the same beginning of motion, namely, that which was in his generation; and that will be the same river which flows from one and same fountain whether the same water, or other water, or something else than water, flow from thence."[22] A ship of war, which has successively changed her anchors, her tackle, her sails, her masks, her planks, and her timbers, while she keeps the same name, is the same.

---

[21]Care and Grimm, *Perception and Personal Identity*, p. 95.
[22]Thomas Hobbes, "Of Identity and Difference," *Concerning Body*, chap. XI, sec. 7. See also Reid's *Essays on the Intellectual Powers of Man*, essay III, chap. 3, sec. ii, p. 246.

Recall, however, that the absent partner, not privy to the ship's evolution, returns and with no difficulty, indeed immediately, recognizes the wooden ship and identifies it as the "Jewelled South." In fact, the name as it originally appeared is still barely visible on the reassembled but faded wood. The situation bears a striking resemblance to the following scenario. Suppose that someone *S* takes her unique vintage car *V* for an overhaul. *S* is told that the entire process will take ten hours. The following events ensue. *S* goes to a nearby motel for the duration of the overhaul. Each unit-part of *V* is systematically removed and replaced one at a time by new and improved substitute parts. Within several hours Twin-*V*, a "teflon" and twice-as-expensive version of *V*, emerges. The parts of *V* are checked and reassembled exactly, all within the advertised time; *S* returns and pays the overhaul bill and drives off with Twin-*V*! A mistake? If so, whose?

This scenario is a speeded-up version of the repair events of the Jewelled South. The developments in *V* and Twin-*V* mirror closely the developments with respect to the wooden ship and its aluminum alter ego. Both are developments over time and involve identity over time. The only marked difference is the rate of change: The activities in the latter case are telescoped and rapid, so that what took a year for the former takes ten hours for the latter.

Is the identity of *V* open to question? Scarcely. The implied rule—the convention according to which a name that continues in use to single out a particular entity as being one and the same in the way described above—does not seem capable of settling the *V* case. The search for the identity of *V* must answer to a different rule, a different convention, one which appeals to *V*'s peculiar character, indeed, its metaphysics. It can be argued that the absent partner, now returned, faces virtually the same situation as that faced by *S* after *S* returned to pick up her *V*. Has Twin-*V* become *V*, or is it the other way around? The wooden ship with his jewels embedded in its planking is ontologically continuous with the ship he recognizes as the Jewelled South. So for this newly returned partner, though defensibly not for those who experienced the ongoing transformation of the original ship, there is, on the one hand, the official Jewelled South and, on the other, the familiar Jewelled South of his intimate acquaintance and memory. Everything he remembers is of the latter. He knows nothing, thus can have no recollection, of the former in its aluminum embodiment.

These cases constitute a particularly interesting identity puzzle, especially as it hints at some of the issues which have come to be associated with the problem of persons and personal identity.

## PERSONS AND PERSONAL IDENTITY

The discussion of identity has so far been restricted to talk about what we uncontentiously refer to as mere physical objects. This strategy has been adopted primarily so as not to prejudge the outcome of the inquiry into the nature of persons or personhood. To do justice, therefore, to the complex project of this inquiry, it is to our advantage that as an introduction, at least, we address the question, What is a person? Or, more precisely, Is there anything in particular that constitutes persons, anything, in virtue of which an individual is a person? The project is worth a try. It may be that no such discovery is there to be made. Following this inquiry, the question we will go on to consider is, How do we determine that any given individual $S$ is, over time, one and the same person? How, again, to reflect Quine, do we decide that two person-stages are stages of one and the same person?

### Of Persons

*Strictly speaking,* we do not bump into persons. We bump into, first and foremost, spatiotemporal things ordinarily talked of as physical objects. These are things, for example, that can get in our way, like walls, shoes, trees, animals, and the like. Indeed, if we did bump into persons, in the way we might be said to bump into any of the foregoing, there would be little point in interminably puzzling over just what constitutes a person. We could solve the problem in much the same way we might go about settling the question of the constitution of a block of wood or some foreign substance. The everyday fact is that from among the objects we encounter, we identify certain ones as entities with qualities associated with being a person. And we *ordinarily* consider members of one and no other class of sensible objects as candidates for personhood, the species-specific class consisting of only humans.[23] A wax or animated replica of Justice Ruth Bader Ginsberg is not considered a person, though Justice Ginsberg undoubtedly is a person. But what exactly is it about Ruth Bader Ginsberg which establishes as true the judgment that she is indeed a person and not a cleverly constituted robot? Our intuitions tell us that it takes a person to recognize a person. Hence if $A$ judges something $B$ to be of the kind $P$—being a person— then it must be on the grounds that $A$ is a person. Person $A$ should be in a position to ascertain what exactly establishes her judgment that object $B$ is of the kind $P$ from the fact that she herself is an instance of the very sort of thing she judges $B$ to be.

But things are not that simple. Unfortunately, and to compound the difficulty for $A$, what she seeks is—with all, due respect to Descartes—neither open to introspection nor to simple inference or demonstration. As Hume so well points out, introspection yields only perceptions without a unifying principle, not a self or a soul or a person. A related difficulty, too, is establishing the premises which would justify the inference that an entity called the person exists. So $A$'s status as a person yields $A$ no privileged or ready access to just what constitutes being a person. *Being* a person does not imply *knowing* what a per-

---

[23]"God," in some religious traditions, refers to a person, presumably nonphysical, that is, spiritual. The possibility that there may be nonterrestrial, nonhuman, but physical creatures who may be considered full-fledged persons cannot be a priori ruled out.

son is. By starting with ourselves, perhaps too close to ourselves, we are brought no closer to a resolution of the puzzle of personhood.

An alternative to this first-person approach is to attempt to make the determination solely on the basis of what we observe of those beings external to us whom we have picked out as persons. But this strategy is doomed. No plausible account can be given which wholly externalizes the investigation to the exclusion of the single entity—the investigator herself. Her claim to being a person, though not clear as to detail, is incontrovertibly established. In these circumstances, the duo of *reflection* and *observation* seems the natural investigating pair. Any account which focuses on the one to the exclusion of the other is likely to encounter intractable difficulties.

It is instructive to glance back a bit and give our inquiry some historical perspective. Locke is one of the earliest to attempt a systematic inquiry into the nature of personal identity and, as part of this project, he provides an account of what he objectively considers being a person. His work, with all its flaws, well exhibits the complexities associated with an investigation of this nature. His views represent an excellent point of departure as we, too, investigate these still very complex and as yet unresolved matters. In considering what a person is, Locke offers the following account:

> This being premised to find wherein *personal identity* consists, we must consider what *Person* stands for; which, I think, is a thinking intelligent Being, that has reason and reflection, and can consider it self as it self, the same thinking thing in different times and places; which it does only by that consciousness, which is inseparable from thinking, and as it seems to me essential to it: It being impossible for any one to perceive, without perceiving that he does perceive. When we see, hear, smell, . . . it is always as to our present Sensations and Perceptions: And by this every one is to himself, that which he calls *self*: It not being considered in this case, whether the same *self* be continued in the same, or divers Substances. For since consciousness always accompanies thinking, and 'tis that, that makes every one to be, what he calls *self*; and thereby distinguishes himself from all other thinking things, in this alone consists *personal Identity*, i.e., the same rational Being: And as far as consciousness can be extended backwards to any past Action or Thought, so far reaches the Identity of that *Person*; it is the same self now it was then; and 'tis by the same *self* with this present one that now reflects on it, that that Action was done.[24]

For the time being we will consider only what Locke identifies as constituting a person. We are told in the passage just given that that which is a person is a being. Not only must the *being* which is considered *the person* be thinking and intelligent, and capable of reasoning and reflection, it must also be able to consider itself as itself; which is to say, it must not only be capable of self-reflection but also of self-identification, to see itself in the relation of object to a subject. It must also be able to regard itself as one and the same self or being both diachronically and synchronically. This it accomplishes, accord-

---

[24]Locke, *Concerning Human Understanding*, chap. XXVII, p. 335.

ing to Locke, through consciousness. A being which cannot do all of these things is not, on Locke's account, a person.

But Locke is fuzzy, if not incoherent, with respect to what the being which hosts consciousness is, or why this being is necessary, given the role Locke gives to consciousness. This is true even when this latter notion is interpreted to mean, as he quite plausibly intends, memory. Locke's view requires the "thinking intelligent Being" to be the immaterial, thinking *host* of the qualities of personhood—to be able, in essence, *to articulate what a person is*. But in determining *personal identity*, Locke resorts to a *property* of that host "Being" and not to the host itself. The host, the immaterial substance, is the bearer of person qualities, but it does so presumably always in association with some material substance.

It is noteworthy that it is in terms of that association, of material and immaterial, that for Locke the notion "Man" has application. He departs from popular usage and clearly distinguishes between the notions "person" and "Man," exhibited in the following passage.

> This also shews wherein Identity of the same *Man* consists; viz. in nothing but a participation of the same continued Life, by constantly fleeting Particles of Matter, in succession vitally united to the same organized Body. . . . For if the *Identity* of Soul alone makes the same Man, and there be nothing in the Nature of Matter, . . . it will be possible, that those Men, living distant Ages, and of different Tempers, may have been the same Man.[25]

By contrast, the identity of persons consists only in continuity of consciousness. Hence Locke's person certainly is not an entity we can point to but rather is the sort of thing which is in some way associated with that which we can point to, a living human body. Indeed, Locke discusses the possibility of one and the same consciousness (one and the same person) inhabiting two different substances. He even thinks there may be several identifiable persons serially inhabiting one and the same substance, one by day and the other by night, but remaining uncommunicating. He concedes: "But if it be possible for the same Man to have distinct incommunicable consciousness at different times, it is past doubt the same Man would at different times make different Persons."[26] In individuating persons, Locke appeals to consciousness only. Locke's person is relegated to insignificance; we are left with the possibility of a disembodied or floating consciousness, had by no human being in particular, and with a career all its own.

Among those who have been critical of various aspects of Locke's account are Thomas Reid and Joseph Butler. Their objections are directed primarily against Locke's conception of personal identity, the subject of the following section. But Reid, in developing his criticisms, presents his own view of what a person is. He defines a person as "something indivisible, and is what Leibnitz

[25]Locke, *Concerning Human Understanding*, pp. 331–32.
[26]Locke, *Concerning Human Understanding*, p. 342.

[sic] calls a *monad.*"[27] Regarding that something, presumably that same thing which in Locke's ontology is referred to as a Being, he says:

> My personal identity, therefore, implies the continued existence of that indivisible thing which I call *myself.* Whatever this self may be, it is something which thinks, and deliberates, and resolves, and acts, and suffers. I am not thought, I am not action, I am not feeling; I am something that thinks, and acts and suffers. My thoughts, and actions, and feelings, change every moment; they have no continued but a successive, existence; but that *self,* or *I,* to which they belong, is permanent, and has the same relation to all the succeeding thoughts, actions, and feelings which I call mine.[28]

Reid's identification of what constitutes the person with Leibniz's monad, to which it bears some striking resemblance, is a curious one, but he does not elaborate. At any rate, whatever its precise nature, the person is, in Reid's ontology, that something without which all talk of personal identity lacks point. It is something which remains immutably the same, and it is on this account that its identity is, in Reid's language, "perfect," not admitting of degrees. For Reid, as well as for Locke, that which is the person is a special sort of thing, a thinking thing, the *I,* or self, something to be strictly distinguished from any material association it may have. It has no parts. In Reid's terminology, "A part of a person is a manifest absurdity."

This is as good a place as any to take a backward glance at the terrain we have so far covered. With respect to its enabling us to fulfill our introductory task of ascertaining, if possible, the necessary and sufficient conditions for the notion person to apply, what does this all come to? It would be extremely odd to suppose that personal identity has little or nothing to do with what we think a person to be. Indeed, it is on this score that Reid most severely castigates Locke. In his account of personal identity, Locke seems to have lost sight of the centrality of the "intelligent being," the being that does the thinking, and instead equates personal identity with one of its features, that is, consciousness, which, for Reid, is merely an indicator of the existence of that being in terms of which alone the notion of personal identity can be understood.

But there are also the materialists who see no need for an immaterial thing and who, as a consequence, offer a radically different account of what it is to be a person. We need the kind of resolution which settles the issue unambiguously between immaterialist and materialist conceptions of the person. Without it, it is pointless, at least at this stage, to attempt a characterization tied to some particular kind of underlying hardware, material or immaterial. To insist otherwise, as a prerequisite to understanding personal identity, we are likely to get nowhere. In the light of this impasse, a more promising strategy is to suspend further treatment for the time being of what a person is and consider the question of personal identity. We can then consider certain qualities persons

[27]Reid, *Essays on the Intellectual Powers of Man,* chap. III, sec. ii, p. 343.
[28]Reid, *Essays on the Intellectual Powers of Man,* p. 343.

are known to have or are capable of having, qualities such as memory and consciousness. From our inquiry, these emerge as, in some sense, necessary to personhood.

So rather than pursuing any further the metaphysical question regarding the nature of persons, we will now seek to discover how an individual human being is over time one and the same person. Intuitively, this seems to be putting the cart before the horse. It does seem wrong-headed not to have in hand some clear notion of what a person is before addressing questions of personal identity, but as should be evident by now, movement in that direction soon comes to a standstill. So let us suspend our intuitions and attempt the indirect route. Let us consider personal identity. It may be that the question of what constitutes a person and the question of personal identity are either the same question or that they are inextricably linked.

### Of Personal Identity

In an essay entitled "Of Personal Identity," Joseph Butler distinguishes sharply between what he calls "the loose and popular," on the one hand and, on the other hand, "the strict and philosophical" senses of identity. The former sense of identity holds for physical objects qua physical objects, and the latter sense for persons only. To say of any physical object $O_1$ at time $t_1$ that it is the same object as $O_2$ at another time $t_2$ is to employ the loose sense of identity. But to say of person $P_1$ existing at time $t_1$ that that person is identical with person $P_2$ existing at another time $t_2$ is to employ the notion of identity in a strict and philosophical sense. Regarding the distinction, Butler says:

> In the loose and popular sense, then, the life, and the organization, and the plant, are justly said to be the same, notwithstanding the perpetual change of the parts. But in a strict and philosophical manner of speech, no man, no being, no mode of being, nor any thing, can be the same with that, with which it hath indeed nothing the same. Now, sameness is used in this latter sense when applied to persons. The identity of these, therefore, cannot subsist with diversity of substance.[29]

Writing largely in support of Butler's view, Roderick Chisholm remarks:

> This thesis might be construed as telling us that there is a very clear sense in which the concept of sameness, or identity, as applied to persons persisting through time, is *not* subject to "defeat" or to "convention"—that there is a very clear sense in which, so far as "defeat" and "convention" are concerned, "the same person" differs fundamentally from "the same ship," "the same house," and "the same railroad train."[30]

[29]Joseph Butler, "Of Personal Identity," in *Personal Identity*, ed. John Perry (Berkeley: University of California Press, 1975), p. 101.

[30]Chisholm, "The Loose and Popular and the Strict and Philosophical Senses of Identity," p. 102.

In Butler's view, therefore, the "Jewelled South," discussed above, is the same ship, though now aluminum, in the loose and popular sense only. After all, and as Thomas Reid would no doubt say, the ship continued to bear the same name with which it began. The pervasive fact of change, to which Hume had earlier called attention—however slight that change might be—renders it such that no physical object can be one and the same object at two distinct times, in Butler's strict and philosophical sense.

But the same is not true of persons. So, following Butler, it is true that many years ago I, H. E. P., lived in a place far removed from where I do now live. It is also true that I, H. E. P., am now seated before a computer and engaged in writing regarding that bit of personal history. But it is no less true that that object which I now refer to as my body has no particle in common with the body which those many years ago I referred to as my body. Hence it is not, speaking strictly and philosophically, the same body. On the other hand, throughout this physical transformation, I—still following Butler—persist as the very same person I was then. Further, I, who clearly recall these details, am the same person; and if that is true, I am not identical with the changing thing which at any given time I call my body. I have persisted while my body of yesteryear has not. The principle seems clear. Where there is change there can be no identity in the strict and philosophical sense. Identity in this sense essentially presupposes qualitative, that is to say, substantial, permanence and persistence of the entity involved.

Before we reflect critically on Butler's distinction, we should consider along with it a similar distinction made by Reid, though along somewhat different lines. Reid says: "The identity of a person is a perfect identity: wherever it is real, it admits of no degrees; and it is impossible that a person should be in part the same and in part different; because a person is a *monad,* and is not divisible into parts. . . . The identity . . . which we ascribe to bodies, whether natural or artificial, is not perfect identity; it is rather something, which for the conveniency of speech, we call identity. It admits of a great change of the subject, providing the change be *gradual;* sometimes, even a total change."[31]

For Butler, as well as for Reid, that sense of identity applicable to persons must be radically distinguished from that applicable to sensible objects. The line of demarcation is an unbridgeable metaphysical one. The sense of identity applicable to persons is strict; the entities considered identical remain substantially and essentially one and the same over time. The sense which applies to sensible objects involves entities which by their nature are susceptible over time to material or substantial modification, however slight. In contradistinction, that which constitutes the person, the subject of psychological experiences, is a self, an immaterial substance. It, this spirit or ego, is permanent. And since, to use Reid's characterization, it is itself a monad, hence by its very nature indivisible, it necessarily has no parts. Nothing can be subtracted from it

---

[31]Reid, *Essays on the Intellectual Powers of Man,* essay III, chap. 3, sec. ii, pp. 244–46.

and nothing added to it. It is immune to any change or modification of this sort. The notion "part of a person" makes no sense. Hence identity as it applies to persons is nothing but the continued existence or persistence of that which cannot but endure as one and the same entity over time.

But what if the metaphysical foundations on which this distinction is based turn out to be insecure? What becomes of the distinction if this particular ego theory turns out to be false? To the complete detriment of the view in question, what if the term "person" does not in fact refer to anything immaterial? Let us reflect for a moment. Perhaps expressing the question in terms of the view turning out to be false is assuming a great deal too much. As we noted earlier in discussing Cartesian dualism, we cannot show *conclusively,* not even in principle, that there is no self or ego in the Cartesian sense. (How would we go about accomplishing this?) We may, of course, argue that the notion of an immaterial substance is incoherent, that nothing recognizably true or false can be said of such a notion. We might say that questions concerning the individuation of selves so interpreted are so intractable as to make the view dangle with no conceivable relief in sight. But arguing thus is not logically equivalent to showing conclusively that the ego view is false. It certainly makes the view appear implausible, even extremely so, but establishing implausibility and establishing falsity are two very distinct notions requiring very different epistemic criteria.

But there remain very real problems for the view that personal identity has to do with an entity, material or immaterial, some unitary something called the person, that the substantive "person" names some one thing. Before we can tackle some of the difficulties it poses, we need to attend to some housecleaning, with respect to consciousness, on the one hand, and to memory on the other.

### Of Consciousness and Memory

Locke maintains that personal identity consists in continuity or sameness of consciousness, to which Reid responds that to think in this way is not only to confuse consciousness and memory but to fail to see what the sheer fact of consciousness presupposes. Consciousness, he argues, is by its very nature momentary and fleeting and can only be of that which is present, whereas memory is of that which is past, acts or experiences which are distinctively and unmistakably ours. And in one of his more charitable moments Reid allows that this is probably what Locke meant but expressed rather ineptly.

The logic of the second half of Reid's criticism amounts to an articulation of the requirement that where consciousness exists something is conscious, to which consciousness (or memory) bears witness. It is precisely with regard to that something that the question of personal identity arises. Recall that Locke identifies that something to be exactly what a person is, "a thinking intelligent Being." But Locke, as both Butler and Reid sternly point out, is not sufficiently attentive to the matter of getting things exactly right. His clumsiness is evident in the following:

> For since consciousness always accompanies thinking, and 'tis that, that makes every one to be, what he calls *self;* and thereby distinguishes himself from all other thinking things, in this alone consists *personal Identity,* i.e., the sameness of a rational Being: And as far as this consciousness can be extended backwards to any past Action or Thought, so far reaches the Identity of that *Person;* it is the same *self* now it was then; and 'tis by the same *self* with this present one that now reflects on it, that that Action was done.[32]

A little reflection here on Locke's part might have sufficed to point up the incongruities. For example, the statement above, which on the face of it *contends* that consciousness *makes* one what is called a self or person, might seem a mere grammatical infelicity rather than a bit of bad metaphysics, after reading the entire text. For as it stands, the contention requires that consciousness, expressed as a constitutive property, be ontologically prior to that of which it is a property, namely, the self or person. That of which any $S$ is constituted is, in order of being, ontologically prior to that $S$. A further muddle concerns the contradiction which necessarily develops if it is asserted on the one hand that the self is simple, that is, indivisible, and on the other that it is constituted. However, if consciousness as it appears in the text is not a constitutive property, but was rather meant to be viewed as the necessary and sufficient condition of personal identity, then Locke's lapse is not very serious. In the ensuing discussion, therefore, we will assume that Locke intended "memory" where he employed the term "consciousness." And in view of the foregoing discussion, we will also assume that memory was employed by him as the sole necessary and sufficient self-identity indicator. These moves now place Locke, Reid, and Butler on a similar footing regarding the role memory plays in determining or ascertaining personal identity.

But exactly how reliable is memory in ascertaining personal identity? Were Locke and others right in locating memory as that psychological phenomenon which alone accounts for the epistemic claim that persons $P_1$ and $P_2$ are one and the same person?

Let us proceed to investigate these and related questions by tackling what seems to many people as intuitively certain. Like you, I recall many things I did when I was growing up. I remember numerous faces and places and occasions, and feelings, too. For many of these, I can fill in the details with a high degree of confidence; for others, the details are a bit fuzzy. But were there to have been preserved a faithful record of them all, though now I have forgotten them, I feel confident that I would now recognize a great deal more as the things which I once experienced, either as having done or had done to me. The record would fill in the memory blanks and I would be back there all over again. Generalizing

---

[32]Locke, *Concerning Human Understanding,* bk. II, chap. xxvii, p. 335.

from my own case, the underlying assumption here is that we cannot remember someone else's experiences as our own. Thus what I recall doing is *my* doing, was done by *me* and by no one else. It follows from this that I who did it is one and the same person doing the recalling. As Reid would say: "If it was done by me, I must have existed at that time, and continued to exist from that time to the present."[33]

This all seems intuitively correct. After all, we cannot possibly *recall*—or so we affirm—what we did not in some way experience. But Reid also holds, as many a person assumes, that regarding "proof" of personal identity, memory "gives undoubted certainty."[34] Let us put memory to the test. Let us see, in what follows, whether memory is (1) according to *Locke,* a necessary and sufficient condition of personal identity, and (2) its deliverances are, following Reid, "undoubtedly certain."

There is a familiar cliché that says that truth is sometimes stranger than fiction. But often technology plays the role of taming fiction. So, in the interest of our investigation, let us suppose that the cases to be discussed next are technologically feasible. The first case is a modification of Derek Parfit's teletransporter thought experiment.[35]

*Case 2.4: Five Uncle Benedicts of Guam?*    Let us suppose the following. You have an uncle living in Guam whose name is Benedict. Uncle Benedict is conned into being teletransported in the following way: Via a teletransported blueprint that covers the distance at the speed of light, an exact replica of Benedict is created on a distant planet. As part of the process, the entire body of Benedict of Guam is completely destroyed so that we now have on this distant planet an exact replica qualitatively indistinguishable from Uncle Benedict. This replica thinks and acts just like Uncle Benedict of Guam. Indeed, in his conversations he recalls experiences he claims he had while he was in Guam and he gives as his name Benedict of Guam. Not only that, he calls you by radio and, in the way characteristic of Uncle Benedict, calls you by your nickname and tells you that he is doing fine.

Now, *is* he your Uncle Benedict? What if there were multiple replications instead of one, say, five; and what if the original Uncle Benedict, instead of being destroyed, were kept alive during the entire process so that there are now an original and five exact replicas? How many uncles do you now have? Is there just one and the same person persisting, namely, Uncle Benedict or do we have six distinct persons? Suppose that four of the replicas and Uncle Benedict of Guam died, and the fifth replica were teletransported to Guam. Is this person your uncle? The answers to these questions are not all obvious. A crucial ques-

---

[33]Reid, *Essays on the Intellectual Powers of Man,* essay III, chap. iii, p. 243.

[34]Reid, *Essays on the Intellectual Powers of Man,* p. 245.

[35]Derek Parfit, *Reasons and Persons* (Oxford, England: Oxford University Press, 1986). pp. 199–204.

tion at this point is whether personal identity, being one and the same person, necessarily presupposes a one-to-one relationship between candidates for the identity relation. Or is the concept of personal identity compatible with a one-to-many relationship?

Before discussing this case, let's add two more hypothetical cases, one of fission and the other of fusion.

*Case 2.5:The Dis/appearance of Linda J.* Imagine that the right hemisphere of Linda J.'s brain is transplanted into the cerebrally vacant head of Daisy D., and the left half is transplanted into the similarly vacant head of Susie B. Now suppose that each hemisphere in its new location functions as though it were an entire brain. Suppose further that Daisy D. and Susie B. can each now recall the sorts of things which only someone identical with Linda J. could possibly have had noninferential access to; all their recollections up to the time of the transplant are of experiences uniquely had by Linda J. and by no one else. Does Linda J. survive as (1) the composite of both Daisy D. and Susan B., (2) equally the one as the other, or (3) only one of them? Alternatively, has Linda J. simply failed to survive?

*Case 2.6:The Amazing Wonderdoc.* Now imagine something like the reverse of the foregoing case. In a mythical Wonderworld, Alice and Jenny fell asleep on a couch. They are visited by Wonderdoc, who anesthetizes the two women and merges their bodies so that there no longer are two but one normal-looking body. Wonderdoc so contrives things that the right hemisphere of Alice's brain and the left hemisphere of Jenny's are integrated to become the new brain of the new person who upon waking, and without any apparent surprise, speaks of and introduces herself as Alijenn. She is extremely articulate. Her memories are free of contradictory details, such as having two unrelated fathers and the like. They are of events and experiences unique to the actual careers of Alice and Jenny up to the time when they fell asleep on the couch. Do we now have the rather odd, if intelligible, case of two persons in one, or do we have the equally odd case of two distinct persons? Have Alice and Jenny survived as one person or do Alice and Jenny coexist? Alternatively, is Alijenn an altogether distinct person, Alice and Jenny having died?

The memory criterion, therefore, understood as the necessary and sufficient condition of personal identity, is in serious trouble. Memory presupposes that which it is supposed to establish, namely personal identity. It poses, as well, a closely related and particularly crucial problem with respect to individuation, as the three cases just presented illustrate.

In all three cases the memory criterion is met, or so it would seem. Yet we have difficulty going from there to make the relevant identifications. Benedict of the distant planet can, presumably, respond to questioning in the way in which Benedict of Guam would have, and provides much the same autobiographical details. But we also know that the body of Benedict of Guam was destroyed. There is in this instance no spatiotemporal continuity between original and replica, though there is qualitative continuity. If Benedict of Guam survives in this new location, the puzzling question is, in virtue of what considerations. The case is rendered still more puzzling when we discover that we have not one but five exact replicas, each claiming to be Benedict of Guam. Exactly who is Benedict of Guam, *your* uncle?

Suppose we attempt to resolve the issue in terms of the continued existence of "that indivisible thing that I call myself," in Reid's view; in terms of some immaterial and indivisible ego or substance, which in this instance is uniquely Benedict's. Then the question of how many identical selves Benedict is capable of having does not arise. Since, presumably, the ego theory permits only one ego per living human body, Benedict alive and his replica cannot be one and the same person. If there are two numerically distinct living human beings, there are two persons. Five claimants to identity with Benedict would necessitate there being five persons. What constitutes a person, as we noted earlier with respect to this view, admits of neither degrees of personhood nor of ambiguity regarding personal identity over time. Person $A$ is identical with person $B$ if and only if numerically one and the same ego persists, that is, remains one and the same from $A$ through $B$. This makes the ego theory entirely determinate in the sense that there are, following this theory, no borderline or tricky cases of persons or of personal identity. Either person $A$ is or is not identical with person $B$.

But this way of resolving our puzzle seems not a little implausible since it appears to imply that there is no dearth of egos to keep pace with advances in technology, should reduplication become technologically feasible. Egos can virtually be multiplied at will. Moreover, settling the issue on the basis of an indivisible and invisible ego alone neglects the sole evidence for the existence of the ego—memory or psychological continuity. Recall that the claimants' autobiographies coincide with Benedict's, so that we cannot pronounce then impersonating frauds: they must have some determinable relation to their ancestry. And on the ego theory, it is memory or psychological continuity which provides the crucial test of personal identity. Of course we can argue in response that the mere existence of more than one individual making the identity claim *a priori* establishes that there is more than one person; indeed, there are just as many egos as there are claimants to identity. But this response merely complicates things. Let us for the moment, however, suspend further consideration of this case until we have had a closer look at the other two cases.

The case of Daisy D. and Susie B.—the fission case—is to some extent like the case of Benedict of Guam at the point where there is not one but five exact replicas of Benedict. The notable difference is that there is qualitative as well as spatiotemporal continuity between what was intimately and crucially a part of Linda J. The continuity concerns her brain and memory contents, and what now are the brains and the memory contents of the two new women, up to the time of the transplant. This spells problems again for the memory theory as well as for the ego theory. Either one ego, Linda J.'s, died and, following the transplant, was succeeded by two distinctly different egos, Daisy D.'s and Susie B.'s; or Linda J.'s ego endures as either Daisy D.'s or Susie B.'s. But either alternative runs afoul of the evident psychological and spatiotemporal continuity in the case. Thus to say that Linda J. died seems indefensibly arbitrary. Alternatively, to hold that the person Linda J. exists as one or the other successor not only leaves us with a multiplicity of egos to account for but also with the seemingly intractable difficulty of determining which ego, Daisy D.'s or Susan B.'s, is Linda J.'s.

The third and final case—the fusion case—also raises problems of a sort similar to the foregoing, though in reverse. Here again, assuming the ego theory described earlier in this chapter, we face the twin problem of ego disappearance or death and ego generation where two become one. Determining personal identity in accordance with this long-standing theory poses what seem to be intractable problems. But this circumstance by no means establishes that there exists no such thing as an ego, that the term "ego" has no referent in the sense required by the theory. We can contend, however, that in making what is essentially an ontological posit, and then relying upon what is so posited as the basis for making personal identity determinations, we go about things the wrong way. To posit the existence of *X*, and to show that *X* actually exists, are distinctly different things; the latter, unlike the former, requires some reliable method of empirical inquiry.

Let us recall from Reid's *Essays*, a passage which is decidedly central to the ego theory we have been discussing.

My personal identity, therefore, implies the continued existence of that indivisible thing which I call *myself*. Whatever this self may be, it is something which thinks, and deliberates, and resolves, and acts, and suffers. I am not thought, I am not action, I am not feeling; and I am something that thinks, and acts, and suffers. My thoughts, and actions, and feelings, change every moment; they have no continued, but a successive, existence; but that *self*, or *I*, to which they belong, is permanent, and has the same relation to all the succeeding thoughts, actions, and feelings which I call mine. Such are the notions that I have of my personal identity. But perhaps, it may be said, this may all be fancy without reality. How do you know—what evidence have you—that there is such a permanent self which has a claim to all the thoughts, actions, and feelings which you call yours? To this I answer, that the proper evidence I have of all this is *remembrance*. I remember twenty years ago I conversed with such a person; I remember several things that passed in that conversation; my memory testifies, not only that this was done but that it was done by me who now remembers it. If it was done by me, I must have existed at that time, and continued to exist from that time to the present; if the identical person whom I call myself had not a part in that conversation, my memory is fallacious; it gives a distinct and positive testimony of what is not true.[36]

Memory, even accuracy of recall, is thus not decisive in determining personal identity. As in the cases discussed above, psychologically overlapping autobiographies where for some given period of time the entire memory contents of two distinct individuals are indistinguishably the same makes memory clearly not a sufficient condition.

But is it a necessary one? No one has direct acquaintance with an immaterial and enduring self that deliberates, but everyone seems freely disposed to introduce many an assertion by expressions like: "I well remember the time when . . . ," "I was there at that time . . . ," and so on. They clearly imply that, in some sense, the *I* then is one and the same as the *I* now. So for all of us, there is a tacit and usually authoritative appeal to memory, not to *assure* ourselves that we are over time one and the same person, or to endorse the existence of a transcendent ego. The appeal serves to underwrite our past. We hold ourselves responsible for what we recall as *our* assertions and *our* acts. For us humans, therefore, memory locates, holds, and fashions the various time-slices of our lives into coherent wholes so that we are able to identify specific biographies as uniquely ours—you, your own; and I, mine. No other feature of our existence seems capable of accomplishing this integration. Hence we may conclude that, so far as autobiographical coherence is concerned, the ability to recall events in our past is a necessary condition. We may, as a corollary to this condition, even venture to hold that total inability to recall our past renders problematic our status as a person. This does not imply in any way that the memory theory is dependent on the existence of a persisting ego.

The issue still remains, though, as to the identity of the individual doing the recalling. Let us grant, at least for the moment, that memory, flawed as it sometimes is, is a necessary condition for personal identity. Recall that both Daisy D. and Susie B., on the basis of their memory contents, are prime candidates for the position of being one and same as Linda J. But they both cannot be. The same is true of the fused individual in the third case.

Perhaps the time has come for us to do some metaphysical as well as some conceptual housecleaning, to call into question commitment to an ontology which seems to make no practical difference. The Reidean *person as ego* is, for all practical purposes, wholly beyond empirical reach. Appealing to it in attempting to resolve cases such as the puzzling ones we looked at above has proven entirely futile. On some accounts memory is the sole evidential access to the self, ego, or person, but it affords no such access and, indeed, tells us nothing definitive about a transcendent self. The ego, so understood, cannot, therefore, be an object of *empirical* concern. In order to come to grips with the very real, rather mundane issue of personal identity, we should treat the term

---

[36]Reid, *Essays on The Intellectual Powers of Man*, p. 249.

"person" as nothing but a figure of speech which we may apply or withhold as our purposes require. We can also attach it to a type of empirically accessible, nontranscendent, object. But to exactly what, and why to just such objects?

Before we proceed with this question, we need to remind ourselves of a number of things. First, that the ego theory has proven ineffectual does not in itself prove that one who remains committed to an ontology which includes egos is mistaken. Second, to secure the claim that the term "ego" refers to nothing in reality, we would need to appeal to appropriate criteria. But no set of criteria can be self-justifying. Any set of criteria presupposes some epistemic system, some set of rules and principles which address the warrantability of the claims made with reference to them. Third, there is no presuppositionless theory of knowledge. In developing epistemic criteria, workability, convention, need, experience, and the like play varying roles. There is no certain Archimedean point available to us to render epistemically secure the systems we appeal to. And when it comes to grappling with crucial matters about our efforts to ascertain what kind of things we are, what kind of place we inhabit, what sorts of things exist, the connection between ontology and epistemology becomes close. By and large, the knowledge claims we make presuppose an orienting ontology which may or may not be fully articulated and which we may or may not be conscious of. But that ontology, too, can only be a matter of commitment, not demonstration. We either provisionally assume an ontology—and in some sense remain skeptically disposed toward it—or we are by default or reflective choice committed to one.

The metaphysical and conceptual housecleaning which we engaged in did not attempt to replace bogus entities like egos with real ones whose existence and nature are beyond question. We did it to help us get securely past our untried intuitions. The world and its furnishings about which we wonder may be quite different from what we suppose, but its physicality, narrowly or broadly defined, is a feature which—some idealists notwithstanding—seems beyond reasonable question. This realization certainly has pragmatic implications.

### The I Reconsidered

In developing an alternative view of what a person is, we do well to consider—and eventually abstract from—those entities or objects with which we are all familiar. These entities we ordinarily, in non-Reidean terms, intuitively designate or pick out as paradigm instances of persons. You and I are such instances. We are first and foremost nontranscendent and empirically accessible things. We are four-dimensional physical objects, the type of thing which, to use G. E. Moore's term, can be "met with in space." Moreover, like Reid's *I*, we are capable of a wide range of psychological states, remembering being one of them. And, again like Reid's self or ego, our *I* is capable of self-reference. It is capable of positioning itself as subject to object. It is able, also, to acknowledge the existence of our selves. In brief, physicality, as well as the ability to engage in deliberative acts, is essential to being the kind of thing we ordinarily describe as persons. As persons, we are capable of regarding ourselves not only as subjects of experience but also as objects among a variety of objects from which we distinguish ourselves.

We do not understand this contention as saying that we are, as persons, constituted as a peculiar amalgam of two distinct substances, the one physical and the other psychological or mental. On the contrary, what the contention minimally asserts is that to be a person at least two conditions must be met. We may refer to the one as the physicality condition—for short, the $P$ condition— and to the other as the psychological condition—the $M$ condition. The contention also intends that the relation between the two conditions be as follows: the $P$ condition constitutes the necessary material possibility of the $M$ condition. That is to say, without the $P$ condition, the $M$ condition cannot be realized. So on this view, there are no disembodied persons, because there cannot be. To speak of a person is always, at some level of reference, to speak of something physical. It obviously also makes reference to an entity with mental capacities—the capacity to reflect, to deliberate, to remember, and so on. Both conditions are necessarily invoked when we speak of persons qua persons. In maintaining this position, we imply nothing of a determinate nature regarding what specific form the physical underpinnings may assume. It is conceivable that the kind of psychology relevant to our investigation of personal identity may be realized in or brought about by a wide variety of physical wherewithal.

In sum then, we are, qua persons, inherently physical systems which are so constituted that we are capable of distinctively mental states and acts. That is, such mental states as do occur are, to borrow an expression of Searle's, "caused by and realized in" the structure and operations of this type of physical system.[37] Identifying the specific entity or structure in the system causally responsible for the psychological phenomena does not much matter at this stage. Whether the psychological phenomena are further reducible will not be discussed at this time. This subject will be taken up in subsequent chapters, in particular when we come to deal with issues having to do with folk psychology and with consciousness.

With this as a working, though admittedly sketchy, view as to what we might consider a person, we now endeavor to see what the puzzles raised by the cases we considered earlier come to. It might be to our advantage to pretend that all the persons named in all the cases are, for the purposes of our investigation, real humans. Hence they are biographically unique individuals, such as you and I presumably are, with respect to their lived lives or experiences, characters, capacities, and abilities. Let us, in consequence, adopt the technical term *bio-print* and use it to stand for such psychological aspects of continuity as make for a person's being uniquely just the person that he or she is. This continuity naturally includes details having to do not only with character

---

[37]John Searle, *Intentionality* (Cambridge, England: Cambridge University Press, 1983), p. ix.

but with capacities and abilities as well. My *bio-print* is uniquely and peculiarly mine, and yours, for the same reason with respect to you, is uniquely and peculiarly yours. It is that which, for each of us, makes you and me the persons that we severally and distinctively are and successfully challenges any candidate claiming to be you or me. Admittedly this characterization can be more precise, but nothing terribly weighty hangs on it at the moment. Our great concern at this stage should be to guard against hypostatizing, that is, "thingifying," one's bio-print so that it is thought of as independent of any physical realization.

We may now, with respect to personal identity over time, posit the following to be necessary. For any person $P$ at a given time, and for any person $Q$ at some future time, $Q$ is one and the same person as $P$ if and only if (1) $Q$'s bio-print is continuous with $P$'s—that is, contains no temporal breaks or discontinuities and (2) the physical stages stretching from $P$ to $Q$ are in an unbroken sequence, and (3) there is no branching; $P$ does not give rise to multiple $Q$'s. The reason for this last condition is that identity is a one-to-one, not a one-to-many relation. Conditions (1) and (2) satisfy the principle of noncontradiction. It cannot be the case at one and the same time and with respect to the same individual that the statements "$P$ does not exitst" and "$P$ does exist" are both true. If at time $t_1$ $P$'s bio-print exists, but at a later time, time $t_2$, it does not, then whatever $Q$ that exists at a still later time, time $t_3$, cannot be one and the same person as $P$. The same would be true for condition (2): Since a bio-print is realized only by a physical realizer, any temporal discontinuity in this realizer entails a corresponding discontinuity in the life answering to that bio-print. Hence, $P$'s discontinuity at time $t_2$, in either of the two respects, is nothing less than the death of $P$.

Let us now return to the puzzling cases sketched above. Let us take the case of Benedict of Guam. Recall that the first time around, the entire body of Benedict is destroyed as an outcome of the teletransporting procedure so that he does not coexist with his absolute replica in the distant planet. Let us, for short, identify the original Benedict by the designation "$B$" and the teletransported version as "$R$." If either of the following is true, the $R$ is not one and the same person as $B$: (a) $R$'s bio-print is not continuous with $B$'s in the sense expressed in condition (1) and (b) the physical medium which realizes $R$'s bio-print is not continuous with $B$'s, as per condition (2). We cannot be sure from the information provided that condition (1) was indeed met, but let us suppose that it was. The stuff which realized $R$'s bio-print was, other than that which realized $B$'s. But here again we are not in a position to tell whether the physicality condition, expressed in condition (2), has been violated since there is no requirement that the physical medium which realizes a bio-print be of a specific nature. The physicality condition can be variously instantiated. Condition (2) requires simply that there be unbroken physical continuity. It follows, therefore, that however indistinguishably alike $B$ and $R$ may be, and $R$'s protestations notwithstanding, failure in either of these two conditions will show that $B$ and $R$ are not one and the same person.

This unhappy conclusion would perhaps be more clearly seen were we to suspend condition (3), the branching condition. Then technology can conceivably multiply as many *R*-instances as it dares to. In that case we have a number of possibilities. We may have either any number of crypto-claimants identifying themselves with *P*, or we may kill off all such claimants save one, or we may simply call a moratorium on the unlimited production of *R*'s. But any of these options yields only a pragmatic solution to the puzzle of bio-replication as it affects personal identity or personal survival. So the identity problem is still with us. Bear in mind, too, that our physicalist view—the present alternative to the ego view—of what constitutes a person disallows the kind of ontology which permits of the existence of physically unrealized, that is, disembodied, bio-prints. I confess here to having an insufficiently supported hunch that, first time around, Benedict was bumped off and *R* was somebody else.

The remaining two cases, the one representing limited fission (where one person is succeeded by two persons) and the other fusion (where just the reverse is true) pose subtle problems. In both these "technologically possible" cases, conditions (1) and (2) are clearly met. Condition (3), the branching condition, is violated by both cases, but in rather different ways. Roughly put, the common question now is who is continuous with whom.

Let us approach these two cases via two scenarios which appear quite a bit less perplexing but which, respectively, seem clearly analogous to the fission and fusion cases. (1) The point *A* marks the source of a river which flows to point *B*, at which place the waters divide and continue in two independent directions, one flowing northeast to point $C_1$ and the other flowing southeast to a point $C_2$. (2) The points $A_1$ and $A_2$ mark the sources of two streams which flow to point B, at which place they merge and become one river and flow thereafter to point *C*. For each of the two scenarios *B* marks the radical turning point. In (1) we have two distinct possibilities: $ABC_1$ and $ABC_2$, with the stretch *AB* in common. In (2) we have three possibilities: $A_1BC$, $A_2BC$, and *BC*.

With respect to (1), we cannot reasonably maintain that the river stretch $BC_1$, and not $BC_2$, is more properly identified with the antecedent stretch *AB*, or vice versa. We could appeal to comparative size, and the like, to settle the issue but this course seems decidedly arbitrary and lacking in rational justification.[38] In a very real sense, *AB* persists in both directions as part of two numerically distinct rivers, and is as much a part of the one as it is of the other. Identity involves a one-to-one relationship and may in this circumstance be out of the question, but not so survival. In (2), one river emerges with *BC* being the river stretch which unites two distinct streams.[39] Again our reasoning is much the same: not a case of identity but one of persistence or survival. The distinct streams $A_1B$ and $A_2B$ survive in some form in the single river stretch *BC*. In each the extent of persistence is indeterminate, entirely a matter of degree. And in

[38]For a description of Robert Nozick's "closest continuer theory," see Harold Noonan, *Personal Identity* (London: Routledge & Kegan Paul, 1989), pp. 152–54.
[39]Derek Parfit, "Personal Identity," *Philosophical Review*, 80 (1971), 327.

either case, which river we say it is is very largely a matter of convention. We cannot reasonably say anything more determinate.

As with fissioned and fused rivers, so with fissioned and fused persons—convention makes the call and keeps the score. Should something approximating fission and fusion technology become a reality, and we are faced with real people as products of such technology, our knowledge of who they are is not significantly improved by having them tell us definitively who they *think* they are on the basis of their unbroken continuity with a biography which has its origin in the distant past. Whatever access to the past they may have as descendants of such an ancestry, they cannot be capable of incorrigible answers regarding their personal identities. Indeed, with respect to determining who they respectively are, they would know nothing more than *we* know. Their identity secrets would, in principle, be a matter of public knowledge. This would be so if our two river scenarios correctly represent the identity puzzles they present. Of course, we may object that rivers unlike persons are not conscious things, and therefore the analogy cannot hold. But it should be responded that while the premise with respect to the possession of consciousness is true, the conclusion clearly does not follow. The analogy does not in any way turn on the assumption of any fundamental similarity between a person and a river. It turns on a formal resemblance between two types of thing. For each of these, though in different senses, the idea of continuous flow is a defining feature—for the former, the flow is psychological, for the latter, material. The analogy is not concerned with the structural content of the two types of thing.

From the discussion of these three cases, we see that we must distinguish personal identity and personal survival. Regardless of theory, personal identity logically presupposes a one-to-one relationship. A single thing $S$ cannot be one and the same as many distinct things, however indistinguishably like $S$ they may be. Identity is not a one-to-many relation. This consideration accounts for the branching condition specified above which rules out identity just in case there are multiple successors in a continuity progression. But, as in the case of persons where, like a river, what $S$ stands for over time may be likened to a flow, $S$ may enjoy unbroken continuity with multiple successors. The persistence of $S$ is then a matter of degree.

We may be puzzled about the identity of a relative who survives a technological transplant. But while, as Reid observed, the notion "part of a person" makes no sense, it might be quite sensible to say that such and such an unnamed brain donor survives, to a greater or lesser degree, as part of the psychological makeup of the person who is now my cousin.

## IN BRIEF

In this chapter we explored Hume's theory of mind as perception—the so-called bundle theory. "For my part," says Hume, "when I enter most intimately into what I call *myself*, I always stumble on some particular perception or other, . . . I never can catch *myself* at any time without a perception, and never can observe anything but the perception.[40] With Hume, therefore, perception takes the place of Descartes's *I*. Hume thus avoids the difficulties of dualism but his perception theory of mind encounters difficulties of its own. Hume was all too aware of this but by his own admission, he was unable to resolve it. Questions about personal identity, perception itself, and memory are among those that pinpoint some of the difficulties with Hume's notion of mind.

A discussion of the notion of identity served as a background for the consideration of personal identity. In discussing both we employed several thought experiments. These cases helped to bring into focus some of the issues which arise in the attempt to come to grips with such notions as identity over time and especially of what constitutes personal identity. In the discussion of personal identity, we gave critical attention to the views of John Locke and Thomas Reid.

## SUGGESTIONS FOR FURTHER READING

### Classical Texts

BUTLER, JOSEPH, "Of Personal Identity," in *Personal Identity*, ed. John Perry. Berkeley: University of California Press, 1975, p. 101.

HOBBES, THOMAS, "Of Identity and Difference," *Concerning Body*, chap. XI, sec. 7, in *The Metaphysical System of Hobbes*, ed. Mary Whiton Calkins. La Salle, Ill.: Open Court Publishing Company, 1963.

HUME, DAVID, *A Treatise of Human Nature*, ed. L. A. Selby-Bigge. Oxford, England: Clarendon Press, 1949. See especially bk. I, parts I and III.

LOCKE, JOHN, *An Essay Concerning Human Understanding*, ed. Peter H. Nidditch. Oxford, England: Clarendon Press, 1979. Particularly see bk. II, chap. XXVII.

REID, THOMAS, *Essays on the Intellectual Powers of Man*, ed. James Walker. Boston: Phillips, Sampson and Company, 1855. See in particular essay III.

### Commentary

ADAMS, E. M., "The Concept of a Person," *The Southern Journal of Philosophy*, 23 (1985), 403–12.

COBURN, ROBERT C., "Personal Identity Revisited," *Canadian Journal of Philosophy*, 15 (1985), 379–403.

PARFIT, DEREK, *Reasons and Persons*. Oxford, England: Clarendon Press, 1984.

SHOEMAKER, SYDNEY, "Critical Notice of Parfit's *Reasons and Persons*," *Mind*, XCIV (1985), 443–53.

———, "Introspection and the Self," in *Midwest Studies in Philosophy, Vol. X: Studies in the Philosophy of Mind*, pp. 101–20, eds. Peter French, Theodore E. Uehling, and Howard K Wettstein. Minneapolis: University of Minnesota Press, 1986.

---

[40]Hume, *A Treatise of Human Nature*, p. 252.

# 3

## Getting Along
## without the I

The inner man wills an action, the outer executes it.
The inner loses his appetite, the outer stops eating. The inner
man wants and the outer gets. The inner has the impulse which
the outer obeys.

—*B. F. Skinner*[1]

## BEHAVIORISM

Human beings are claim-making entities. We are given to making assertions
about the world and its contents. We express this characteristic through language. There is no limit to the things about which we may make claims, and
correspondingly no limit to the number of claims we may make about any given
thing. But claims do not all share the same epistemic standing. We distinguish
between true claims and false ones, between reliable claims and unreliable ones.
We discriminate among claims primarily in terms of their warrantability, in
terms, that is, of standards and principles with which we suppose they should
comply. Hence the rational virtue of a claim resides only *derivatively* in the authority of the utterer or in the nature of the claim itself, but *originally* in the
character of the system of principles to which appeal is implicitly or explicitly
made with respect to the claim. In the final analysis, therefore, the acceptability of a claim is a function of the system which gives it warrant. To inquire, for
example, whether, any given statement $S$ is true or worth making is, in a round-
about sort of way, to inquire regarding its epistemic standing, to inquire re-

[1]B. F. Skinner, *Science and Human Behavior* (New York: Macmillan Company, 1953), p. 29.

garding its prospects vis-à-vis some grounding set of principles. We sometimes speak of pseudoclaims—as when, for example, claims refer vacuously yet are mistakenly thought by the claimant to refer to actual existents.

The earliest motivation for the closely related views which today we refer to as "behaviorism" seems to have been scientific. The aim was to make claims about mind rationally, that is, scientifically, defensible. As such, the motivation was both epistemic and metaphysical. J. B. Watson, in the 1920s, attempted a bold and radically new approach to the study of mind. He reacted against an "inner-outer" metaphysics of human nature according to which inner but unobservable causes issuing from an inscrutable mind produced outer and observable effects. The old ego-entrenched metaphysics was hopeless. It had so far yielded only pseudo- or nonverifiable claims. As a consequence we could not be said to know anything significant about human thought or behavior. Moreover, since humans are nothing but complex physical systems (or so it was thought), their behavior should on that account be thoroughly accessible to scrutiny via the established methods of the physical sciences. There should be no need to regard humans as a special case requiring a peculiar set of explanatory principles to account for their behavior. In the above quotation, Skinner tersely expresses the myth which Watson before him and he soon after are at pains to explode by this new and radically uncompromising behaviorism.

Not only is the *I* of Cartesian dualism a grave metaphysical mistake, but mental states as inner and causal are alike greatly misconceived, hence misidentified. Instead, all there is to mind, and derivatively to mental states, is described or explained entirely in terms of the interaction between external physical stimuli, or what Skinner sometimes referred to as independent variables, on the one hand, and, on the other, observable responses—dependent variables—of the human organism. The true explanation of mind is a functional or causal one. It is functional, or causal, in the sense that behavioral responses—the dependent variables—are brought about by, or are a function of, external stimuli—independent variables. Understanding the roots or causes of human behavior involves understanding the complex ways in which variables of both types interact. Essentially, to understand behavior is to understand mind. There is nothing over and above behavior to complete the study of mind. Thus the true account of mind, on this view, is one that rests solely on that which is public and wholly accessible to scientific control and investigation. Mind is behavior, and behavior is overt.

The strength of the emphasis on that which is observable owes much to the strong influence of the Vienna Circle of the 1930s. The logical positivists, as members of the Circle came to be called, included Rudolph Carnap. Ludwig Wittgenstein, though at times associated with the Circle, was not a member but, from different perspectives, and in distinctive ways, both he and Carnap made significant contributions to *logical behaviorist* thought. The logical positivist principle of verifiability, for example, according to which the meaning of a statement is its method of verification, had, as one of its motivations, the need to undertake a long overdue bit of metaphysical housecleaning. The thoroughness of this endeavor meant that the Cartesian ego and its mentalistic accoutrements would have to be thrown out. Indeed, metaphysics *in toto* must go. A science of mind must accord with rigorous scientific practice, which means that all its claims have to be verifiable, at least in principle.

But it soon became apparent to some that the exclusive emphasis on overt behavior and on that which is publicly observable seemed to distort things severely. The refusal to recognize the existence of inner causal states—beliefs, desires, and the like—struck many as seriously mistaken. This refusal amounted to ignoring what seemed to be the causes of human behavior. After all, people do act upon particular beliefs or desires which they have. They do seem at times to act deliberately and voluntarily. Further, the new model also seemed incapable of accounting for those decidedly mental phenomena—perception or anger, for example—which, in certain circumstances, not only did not issue in any *observable* behavior but were accompanied by *no* behavior at all.

Partly in response to these and other criticisms of this pioneering form of behaviorism (variously referred to as radical, scientific, or metaphysical behaviorism, depending largely on emphasis) emerged the refinement known indifferently as logical, analytic, methodological, or philosophical behaviorism. Not only overt behavior but *dispositions* to behave now entered into the account of mind. On the face of it, this new form of behaviorism expresses a semantic theory regarding the way to understand mentalistic terms. Gilbert Ryle, one of the foremost proponents of this refinement, writes: "To possess a dispositional property is not to be in a particular state, or to undergo a particular change; it is to be bound or liable to be in a particular state, or to undergo a particular change, when a particular condition is realized."[2] A disposition on this account would be expressible as a conditional of the form "if $p$ then $q$." The antecedent, $p$, of the conditional would express the coming together of such conditions as, presumably, were on any given occasion sufficient to bring about a desired response or behavior. The consequent, $q$, would express the behavior itself. Note especially that on this view the antecedent conditions—the independent variables—are all external and observable; they stand in a causal relation to the behavioral response—the dependent variable. Mental terms are in this way eliminated. To say, for example, "$X$ is thirsty" is to express nothing but an extended conditional. It would be a form something like: "If $X$ were presented with water, and if that water were safe to drink, and provided that . . . and if . . . " —the dots to be replaced by antecedents indicating specific conditions—followed by the appropriate consequent, "$X$ would drink."

One drawback of this way of expressing the meaning of mental terms is that the antecedent conditions, possibly infinite in number, will always be subject to interminable qualification. Hence the definitions in our dictionary of

---

[2]Gilbert Ryle, *The Concept of Mind* (London: Hutchinson & Co., 1960), p. 43.

mental terms must remain open, since they are impossible to complete. We are hardly ever in a position to predict reliably that any specific set of conditions is sufficient to bring about a particular behavioral response by a particular organism. The more complex the organism, the more difficult reliable prediction becomes. We may be able to lead a horse to water and ensure that drinking will indeed occur, as Skinner maintained,[3] but an intelligent human may refuse to go along at all costs.

This is a narrow definition of what it is for an organism to possess a disposition. It is restricted to conditionals expressive of a direct causal link between external stimuli and behavioral response. It seems to turn on what common sense would regard as a simple but serious mistake. The mistake consists in supposing that the causal link that accounts for human behavior can be completed without any reference to inner states of the behaving system. Like anyone else, for example, when I am angry or thirsty or suspicious, I am aware that there is something going on in me. True, I may not be able to provide the details of all that is occurring within me. What is certain is that I am, on those occasions, in a state which inclines me to any of a range of observable behaviors which I may or may not engage in. I may, for example, be seethingly angry but, out of prudence dictated by my values and my beliefs, do nothing observable about it. Such predisposing states, familiar to all of us and decidedly inner, should figure in any attempt to provide a complete causal explanation of behavior. But, as the passage from Ryle indicates, the logical behaviorists deny that inner states are causally relevant in dispositional accounts of behavior.

To illustrate what is meant by the notion "disposition," the brittleness of glass has been a standard example. Let us take a look. No careful examination of what goes into the making of glass reveals brittleness as a constituent element. But it is, nonetheless, a real feature which supervenes upon the constituent properties of such objects. Put another way, things like glass are so constituted with respect to their microstructure that under certain specified circumstances, such as being lightly struck, they are likely to shatter. They are just that kind of thing—always in a state of readiness to go to pieces. Properties of this kind may be described as dispositional. A perfectly sound piece of crystal is, nonetheless, a brittle piece of crystal. And, correspondingly, the brittleness of any brittle thing is never the cause of its breaking. Were this not true, there would exist no brittle things; but obviously there are such things. Hence brittleness is a predisposing feature, not the cause of the demise of things of which it is a feature.

The term "disposition" may, of course, apply to that which is a permanent feature of certain kinds of things, or to features which are relatively short-lived. As applied to things like glass, the term picks out a permanent characteristic, whereas for humans it usually picks out what is temporary. Episodes like anger, or fear, for example, come and go. It is this latter application of the no-

[3]Skinner, *Science and Human Behavior*, p. 31.

tion which has been of special interest to the logical behaviorist. But the semantic view interprets mental terms, ordinarily presumed to be descriptive of mental states, as telescoped conditionals, so that anger, fear, thought, and the like are nothing but disguised conditionals referring to nothing inner. In this way, both logical behaviorism and its metaphysical predecessor disregard any reference to inner mental states.

It is difficult to see what was gained by regarding dispositions in this way. The externalizing of mind is purchased at much too high a price. Once we admit dispositions to behave, it becomes an easy step to acknowledging that some dispositions can be inner. The flight which on occasion is associated with fear, for example, has to be accounted for, in terms of subject's *interpretation* of the object of fear. The object is *seen as* meaning such and such, or *standing for* so and so. Some inner processing of information is occurring based in part, quite naturally, on the existence of a particular set of external stimuli. To omit this inner phenomenon from the account of flight is to omit something very crucial to the explanation of the behavior. The cause of flight is, in part, an inner state, resulting from what the subject at a given time and in a particular set of circumstances takes to be a threatening situation. As glass, being brittle, may shatter, dispositional states of being in humans—fear, anger, and the like— render them liable to specified behaviors. They are mental and internal, and they contribute causally to behavior.

Much can be said in defense of behaviorism. Not only has it been of revolutionary importance to the program of scientific psychology, as Ryle observes, it has also been one of the main sources of the suspicion that the two-worlds story, one world material and the other immaterial, might be a myth. It attempts to remove psychology from the realm of mystery and frame its concerns squarely within the reach of empirical methodology. True, and to its detriment, it vastly exaggerates the connection between mind and behavior, reducing the former to the latter. But the claim that the study of mind cannot be isolated from the study of behavior remains an important one. Its metaphysical commitment seems through and through materialist. Thus the contention sometimes made that logical behaviorism is not a metaphysical theory, seems calculating.[4] While it is true that it is nowhere expressly stated as a metaphysical theory, it very clearly presupposes one. Indeed, some have observed with justification that philosophical behaviorism is nothing but metaphysical behaviorism in disguise.[5] Certainly its motivation as well as its strategy for eliminating mental terms from psychological discourse strongly support this view.

The view that mental terms refer to nothing inner, that mind is external, makes behaviorism's account of mind implausible and flawed. We will now discuss other developments in the study of human behavior that focus on inner states.

[4]Paul Ziff, "About Behaviorism," *Analysis*, 17, no. 2 (October 1956), 132–36.
[5]See Jerry Fodor, "The Mind-Body Problem," *Scientific American*, 244, no. 1 (January 1981), 114–22.

## IDENTITY THEORY

Logical behaviorism, as we have just noted, refuses to acknowledge the existence of inner causal states. All talk about mental terms, so the claim goes, is reducible without remainder to talk about behavior, and all behavior can be accounted for as the direct result of environmental, hence external, causes. But in construing the cause of behavior so narrowly, logical behaviorism finds itself out of step with standard accounts of causation in the physical sciences. It is not unusual in those sciences to regard two observable events as related by cause and effect yet connected by several intervening though unobservable causal stages or links. What came to be known as the identity theory, or central state materialism, was introduced by people sympathetic to logical behaviorism but who, at the same time, sought to remedy what were seen as some of its crucial shortcomings, notable among which was its denial of causal efficacy to mental states. Indeed, at the outset the theory applied primarily to such mental phenomena as seemed especially resistant to translation in logical behaviorist terms—notions like consciousness, sensation, mental imagery, for example—but it later came to apply to all mental phenomena regardless of kind.

The basic claim of the theory is that any and all mental states are identical with brain states, or as the central state materialists would say, with states of the central nervous system. This claim is a *scientific* thesis, not a *semantic* theory having to do with the meaning of terms—the truth of which can be established by empirical investigation. This is a bold claim. What it asserts is that the mental is in reality physical. So there is nothing distinctively or peculiarly mental.

Three versions of the theory ought to be identified. The earliest, pioneered by the Australians U. T. Place and J. J. C. Smart, identifies mental states with material states, with states of the central nervous system. This would mean, for example, that consciousness, sensation, thought, beliefs, desires, and the like are nothing but material states. The second is due largely to Herbert Feigl. The following passage from his essay "Mind-Body, *Not* a Pseudo-Problem" gives terse expression to his view. Note that this version, unlike the preceding, does not expressly identify the mental with the material. Indeed, Feigl's is an *identity of referents of two sets of terms with widely differing senses*. To resolve the mind/body puzzles, he says:

> The solution that appears the most plausible to me, and that is entirely consistent with a thoroughgoing naturalism, is an *identity theory* of the mental and the physical, as follows: Certain neurophysiological terms denote (refer to) the very same events that are also denoted (referred to) by certain phenomenal terms.
> . . . Utilizing Frege's distinction between *Sinn* ("meaning," "sense," "intension") and *Bedeutung* ("referent," "*denotatum*," "extension"), we may say that neurophysiological terms and the corresponding phenomenal terms, though widely differing in *sense*, and hence in the modes of confirmation of statements containing

them, do have identical *referents.* I take these referents to be the immediately experienced qualities, or their configurations in the various phenomenal fields.[6]

Unlike the Australian version of the identity theory, which is straightforwardly reductive—the mental *is* material—this version recognizes the legitimacy of phenomenal or mental terms in our dictionary of referring terms.
Phenomenal terms, like physical terms, genuinely refer. They may in principle
be eliminable, but they do refer to the same sorts of things as are picked out
by the neurophysiological terms. These common referents are, nonetheless,
physical. For both versions of the theory, however, the identity defended is that
of strict identity, not of logical necessity having to do with the meanings of
terms. The identity in question is such that it can only be known *a posteriori.* As
such, the truth of the identity claim is thought to be discoverable by scientific
investigation.

The third version of the identity theory is one which Richard Rorty[7] calls
the *disappearance* form to distinguish between it and what he speaks of as the
*translation* form. Unlike the standard, or translation form, it questions the legitimacy of mental talk and would replace it by language that is scientifically
appropriate. So instead of talking of headaches, for example, you speak of the
firing of C-fibres. You might, and for the same reasons, eschew talk of possession by demons in favor of the scientifically more apt possibility of epileptic
seizures. According to this view, shared also by Paul Feyerabend, all mental talk
is entirely eliminable without remainder and without loss.

Now what are we to make of the identity claim that mental states are nothing but states of the central nervous system?[8] The identity in question, since
*strict,* is expressible in terms of Leibniz's Law, the indiscernibility of identicals,
to which we called attention in Chapter Two. The formula, recall, is as follows:
$(x)(y) [(x = y) \supset (F)(Fx \equiv Fy)]$. So *A* and *B* are in reality one and the same
thing if and only if whatever property is had by *A* is equivalently had by *B*. But
this formulation poses a number of problems for the mind/brain identity theorist, not all, admittedly, equally serious. For one thing, if some given referent
*A* is in fact identical with a referent *B* in the sense of the foregoing, then with
respect to both referents, *A* and *B*, it does not matter which referring term appears to the right or to the left of the identity marker in an expression defining the identity relation. So the proposition "Phosphorus is identical with

[6]Herbert Feigl, "Mind-Body, *Not* a Pseudo-Problem," in *The Mind/Brain Identity Theory,* ed.
C. V. Borst (New York: St. Martin's Press, 1970), p. 38.

[7]Richard Rorty, "Mind-Brain, Identity, Privacy and Categories," in *The Mind/Brain Identity
Theory,* ed. C. V. Borst (New York: St. Martin's Press, 1970), p. 138.

[8]For Saul Kripke's discussion of identity and his brilliant critical analysis of one form of the
mind/brain identity thesis in terms of the notion of rigid designators, and for A. J. Ayer's critique
of Kripke's analysis, see respectively: Saul Kripke, *Naming and Necessity* (Cambridge, Mass.: Harvard
University Press, 1980), pp. 3–155; and A. J. Ayer, *Philosophy in the Twentieth Century* (New York:
Vintage Books, 1982), pp. 265–66.

Hesperus" expresses exactly what is expressed by "Hesperus is identical with Phosphorus." The terms "Phosphorus" and "Hesperus" may interchange places without thereby changing the truth value of the original proposition. But for the identity theorist to permit this logically proper move with respect to the identity claim in question is to run afoul of the motivation for making the identity claim in the first place. That motivation was the eliminability of the mental term on the left of the equation in favor of the physical term on the right. This is because all talk of mental states is in reality nothing but talk about something different, of states of a material system, the central nervous system.

The situation is roughly analogous to finding ourselves saying things like "ghosts *are really* . . . ," without our wanting to admit to the reality of ghosts in order to make them *really* so and so. We do not want to suggest there are ghosts since no ghosts exist. Indeed, by saying "ghosts *are really* . . . ," we are denying the existence of ghosts. The difficulty of this sort of disguised ontological denial accounts in part for Rorty's proposing a "disappearance" form of the theory. Rather than being explicit, the identity becomes tacit. No equation is produced, hence no terms as such are equated. Mental terms simply disappear from standard discourse about mind, their place being taken by neurophysiological terms.

But the identity claim, as we noted, is not intended to express a linguistic or a metaphysical *preference* but a discoverable fact, that mental states are nothing but states of the central nervous system. The problem is analogous to discovering that heat is *nothing but* mean kinetic energy, or that lightning is *nothing but* the sudden discharge of electrical energy due to the ionization of water vapor molecules in the atmosphere. One obvious problem with this translation is that it may apply equally to practically anything whatsoever which is physically or phenomenally reducible, but with very dubious ontic or epistemic benefits. Indeed, we could, in this way, make just as good a case for materialism as for idealism. We could quite defensibly hold, for example, that objects like tables and chairs are nothing but constructions out of sense data. We could just as defensibly hold that tables and chairs are nothing but huge concentrations of microparticles in mutual attraction. But one and the same thing A cannot be nothing but B *and* nothing but C, if B and C are not one and the same. With no uncontroversial way of assessing the merits of incompatible translations, or reduction, we may simply have to opt for a view which, following Quine, fits our ontological commitment. So translation does not in and of itself render discovery easy: The left-hand term of the identity equation is still legitimate, if not permanent, in our ordinary discourse.

But perhaps we can still get the better of this troublesome term on the left of the identity equation by regarding it "topic-neutrally." It may be a very imprecise symbol or place-holder in much the way that the terms "someone" or "something" are imprecise and in this way *neutral.* This is suggested by J. J. C. Smart. "When a person says, 'I see a yellowish-orange after-image,' he is saying something like this: '*There is something going on which is like what is going on when* I have my eyes open, am awake, and there is an orange illuminated in good light in front of me, that is, when I really see an orange.' "[9] Notice that Smart does not intend to say that the orange after-image is a brain state but that the experience of "seeing" it is. Thus the italicized words expressive of this state or series of states are topic-neutral. The autobiographical reporter in question knows only that something is going on, but does not know exactly what. What is going on is not something mental but something altogether material. The purpose of proposing this hygienic agnosticism is to undermine any independent ontic standing mental designata may seem to have. All mental designata would therefore be accounted for in this way.

But this approach is problematic. How exactly does translation advance the identity inquiry? Translating is not itself a form of discovering. It is one thing to dislike talk about ghosts, or orange after-images; it is quite another to establish their nonexistence. The true nature of the "something going on" has not been fully established. On the basis of independent observations, we discover that the Morning Star is in fact the same star as the Evening Star. But what conceivable experiment or set of independent observations would establish the claim in question that mental states are in reality nothing over and above brain states or states of the central nervous system? This would seem to be by far the most difficult question for the identity theorist. Perhaps the identity claim was not an empirical hypothesis after all.

But suppose, as with the Morning Star/Evening Star example, independent observations were possible. What exactly would the finding settle? What, that is, beyond the fact that, as with the foregoing example, the terms in the claim are now, reversible? There would then be little point in refraining from employing phenomenal terms from our discourse. No doubt one possible advantage would be that we would now possess the *explanations* of mental phenomena. But the issue which the theory attempts to address is one of identity and *not* one of explanation: What explains *X*, and what *X* is, are distinct questions.

There are two other criticisms, one relatively minor, the other quite serious. The first has to do with the application of Leibniz's Law, the principle of the *indiscernibility of identicals*, to the mind/brain identity claim. By Leibniz's Law, if *a* is identical with *b*, any property which *a* has *b* has, and any property which *b* has *a* has. Whatever we assert about *a* we also assert about *b*, and vice versa. If assertions suited to the one are not suited to the other, we might validly infer that *a* and *b* are not one and the same thing. The claim that mental states are identical with brain states has been challenged on the ground that some assertions fitting mental states are ill-suited to describing brain states. We speak, for example, of *sharp* or *shooting* pains and *intense* desires, which seem clearly inappropriate to the description of physical states. Statements which apply to mental states cannot apply to states of the central nervous system, and vice versa.

---

[9] J. J. C. Smart, "Sensation and Brain Process," *Philosophical Review*, 68 (1959), p. 149.

But if mental states are indeed nothing but brain states or, more generally, states of the central nervous system, we are faced with a linguistic inconvenience rather than with a metaphysical problem. To remedy the problem requires nothing more serious than a change in our linguistic conventions and practices. The way we talk is no sure index to the way things are in reality; when the two are in conflict, if either must give way, it must be talk.

Further issue is sometimes made in terms of so-called "intensional" properties which may on occasion be true with regard to *a* but false of *b*, or the other way around. We may, for instance, believe, assume, or fear, that the Morning Star is a god without at the same time believing, assuming, or fearing, that the Evening Star is a god, even though they are one and the same star. [But our believings or assumings are not constitutive or defining characteristics of things. They are therefore not among a thing's intensional properties. Properties of things are their characteristics.] Being believed to be an actor is not a property of actors. The Morning Star is extensionally or denotatively identical with the Evening Star because they are one and the same entity characterized, as a consequence, by one and the same set of constitutive or defining properties. Identity has to do with the intersubjectively describable features of objects and not with the thoughts and feelings we have toward them.

The second, and certainly the more serious criticism, is a functionalist one: that the mind/brain identity is conceived much too narrowly. The characterization of mind is unacceptably narrow, for it excludes the possibility that mental states might be nonbiologically realized. Entities without a central nervous system might, nonetheless, have or be capable of mental states. In that case it would be incorrect to identify mind with what stuff it happens to be appearing in. Consider, for example, the possibility of a race of Extraterrites or a breed of manufactured Sillykytes with nothing remotely analogous to a nervous system but who exhibit intelligent behavior. There is no good reason to refrain from making mental ascriptions regarding them. It is one thing to show that mind *is* biologically realized; it is quite another to establish that it can *only* be so realized. To identify mental states, hence to translate mental talk, exclusively in terms of neurophysiological states would go beyond what can be confidently asserted of mind.

The foregoing is certainly a functionalist criticism. We should, however, note that within the ranks of identity theorists, there are two schools of thought answering respectively to *type* physicalism and *token* physicalism. The former holds the narrow or chauvinist view, the latter an inclusive view. The former insists that things like "smart" computers or robots cannot be said to have mental states for they are not constituted of the right stuff. They do not possess neurons—they are nonbiological entities and therefore excluded from the entire class of minded things. Token physicalists, on the other hand, allow for the possibility that the class of minded things may transcend the instances with which we are now familiar to include things like "smart" computers and entities like Sillykites. We will pursue this functionalist line of thinking in the section which follows.

As we noted earlier in this section, Rorty preferred his alternative, the *disappearance* form, over what he termed the *translation* form. The term "translation" was not used with contempt. On the contrary, it characterized the standard topic-neutral attempt to express how to interpret the claim of mind/brain identity, following Leibniz's strict identity principle. More exactly, it showed how to understand the left-hand term in the identity equation. As we saw from the discussion above, the attempt at clarification yields its own crop of problems. Rorty's solution—dissolution, we may say—is to deny that the identity in question is strict, in which case Leibniz's principle presumably would not apply. The advantage of this move is that the hauntingly troublesome left-hand term of the identity equation can now be exorcised. All mental terms without exception simply disappear from serious discourse, their places taken by expressions describing only neurophysiological phenomena. Armed with the disappearance form of the theory, Rorty says: "[T]he relation in question is not strict identity, but rather the sort of relation which obtains between, to put it crudely, existent entities and non-existent entities when reference to the latter once served (some of) the purposes presently served by reference to the former—the sort of relation that holds, for example, between "quantity of caloric fluid" and mean kinetic energy of molecules."[10] This move involves nothing short of a total ban on the whole sorry lot of mental terms, no more useful in serious discourse than talk of caloric fluid, ghosts, gremlins, and demon possession. Scientific replacements now suffice in every instance where phenomenal talk was habitual.

But this move seems extremely weak. For one thing, if *only* the terms on the right of the equation, the neurophysiological ones, survive the Rorty maneuver, in what sense is the resultant theory seriously a form of the identity theory? Rorty's response, of course, would be that the identity was never strict, but nominal or, at best, heuristic. If we grant this move, we should be at a loss to know what exactly to make of the more fundamental claim that mind/brain identity theory—that mental states *are* brain states—*is* a scientific hypothesis. To avoid any commitment to an ontology based on the referring use of mental terms, Rorty would say, "What people called . . . are nothing but . . . ," and he would, in place of the first set of dots, insert the mental term or terms in question.[11] So pains and thoughts would go the way of ghosts and caloric fluid. But the maneuver which yields this result looks very like a recommendation in need of scientific warrant. It is altogether too facile, for it appears to explain away rather than explain the mind/brain identity claim. Unfortunately for the disappearance form, the issue of identity in the strict sense persists, albeit tacitly, and it is identity in that sense that has to be clearly and unequivocally established.

It is also a matter of contention as to whether pain talk and talk of ghosts and caloric fluid are on the same ontic level. Some people and cultures talk of

---

[10]Rorty, "Mind-Brain, Identity, Privacy and Categories," p. 138.
[11]Rorty, "Mind-Brain, Identity, Privacy and Categories," p. 194.

ghosts and take them to be real, fewer talk of the reality of caloric fluid, but *everybody* talks about pains. We feel them and we seek remedies for them. Some of these remedies work and some do not, but when they do we know. We spend a good deal of our resources in an effort to rid ourselves of pain-producing conditions. So universal an experience can hardly be dismissed without much ado. The phenomenal, as distinct from the neurophysiological, reality of pains is something all seem to experience so directly that a causal account of our phenomenal experiences does not per se render the phenomena reported nonexistent. Something similar may also be true of other mental terms. This possibility will be discussed in the following section on functionalism.

But, by and large, for all its shortcomings, the identity theory, at least in its so-called translation form, has the clear merit of having taken psychological states seriously, understood, of course, as states of the central nervous system. They thus figure causally in human behavior. In so doing, unlike logical behaviorism, it manages to keep its causal accounts in line with standard scientific practice.

## FUNCTIONALISM

Its attractiveness notwithstanding, the mind/brain identity theory sketched the boundaries of the mental much too narrowly. By identifying mental states with brain states, the theory required that only entities possessed of brains could have mental states. But the possibility could not *a priori* be ruled out that entities, say, for example, a race of Extraterrites neurophysiologically very unlike us, or entities with nonneural systems, might have mental states as well. An adequate theory of the mental has to be comprehensive enough to accommodate such possibilities. The theory known as functionalism represents the attempt to develop a way of understanding the mental that can meet challenges of this sort. In actuality it is not a single theory, as will become apparent below.

As with most movements, functionalism has its subgroupings representing different ways in which a common theme or protocol is conceived and, as a consequence, differences regarding its implementation. So it is not a simple thing to say exactly what functionalsim is. I adopt functionalist Ned Block's cautious description. He says: "One characterization of functionalism that is probably vague enough to be acceptable to most functionalists is: Each type of mental state is a state consisting of a disposition to act in certain ways *and to have certain mental states,* given certain sensory inputs and certain mental states."[12] This designation resembles that of logical behaviorism, but there is a crucially important difference. Unlike logical behaviorism—which is a semantic theory regarding the meaning of mental terms—functionalist theory fully recognizes the existence of mental states as causal constituents of behavior. So instead of

---

[12]Ned Block, "Troubles with Functionalism," in *The Nature of Mind,* ed. David Rosenthal (New York: Oxford University Press, 1991), p. 211.

mental states being identified with dispositions to act, they are associated with dispositions to act.

But what then is a mental state if it is neither a brain state nor a disposition to act? We have not definitely said. True, functionalists regard it as playing a causal role in behavioral output. To avoid the narrowness to which the mind/brain identity theorists fall victim, the characterization of a mental state has to transcend that state's material realization. The account given of a mental state should hold for any and all its instances independent of the "stuff" in which it is exhibited. Thus no particular stuff can form part of its characterization. This would mean that the level of specification has to be stuff-neutral, and for the functionalist, that specification is provided at the level of function or causal role. Precisely because of this stuff-neutrality, functionalism is compatible with both materialism and dualism.

For a theorist like Hilary Putnam, as presumably for most functionalists, a mental state is a functional state of the whole organism, not of a narrowly defined region of it. This move escapes one of the narrow confines of materialist identification of mind. Pain in humans, for example, though we may be inclined to localize it is, qua mental state, a state of an entire system. It is a state of the system or organism which causes the system to bring about any of a range of *probable* outputs. Of course, a system can be in more than one identifiable state at any given time. We can be angry and hungry and in pain at one and the same time.

As we noted previously, functionalists do not agree on details of the position. They differ, for example, on how to functionally characterize mental states—pain, for example. While they all express inputs and outputs in physical terms, they differ with respect to what is permissible in those two categories. To get a good handle on functionalism, therefore, it would be useful to make some classificatory distinctions. Thanks to Block, we may usefully distinguish between those theories expressed in terms of a Turing-machine model and those that are not so expressed. We may also distinguish between those theorists who express functional identities in terms of *a priori* psychology and those who express them in terms of scientific psychology.

At its simplest, a Turing-machine is a device whose "table" lists machine states, inputs and outputs. Outputs are determined solely by machine states and inputs. A pop machine explains this quite well. Assume a pop machine in good repair and in service. At any given time the machine is in some particular state, and whether or not it dispenses a bottle of pop depends on what inputs it receives, the exact sequence of nickels, dimes, quarters, or other permissible currency. From initial state to output state, the machine goes through intervening states—its *transitions*—each determined by the preceding. For example, the input of a dime followed by a quarter disposes the machine to move from an existing state, say $S_1$, to the next state, say $S_2$, and so on, the final state in the process being the output state. The output executed, the machine returns to the initial state. For such a machine the states are finite—without this stipulation, quite possibly no pop! The inputs and outputs are explicitly specified: no rubber coins and the like as input, but nickels, dimes, and quarters, or other as specified—and strictly bottles of pop, not bagels, as output. So the machine—which is to say its transitions—is fully deterministic. Its transition contingencies are fully expressed as conditionals of the form: "If machine is in state $S_1$ and there is input $I_1$, then it will go to state $S_2$," and so on to the final output $O_n$.

Admittedly, humans are not exactly like pop machines. We feel, we have beliefs, and we consider ourselves as entities capable of self-directed or autonomous activity. And there is no predicting with certainty what any Leslie may do with a baseball bat if provoked. She may, just may, walk back into the dugout. But then she may not. But humans *are* like pop machines in the sense that they *can* be described at least in terms of states, inputs, and outputs. Indeed the Turing-machine functionalists identify some mental states as functional states. So humans are like a Turing-machine, arguably not a deterministic one in any ordinary sense but a probabilistic one. A T-machine functionalist can therefore say that humans are probabilistic automatons. This is so primarily because the machines that we are permit us, unlike the pop machine, to exercise a great degree of control over the "machine tape." It would thus appear that inputs and internal parameters seem, in a sense, to underdetermine output. The contingencies are so many that predicting output would be a pretty chancy affair.

It should be borne in mind that there is nothing about T-machine functionalism that requires that the realization of a Turing-machine be physical. Mental states, understood functionally, can appear in a diverse array of types of entity. Indeed, it is this characteristic which makes functionalism compatible with dualism.

Then, too, we may think of functionalism along the lines of those who, like Smart and Lewis, individuate functional identities in terms of *a priori* psychology and those who, like Putnam and Fodor, view them in terms of empirical psychology. What exactly is the difference? Of these two types, Block says: "The a priori functionalists . . . are heirs to logical behaviorists. They tend to regard functional analyses as analyses of the meanings of terms, whereas the empirical functionalists . . . regard functional analyses as substantive scientific hypotheses."[13]

Let us try to understand this. Bear in mind that functionalism is an identity theory. It claims that mental states *are* functional states. Just what is entailed in this claim has yet to be made clear. But identities as we know can prove troublesome. Recall the difficulty the mind/brain identity theorists encountered in trying to express the identity they conceived of in terms of Leibniz's Law, the indiscernibility of identicals. At any rate, the trick turns upon the challenge of successfully eliminating mental terms to accord with the requirements of the new theory. That is not particularly easy.

[13]Block, "Troubles with Functionalism," p. 213.

To meet the challenge, some functionalists, Block, for instance, have attempted to express functional identity by employing a rather elegant translation device, really a strategy, known as the Ramsey sentence—after the Cambridge mathematician and philosopher Frank P. Ramsey, with whom the device originated. Technicalities aside, here is how roughly in Block's terms the strategy works for functionalism in both its *a priori* and scientific versions. Let us say we have a theory *T* about a mental state, say, pain, which we want to express in functional terms. Our pain theory, of course, has the form of a lawlike generalization. In essence a Turing-machine routine, it specifies something formally like: Whenever anyone *E* is in state *p* and receives input *q*, *E* gives output *r* and enters state *s*. Suppose we represent *T* in the following way: $T(S_1 . . . S_n, I_1 . . . I_k, O_1 . . . O_j)$ where *S* stands for mental state terms and *I* and *O*, respectively, for inputs and outputs. Now the Ramsey translation of *T* will not contain any *mental* state terms. All such terms as are identified by $S_1 . . . S_n$, in our theory *T* will be eliminated and replaced by variables—to be exact, existentially quantified variables as follows: $\exists F_1 . . . \exists F_n$. So in the Ramsey sentence which expresses our pain theory, there will be a variable replacing the mental term "pain," and so on for each mental state term in the theory. The Ramsey sentence which thus defines pain will therefore have as its predicate an expression consisting of the specific variable which replaces the term "pain" in our theory, plus other terms picking out specific inputs and outputs. So being in the complex of states picked out by the predicate of the Ramsey sentence is what functionally defines pain. It is, in the language of the functionalists, the Ramsey functional correlate of pain.[14] (Note that for a probabilistic, as opposed to a deterministic, Turing-machine, precise specification of some mental states would be well-nigh unachievable.) Through this strategy presumably all, or most, mental state terms can be functionally reduced, the reduced expressions containing only terms descriptive of causal relations. Presumably, these terms pick out nothing over and above their Ramsey functional correlates.

Now the difference between the *a priori* and the scientific functionalists may be expressed by saying that with respect to the Ramsey sentence, the former interpret inputs and outputs in terms of *commonsense* psychology, whereas the latter treat them from the standpoint of *scientific* hypotheses. For the former, but not for the latter, inputs must be observable and refer standardly to, as in the case of pain, such things as cuts and bites and to the standard outputs like winces and yells. The latter have recourse to internal parameters whereas the former are precluded from any such consideration. For both, of course, inputs and outputs are physically specified.

A good example of the former is provided in two imaginary scenarios presented by David Lewis in his essay "Mad Pain and Martian Pain." Lewis has us imagine a strange kind of person who feels pain just as we do, but whose pain differs greatly from ours in its causes and effects. For example, whereas pain for us is caused typically by cuts and bruises this person's pain is caused by mod-

---

[14]Block, "Troubles with Functionalism," pp. 213–15.

erate exercise on an empty stomach. Further, whereas for us, pains are distracting, this strange person's pain inclines him to mathematics; indeed, they aid in his concentration. Intense pain produces none of the reactions with which we are familiar, nor is he the least bit motivated to prevent or get rid of it. Call him the madman with a mad pain. Next, Lewis has us imagine a different character, a Martian, whose pain also differs from ours but this time with respect to its physical realization. His mind is hydraulic and contains nothing like our neurons. Physically, he is outfitted in radically unfamiliar furnishings—with valves and inflatable cavities and such. Having observed that a credible theory of mind must be broad enough to allow for both mad pain and Martian pain, Lewis says, "[T]he lesson of mad pain is that pain is associated only contingently with its causal role, while the lesson of Martian pain is that pain is connected only contingently with its physical realization." Then he asks: "How can we characterize pain a priori in terms of causal role and physical realization, and yet respect both kinds of contingency?"[15]

One thing to notice in this transworld thought experiment is that Lewis is employing the term "pain" in a more or less standard everyday way according to which the *connotation* of the term is antecedently, more or less, fixed in terms of commonsense sorts of inputs and outputs. In a sense, we know what to make of the term, thus we know at any given time what we are looking for. The issue is finding it or, perhaps better, making it adequate in all worlds. Indeed, with respect to "pain" Lewis says: "It is the concept of a member of a system of states that together more or less realize the *pattern of causal generalizations* set forth in commonsense psychology."[16] But it would seem not a little puzzling as to just how, on either side of the world-divide in the mad pain scenario, we can determine that pain is occurring. What is there to give it away? Indeed, how can the notion of pain be intelligibly communicated across the divide?

### The Pros and Cons of Functionalism

Functionalism has had, and continues to have, considerable appeal, especially among researchers in the fields of cognitive psychology and artificial intelligence. Certain of its merits are not hard to discern. In the first place, metaphysical behaviorism attempts to account for mind much too simplistically solely in terms of environmental inputs and behavioral outputs. Functionalism recognizes, *in addition* to inputs and outputs, the uneliminable causal roles played by internal states of a behaving system. In this way, functionalism avoids the liberalism of behaviorism whose bloated universe can include practically any and all input-output systems. This is incongruous, since included along with humans in this mental universe would be highly unlikely members such as

---

[15]David Lewis, "Mad Pain and Martian Pain," in *Readings in Philosophical Psychology: Vol. I.*, ed. Ned Block (Cambridge, MA: Harvard University Press, 1980), pp. 216–17.

[16]David Rosenthal, ed., *The Nature of Mind* (New York: Oxford University Press, 1991), p. 217. [Emphasis mine.]

drums and mouse traps. In the second place, functionalism avoids the chauvinism entailed by the mind/brain identity theory by conceiving of mindedness as a feature which may be true of systems entirely devoid of neurons. Indeed, by conceiving of mind at the level of function rather than at the level of material realization, functionalism is, as we noted earlier, compatible with dualism (though as a matter of fact most functionalists are committed to some form of materialism).

But, functionalism has its difficulties. Perhaps the ones which have received greatest attention are the properties known as mental qualia (singular: *quale*). Some regard the possession of qualia as a feature characteristic of only conscious entities.

Since so much is made of this issue, we will need at least to have a good working notion of what a *quale* is. We might contrast the notion of a *quale* with that of a quantum. The latter is concerned with the question "How much?" —matters of quantity, measurables like length, weight, duration, and so on. The former, on the other hand, is a qualitative notion and has to do with the question "What is it like?" —considerations like what it feels like to be in pain, or to such things as what it is like to sense the redness or fragrance or delicacy of a rose, or the beauty of a sunset. In short, *quale* has to do with the subjectivity or phenomenological character of our experience, what we cannot know unless we have had the relevant experience.

The qualia difficulty typically takes two forms. One form—call it the problem of the inverted spectrum—is illustrated by conceiving of two persons functionally identical but one of whom experiences light spectra as inverted so that she sees green where the other, as standardly is the case, sees red. The other form, sometimes referred to as the absent qualia problem, is illustrated by any system deemed to be functionally equivalent to a human being but from which qualia are absent, or so it is claimed.

With respect to the inverted spectrum, we may express the problem facing functionalism as follows. If person *A* and person *B* are functionally identical yet it is conceivable that the spectral experience of the one is the exact reverse of the other's such, for example, that the phenomenological character of the one's experience is that of red-seeing and that of the other that of green-seeing, then it would seem to follow that functionalism does not constitute an adequate theory of mind. If functionalism is correct, how can it be that two *functionally identical* individuals can have two widely *different* qualitative experiences? Functional identity and identity of qualitative experience should, if the theory is correct, go hand in hand; that is, the one should be isomorphic with the other.

One response to this particular version of the qualia problem takes issue with the isomorphism presumed to hold between functional identity and qualitative experience. What makes an experience seeing red one and the same experience as that of seeing green has nothing to do with the qualitative or subjective uniqueness of the experience but with its functional and holistic character. What crucially matters is how person *A* and person *B* relate holistically to the environment in which color discriminations are made. Presumably their color discriminations are identical and that establishes the claim of functionalism as a viable theory of the mental. A related response regards qualia as epiphenomenal side-shows, their peculiar character entirely contingent upon the particular functions which give rise to them.

Indeed the former response seems to beg the question in favor of functionalism, for it seems to assume precisely what it is supposed to establish by argument. It says, in essence, that the conceivable difference in qualia, given functional identity, is accounted for by the fact that associated qualia do not have to be identical! This ploy seems to be at one and the same time a nod of acknowledgment to the reality of qualia but their summary dismissal as well. But the phenomenological character of our experiences is a feature so real to our mental life as human beings that any adequate theory of mind will have to consider it seriously. In this regard functionalism needs to do a lot more thoughtful homework. It will not do merely to insist that given materialist presuppositions qualia are reducible to or explicable in terms of neurophysiological events. It is necessary instead to demonstrate this.

The other problem for functionalism is the absent qualia problem. Several thought-experiments illustrate this particular difficulty. In these experiments, the imaginary system in question, social or mechanical or some other, is functionally a virtual duplicate of a human being. However, qualitative mental states are absent from it. Some have imagined the population of China—something in the order of four billion—to comprise the constituents of such a system; others have conjured up a system constituted entirely of sentient microparticles (*homunculi* or little men), or an assortment of sentient beings to do the trick. The issue, in brief, is: If it is possible to develop a system functionally isomorphic with that of a human being yet from which qualitative experiences are absent then functionalism as a theory of mind is either incomplete or simply false. We choose human, since we know incontrovertibly that humans do experience qualia in the course of their mental lives. It will not do, of course, to contend that functional identity is all that crucially matters in determining the type-identity of mental states. That is, once it is determined that two systems are entirely functionally identical, that similarity or the presence or absence of qualia is at best a peripheral issue. That is precisely what needs to be shown.

Theoretically at least, the functionalists are in a much better position in responding to the inverted spectrum problem than they are with respect to the absent qualia problem. With respect to the former, even now introspection is hardly an objective arbiter in settling the issue of sameness of qualia of two human perceivers. It may well be the case that no two humans confronted with the same colored object ever have the same qualitative experience. And we simply have no way of finding out whether they do or do not. I do not know what "redness" my keen-eyed colleague experiences when we both clearly perceive the same "red" patch we associate with the same red apple. For all I know, we both may be making the same noise, "red apple," in the same circumstances but visually may be experiencing the apple in qualitatively divergent ways. Qualitative peculiarities are inevitable and are always supervenient upon specific functional organization. Let us grant that much for the sake of argument.

The total *absence* of qualia from a system, however functionally equivalent to a human being's, is an entirely different affair. That human beings experience qualia is beyond dispute. The question remains as to whether functional isomorphism of the sort discussed constitutes a sufficient condition for establishing the occurrence or the identity of qualitative mental states. In defense of functionalism, if physicalism, or some version of it, is the correct view of what there is, then it should be possible to account for qualia in terms of the operations of whatever physical system they happen to appear in. But, recall, functionalism is not per se a physicalist theory, though, as has also been noted above, most functionalists are as a matter of fact materialists. So the reduction of qualia to manifestations of the *physical* depends on the assumption of a materialist ontology. It follows, therefore, that this reduction leaves functionalism open to the charge of chauvinism, the very charge which had rendered the mind/brain identity theory untenable and which in no small measure had inspired the move to functionalism.

It is fair to say that attempts to meet the chauvinism/liberalism charges, as well as the qualia problem, have not been very successful. Indeed, some consider them abysmal failures. The qualia problem has proven the most intractable, and every attempt to avoid the Scylla of chauvinism seem to guarantee an inevitable encounter with the just as menacing Charybdis of liberalism. One way out of the Scylla/Charybdis dilemma, is to argue that *if* physicalism is the correct view of what there is, then to hold that any functional organization whatever must be physically realized is entirely defensible, indeed is entailed by the physicalist ontology. So what appears to be chauvinism with respect to the stuff necessary to functional realization is in reality an ontological requirement. But assuming the truth of the argument that what there is is physical leaves the dualist justifiably unimpressed. For one thing, it seems to settle the mind/body problem by fiat rather than by effort; for another, the scope of the physicalist claim goes well beyond the immediate issue of the mind/body problem to embrace all reality, so that Leibniz's God, if He exists, is physical. If we are not sure of the claim, we cannot be sure of the chauvinism it is invoked to defend. Thus the dilemma remains.

Because of its intimate connection with consciousness issues, the qualia problem is of significance especially for those who see it as getting at the heart of what it is to be a human being. All conscious human beings have qualitative states. If functionalism as a theory of mind is true, then anything which is in every detail functionally equivalent to a human being with respect to possession of mind must experience such states. Negatively expressed, the absence of qualitative states from any entity functionally equivalent to a human being is *prima facie* reason to reject the supposed equivalence. And just as it will not do to insist that the equivalence holds in spite of the absence of qualitative states, it also will not do to maintain that the qualitative states are in reality present since implied by the assumption of functional equivalence. One interpretation of functional equivalence holds that $A$ is functionally equivalent to $B$ with respect to some $C$. This is a stipulative claim which permits as a consequence no empirical disconfirmation. But there is also an *a posteriori* interpretation according to which the supposed equivalence is nothing but a hypothesis. Functionalists cannot espouse the former, for obviously that recourse would render functionalism arbitrary. A functionalist cannot simply lay it down that, so far as mind is concerned, a "suitably" or "appropriately" designed machine is the functional equivalent of a human brain. And to espouse the latter interpretation requires that the hypothesis pass the qualia test. After all, it is functional equivalence to the mental life of humans—qualitative states and all—that is at issue.

But perhaps there is yet another way out of the qualia impasse. Some say the so-called qualitative states are not functionally reducible but are, reminiscent of epiphenomenalism, a sort of efflux of the physical functions which underlie them. So while they may not be characterized in functional terms, they are nonetheless accounted for entirely in terms of a functionalist theory of mind. They result from physical functions, in the final analysis are physical phenomena of some sort, but are not themselves functions. It would also seem to follow from this line of attack that their nature or existence is of peripheral importance only. True, we are introspectively aware of our qualitative states and think their possession essential in some way to our mental life as humans. After all, knowing what pain is like seems to play no small part in motivating us to avoid pain-threatening situations. But, our intuitions to the contrary, such qualia do not much matter.

The prospects for a convincing resolution to all the difficulties presented above do not seem to be especially good, though there are many who remain sanguine with regard to the viability of functionalism as a theory of mind. Indeed, the functionalist conception of mind has inspired a great deal of experimental activity in the field of cognitive psychology and in the related field known as artificial intelligence (AI, for short). These fields represent ways in which theory and technology join hands to develop devices—primarily computers—which will simulate or, more ambitiously, duplicate the mental life of intelligent biological systems.

## ARTIFICIAL INTELLIGENCE

At first glance, the expression "artificial intelligence" seems an oxymoron. After all, the second term in the expression is normally predicated of certain naturally occurring entities, of certain biological systems, things *found* in nature— such as dogs and men and dolphins. In contrast the term "artificial" is normally predicated of things which are *fabricated* out of lifeless stuff, such as cars and thermostats and calculators. The classes these two terms pick out seem to be exclusive: Membership in the one seems to preclude membership in the other. If $X$ is intelligent, then $X$ is not artificial; and if $X$ is artificial, then $X$ is not intelligent. The principle which motivates AI calls this intuitive distinction into question. Tersely, it asserts that mental processes such as perception, learning, understanding or, more generally, intelligence and cognition are, strictly, formal computations over physically encoded representations in the brain. It is easy to see that if this is indeed the true account of the nature of these and all mental processes whatsoever, then nothing in principle prevents such processes from being mechanically put into artificial systems such as computers. For any process whatever, once that process can be discretely specified then, in accordance with the Turing principle, there is a machine program, a universal Turing-machine, which can precisely enact it. AI proponents hold that any intelligent system, human beings being examples, is nothing but an information-processing system. All such processing is entirely formal, computational, and representational, hence capable of simulation by a universal Turing-machine. On this account, intelligence can properly be predicated of any *suitably programmed* machine, and in this way one intuitive distinction between the natural/biological and the artificial is removed. The gap is functionally bridged.

Before going any further we should, following John Searle, distinguish between what he calls strong AI and weak AI. The latter claims only that machines suitably programmed can *simulate* human cognition. The proponents stop short of maintaining that such machines can actually *duplicate* human cognition without remainder. Strong AI, in contrast, does make this further claim.[17] For strong AI, a suitably programmed computer is literally capable of mental states; it can, for example, understand the stock market, appreciate a good joke, and so on. In his essay "Computation and Cognition: Issues in the Foundations of Cognitive Science," Zenon Pylyshyn contends that "there is no reason why computation ought to be treated as merely a metaphor for cognition, as opposed to a hypothesis about the literal nature of cognition."[18] Moreover, argue some, it is ontologically feasible that terms like "person" can come to have unattenuated application to a suitably programmed computer.[19]

As might be expected, the most interesting philosophic issues associated with AI are encountered at the level of strong AI, and to certain of these we now turn. We will look first at how a number have been identified and resolved.

Some accounts of mental activity, the activity of understanding, for instance, almost seem to require that there be somewhere in our insides a kind

[17]John Searle, "Minds, Brains, and Programs," *The Behavioral and Brain Sciences*, 3 (1980), 417–24.

[18]Zenon Pylyshyn, "Computation and Cognition: Issues in the Foundations of Cognitive Science," in *The Tradition of Philosophy*, eds. Harrison Hall and Norman E. Bowie (Belmont, Calif.: Wadsworth Publishing Company, 1986), pp. 244–52.

[19]Paul Churchland, *Matter and Consciousness* (Cambridge, Mass.: MIT Press, 1988), p. 120.

of "understander"—a homunculus—responsible for doing the understanding. Daniel Dennett exorcises all such homunculi by proposing that psychological phenomena can be fully described by the simple strategy of "top-down," progressive decomposition of those phenomena. By "top," of course, Dennett is referring to the highest levels of psychological organization or attribution. For example, the phenomenon of "understanding," which we encounter at those levels, can be broken down into progressively more simple and thus more stupid units to the place where, at the lowest and most elemental level, the tasks performed are the most humdrum and mindless. The elemental units at this level of computational descent assume one of two possible modes: They are either "on" or "off." Thus in the final analysis, understanding is fully accounted for in terms of the configurations of "on/off" switches. The same would be true, for any and all other psychological phenomena. Note that this decomposition more or less mirrors the way computers operate. At the basic machine-language level, the units are 1s and 0s. It is entirely as configuration of these binary units that the central processing unit of a computer—its brain, so to speak—receives its input from the keyboard, executes all its internal procedures, and effects its output. The output of the computer, however spectacular, is traceable down the constitutive line to its machine program, which consists of nothing but ones and zeros.[20] Well, so much for those pesky homunculi. We will judge of that a bit later in this section.

Strong AI proponents have a typical strategy in pressing the functional nature of the mental. They hold—perhaps *insist* would be an apter term—as an empirical hypothesis that the operations characteristic of human mental processes are isomorphic with the formal operations carried out by a suitably programmed computational system. Those operations are not only formal but representational as well, by virtue of their involving a symbolic code. Mental computations do not occur willy-nilly. Computations are of necessity rule-governed or formal, hence *syntactic.* But these computations are about actual things, objects, or states of affairs in our environment. They have to do with what we think, what we believe, what we do, and so on. In a sense, our survival as humans depends on them. Thus the computations are not in any sense meaningless. They have *semantic* content; they mean this or that. They are directed toward something or other and by virtue of this quality are said to be *intentional.* Take the phenomenon of perception, for instance. Physical phenomena *presented* to the input terminals of the central nervous system become physically encoded, that is, *re-presented,* in the brain's symbolic system. This encoding which is effected in the brain is entirely computational. So the world of our meanings, the world we ponder, interpret, bump into, and remark about via our language—our semantic world, if you will—gets syntactically enmeshed in the functional architecture of the brain. The proof of the hypothesis requires mov-

[20]See Daniel Dennett's "Artifical Intelligence as Philosophy and as Psychology," in *Philosophical Perspectives in Artificial Intelligence,* ed. Martin Ringle (Atlantic Highlands, N.J.: Humanities Press, 1979), pp. 57–80.

ing from the level of talk to the level of creation—creating a device which embodies the truth of the claims central to AI.

It was thought, quite early in the history of AI, that all that stood in the way of demonstrating the viability of the computational hypothesis of mind was the absence of the technology required to develop a device capable of phenomenal computational speed and a vast memory. Those obstacles have largely been removed. Speed and memory capacity are no longer barriers. But nothing like the success which the early AI enthusiasts envisaged has been realized. Devices—special task robots and the like—simulating specific mental skills have performed unconvincingly, even as judged by strong supporters of the notion of artificial intelligence. The prospects for a device inspired by AI premises that simulates, to say nothing of duplicates, human cognition seem rather gloomy.[21] Something seems congenitally wrong with the conception of mind in terms of serial computing. The functional operations required of serial or digital programming seem incapable of actualizing human cognition. Human cognition seems to work along rather different lines.

Let us now look at a number of issues or problems which seem resistant to convincing resolution and which as a consequence appear to cast very serious doubt on the computational conception of mind. Let us begin with Dennett's attempt at homuncular exorcism.

Recall that for Dennett, the homuncular issue is easily resolved by the simple strategy of "top-down" or recursive decomposition. So by going backwards and tracing the genealogy of a cognitive act to its radical and elemental level, nowhere would one find an "understander" whose ministrations make for understanding, or find a hidden "perceiver" whose doings render perceiving possible. No homunculus is ever found, not because it is invisible but because in the computational idea of mind any such entity is superfluous. Homunculi are as good as nonexistent.

But this exorcism seems too easy. Through what *findings* has it been established that computation is a naturally occurring phenomenon? To contend strongly that cognition *is* computation, rather than the weaker contention that it is *like* computation, is to be committed to what is entailed by this stronger claim. Included, crucially, is the corollary that the truth of the claim is open to *discovery*. But to date there is no such finding, and there is not likely to be any. The reason for this failure rests on a confusion of conceptual categories: between, in Searle's terms, that which is "intrinsic," and that which is observer relative. It is between that which is "out there" because it naturally occurs independent of our presence or machinations as humans, and that which is not. Computation seems clearly to belong to the latter category and not to the former.

---

[21]See Drew McDermott, "Artificial Intelligence Meets Natural Stupidity," in *Mind Design*, ed. John Haugland (Cambridge, Mass.: MIT Press, 1981), pp. 143–60; and Hubert Dreyfus, "Misrepresenting Human Intelligence," *Thought*, LXI (1986), 430–41.

The notion of computation, taken literally, presupposes some symbolic system and specific rule-governed relationships between symbols. This AI proponents readily grant. But symbols in this sense are not naturally occurring devices, and if they are not, nothing presumed to be built out of them can be naturally occurring either. So, by entailment, *syntax gets the ontic axe.* There is no natural syntax constituted of symbols because there are no symbols in nature—they do not feature in any strictly physical description of what there is. And if there are no symbols or syntax, then there are no computations in nature; and if no computations, then clearly no computation which happens to be cognition or anything else, for that matter. It seems clear, therefore, that the claim that mental acts are in reality nothing but physically encoded computations begs the question. It presupposes what it must exhibit.

But clearly the observer-relative notion of computation, however misassigned by AI, does intimate that there is at least a homunculus (the size or number of such creatures does not really much matter) somewhere in the offing. Some knowing entity, capable of deliberately creating symbols, axioms, a suitable syntax, rules of transformation, and a program, is responsible for each *bona fide* instance of computation that there is. The computational reduction of mind indeed *requires* rather than eliminates the pesky, plotting "understander." On the view that cognition is literally computation, Dennett's thinking merely shows what no one these days doubts, that there is no need for homunculi *within* the workings of digital computers to account for their operations. It does not show that *no* homunculi are necessary to the functioning of such systems. You and I are the "knowers" and "understanders." We are physically outside the system but effectively within it in the sense that it is the physical expression of our intentions and purposes.

This brings us to a closely related consideration. In keeping with the AI functionalist model of mind, it seems excessively generous to regard digital computers as "information processing systems" in exactly the same sense in which human beings are said to be processors of information. Ordinarily, to say that a person *P* was informed of her rights *R*, and that *P* took appropriate steps with respect to *R*, is to imply a great deal. It suggests *P*'s grasp of what it is to possess a right. It implies understanding of the concept *R* and numerous related concepts, a vast network of social institutions and agencies, and relationships of a conceptual, legal, moral, political sort, and so on. These are notions that draw upon life as lived and experienced in the context of a rather complex system. *P*'s acting intelligently with respect to *R*, by taking appropriate steps, would indicate that *P*, among other things, understood and valued, to some extent at least, what she was involved in. In brief, the notion of information presupposes so much of these sorts of global understandings, it is highly doubtful that a deliberately programmed digital computer will ever be able to "process information" in any but a strictly instrumental sense. Cognition is not identical with computation.

But in holding that human cognitive acts are not in fact digital operations, the question remains as to whether a "suitably programmed" computer of an entirely different sort would be capable of genuine human intelligence. Beyond the altogether bland acknowledgment that humans are precisely such computers, the question is, Is *artificial* intelligence yet a possibility?

Note that in keeping with its strictly functionalist view, AI has always placed exclusive emphasis on the program or software. But programs must be realized in something or other, some hardware. No one seems commited to disembodied programs. Unresolved, therefore, is whether the condition expressed by the term "a suitably programmed computer" can be met without regard for the physical nature of the hardware. Our ascription of intelligence to any particular thing depends on our using our own case as an example. In the final analysis, therefore, we are looking for not mere simulation but literal and genuine duplication of human intelligence. The question then has to be whether human cognition is fully accounted for exclusively in terms of functional operations, without any regard to the character of the realizing medium. Is the possession of something akin to biological hardware—as Searle, presumably, might maintain—a necessary condition for realizing intelligence of the human sort? Or is that feature merely a peculiarity only of certain systems? As we noted, part and parcel of what it is to instantiate human intelligence and cognition is the capacity to *experience* the world in peculiar ways. These ways have so far been peculiar to biological systems. This might suggest that an adequate conception of mind needs to be attentive to considerations of hardware. If this is so, it will require that mind be conceived along somewhat different lines from those proposed in strong or weak AI. And this possibility leads us now to the consideration of an approach to the scientific study of the mental referred to as "connectionism," or "parallel distributed processing" (PDP).

## CONNECTIONISM

Connectionism represents an alternative to the computational view of human cognition modeled after the digital computer. Whether the alternative constitutes a radical departure from the computational view depends on whom you talk to. Advocates of the view range from the "wild," those who see the new turn as logically inconsistent with the computational model, to the "conservative," who see the two views as compatible in some limited respects.[22] We will look at some of the specific differences a little later. The computational view championed by classic AI conceives of mind in terms of a central processing unit (CPU) operating on symbolic representations. Connectionists, by contrast, using the brain as the model, view cognition as distributed over a vast array of interconnected nodes. Connections between nodes vary in strength or weight, so that the function a node performs at any given instant depends upon its ac-

[22]See James Garson, "What Connectionists Cannot Do: The Threat to Classical AI," in *Connectionism and the Philosophy of Mind*, eds. Terence Horgan and John Tienson (Dordrecht: Kluwer Academic Publishers, 1991), pp. 113–40.

tivation level or the weight it gets assigned to it. Hence some nodes function as activators and others as inhibitors depending on the weight or connecting strength of incoming signals. Connectionist networks are therefore dynamic in the way they operate.

Notably absent from this model of mind is any semblance of central processing, a feature crucial to the computational model, as well as *symbolic, syntactic* representations. Syntactic representations are strings of symbolic representations. On the connectionist view of cognition, mental activity is extremely widely dispersed and redundant. It is redundant in that a given input, for example, is distributed throughout the system in parallel networks rather than along a single neural route. There is thus considerably greater efficiency in handling input and structuring output than seemed possible under the typically serial architecture of the computational model. Indeed, devices based on the computational model of mind have been strongly criticized for their inability to execute commonsense tasks, or to recognize patterns efficiently. Devices designed on connectionist lines, on the other hand, seem to be able to do remarkably well in both respects. And perhaps more interesting, they have also displayed an impressive capacity to "learn." We do not so much *write* a program, at least not in the traditional sense, for a connectionist device, but we develop a "training regimen from which it *learns* to solve problems."[23]

For connectionism, cognition is activity within a neural system; for the classic AI model to which it is considered an alternative, cognition is the manipulation of symbols. Both views are strongly representational. Advocates of both views treat perception, for example, in terms of mental representations. Cognitive states are representational. Our perceptions are, in some important sense, *re*-presentations. But recall that symbols do not form an essential part of the connectionist theory of cognition. So the account of how any feature of the world is represented cannot be in terms of symbols. The proponents of connectionism must specify exactly how representation occurs, since it is not symbolic. Moreover, what is it that discriminates a given activity within a neural system as cognitive as opposed to something else? It is not sufficient to say that cognition is activity *within* a neural net. The peculiar character of that activity needs to be specified, as well as the precise sense or nature of representation.

The question of representation has been a difficult one for connectionism. The difficulty has perhaps nowhere been better dramatized than in a challenge mounted initially in an essay by Fodor and Pylyshyn and subsequently reiterated by Fodor and McLaughlin, "Connectionism and the Problem of Systematicity."[24] The challenge is based on the notion of the systematicity or rule-governedness of cognition. Cognition, they argue, is systematic. What is

---

[23]See Tienson's introductory essay in *Connectionism and the Philosophy of Mind*, pp. 1–28.

[24]Jerry Fodor and Brian P. McLaughlin, "Connectionism and the Problem of Systematicity: Why Smolensky's Solution Doesn't Work," in *Connectionism and the Philosophy of Mind*, eds. Terence Horgan and John Tienson (Dordrecht: Kluwer Academic Publishers, 1991), pp. 331–53.

systematic is syntactic. Therefore cognition is syntactic. They offer a straight-forward, commonsense defense of the minor premise, the contention that cognition is systematic. You do not find, they observe, an organism capable of learning to prefer a red square to a green triangle, but which cannot learn to prefer the red triangle to the green square. Similarly, you do not find organisms that can infer $P$ from $P$ & $Q$ & $R$, but which cannot infer $P$ from $P$ & $Q$. Fodor and his colleagues therefore hold that cognition, wherever it occurs, is systematic, and that systematicity is nomologically invariant for all instances of cognition. If $X$ is not systematic, then whatever else may be true of $X$, $X$ is not an instance of cognition. Mental representation qua representation, if cogni-tive, is systematic. And if this is the case, there must be, they hold, some psy-chological mechanism in virtue of which cognitive capacities are systematic. An adequate theory of cognition should exhibit this fact.

Now if systematicity entails a syntax of some sort, then by being system-atic a theory of cognition is syntactic as well. But if all this holds, then connec-tionism as a *bona fide* theory of cognition is questioned since syntax plays no essential role in its account of cognition. Indeed, Fodor and Pylyshyn say that, if connectionism constitutes a *genuine* theory of cognition, it is syntactic, and in being syntactic, it can be viewed merely as an *implementation* of, and not an alternative to, the classical computational model of cognition. On the other hand, if it is not syntactic, it does not qualify as a genuine theory of cognition. This is indeed a troubling dilemma for connectionism, one that has evoked and continues to evoke a large volume of responses. It might be noted here, too, that in Fodor's view of cognition, the syntax of mental representations—in the language of thought—mirrors the syntax of ordinary sentences of nat-ural languages. We may further maintain that a system is cognitive if and only if it is syntactic in the sense that it is algorithmic, that is, that its operations con-sist of manipulations of symbolic representations in the manner discussed ear-lier. Then connectionism is *a priori* ruled out as a theory of cognition.

But connectionism need not concede that representation must of neces-sity be syntactic in the sense required by the computational theory. It may, as it has done, argue for some form of pictorial and holistic representation.[25] But this view sooner or later runs into serious difficulty in attempting to describe how exactly in pictorial terms certain levels of inference are possible. The pic-torial/holistic account seems implausible beyond the level of "basic" percep-tual episodes. Further, the syntax which connectionists are willing to grant as occurring at a higher level of abstraction seems to the computationalists to come too late in the account of how cognition is possible.

So there seem to be two equally unwelcome consequences to admitting to syntax. On the one hand, if syntax is admitted, connectionists seem to be im-paled on one horn of the Fodor/Pylyshyn dilemma. Connectionism becomes

[25]See Andy Clark, "Systematicity, Structured Representations and Cognitive Architecture: A Reply to Fodor and Pylyshyn," in *Connectionism and the Philosophy of Mind*, pp. 198–217.

nothing but an *implementation* of the classic computational model. On the other hand, and no less serious, the characterization given to syntax, and the level at which it is admitted in connectionist theory, raise questions as to its functional efficacy. If cognition is indeed *fundamentally* syntactic, as classic AI holds, then by denying syntax at the fundamental level connectionism denies that it constitutes a new, that is, alternative theory of cognition. It is impaled by the other horn of the dilemma. Either way, connectionism is nailed.

Searle says that, metaphysically at least, our inquiry into the nature of mind is off to a very bad start when we frame the issues in terms of symbols and syntax. These are notions which are entirely observer relative, that is, picking out no "intrinsic" physical referent. If Searle is right, then there would seem little ground for choosing between connectionism and AI. Put somewhat differently, if connectionism turns out to be syntactic in the classic AI sense, then Searle's criticism, if sound, holds as well for both views, for both would be flawed in the same way. But, perhaps, connectionism can come up with an account of syntax—not, as in classic AI, a primitive—which is capable of handling complex instances of cognition. Then its claim to being a genuinely new theory of cognition will be met in large part. The crucial issue revolves around the notions of representation and syntax and how exactly these notions are filled out and implemented.

Enough has been said to exhibit something of the character of the issues at stake in the classic AI/connectionist encounter. Let us now take stock.

### Goodbye to the I

Our discussion has placed us in the center of what is at present a lively debate of particular interest to the philosopher of mind. In classic AI and connectionism we are presented with two models of mental architecture. We may even view them as attempts to implement a broadly functionalist conception of mind. But to say that they are attempts may be to understate things. The computationalists seem to think that in conceiving of mind after the model of the digital computer, they have captured the erstwhile elusive mind, they have "got it right." The connectionists for their part are intent on making the same claim; they, too, have "got it right," but in terms of neural nets. If these are logically inconsistent alternatives, they cannot both be right, though they may both be wrong. But let us suppose that one or the other is on the right track. Let us then suppose that a species of, say, "anthrobots" is in the offing. Let us suppose, further, that with reference to this species the ascription of its being intelligent is, by common agreement—based on tests of one kind or other—practically justified. Would we have, in virtue of such exhibits, solved the mind/body problem? Would we have created a species of persons? Would an anthrobot have convictions in the same sense in which humans are said to have them? Would an anthrobot be capable of genuine self-reference? What should we make of its employment of pronouns such as I and we? What becomes of the by-now-familiar qualia problem?

In short, what becomes of the cluster of concepts—consciousness, belief, conviction, desire, and the like—which are associated with what has come to be called folk psychology? What, if true, does the claim that $X$ is an artificially intelligent being entail? It is to specific questions of this sort that the remaining chapters of this book will be devoted. We turn next to issues of consciousness and to a consideration of closely related notions.

## IN BRIEF

This chapter represents a watershed in the organization of this book. In it we completed our historico/theoretical ascent. We did so by presenting and closely examining the currently leading theories of mind and their variations. As with the views we discussed in the preceding chapters, we sought to identify the merits and strenghs as well as the perceived weaknesses of these several theories. These included in their many versions behaviorism and mind/brain identity theories, and also functionalism, artificial intelligence, and connectionism, the newest theory. These theories have this in common, at least so far as their theoretical statements go: the $I$ of Cartesian dualism is an entirely unnecessary feature.

## SUGGESTIONS FOR FURTHER READING

AYER, A. J., *Philosophy in the Twentieth Century*, pp. 265–67. New York: Vintage Books, 1984.

CAM, PHILIP, "Searle on Strong AI," *Australasian Journal of Philosophy*, 68, no. 1 (March 1990), 103–8.

DRETSKE, FRED, "Machines and the Mental," in *Philosophy, Mind, and Cognitive Inquiry*, pp. 75–88, eds. David J. Cole, James H. Fetzer, and Terry L. Rankin. Dordrecht: Kluwer Academic Publishers, 1990.

FETZER, JAMES, *Artificial Intelligence: Its Scope and Limits*. Dordrecht: Kluwer Academic Publishers, 1990.

HORGAN, TERENCE, AND JOHN TIENSON, eds., *Connectionism and the Philosophy of Mind*. Dordrecht: Kluwer Academic Publisher, 1991. In particular, see the following papers: Robert Cummins and Georg Schwartz, "Connectionism, Computation, and Cognition," pp. 60–73; James W. Garson, "What Connectionists Cannot Do: The Threat to Classical AI," pp. 113–39; and D. E. Bradshaw, "Connectionism and the Specter of Representationalism," pp. 417–33.

KRIPKE, SAUL A., *Naming and Necessity*, pp. 43–155. Cambridge, Mass.: Harvard University Press, 1980.

LYCAN, WILLIAM G., ed., *Mind and Cognition*. Cambridge, Mass.: Basil Blackwell, Ltd., 1990. Especially see paper number 5, "Putting the Function Back into Functionalism," by Elliott Sober.

MOODY, TODD C., *Philosophy and Artificial Intelligence*. Englewood Cliffs, N.J.: Prentice Hall, Inc., 1993.

PHILLIPS, HOLLIBERT E., "On Appealing to the Evidence," *Philosophical Forum*, 22, no. 3 (Spring 1991), 228–42.

POLLOCK, JOHN, *How to Build a Person: A Prolegomenon*. Cambridge, Mass.: MIT Press, 1989. See especially the first four chapters.

ROSENTHAL, DAVID M., ed., *The Nature of Mind*. New York: Oxford University Press, 1991. In particular, see the following papers: Hilary Putnam, "The Nature of Mental States"; Ned Block, "Troubles with Functionalism"; Paul Feyerabend, "Mental Events and the Brain"; and Sydney Shoemaker, "Functionalism and Qualia."

WECKERT, J. "Functionalism's Impotence," *Philosophical Inquiry*, 12, nos. 1–2 (Winter–Spring 1990), 32–43.

# 4

## Consciousness without an I

The most unavoidable feature of our consciousness is the
initiation of change at will. . . . The idea of a thinking observer
who could form from his experience no notion of making a
movement, or, more generally, of doing something, is one that
can scarcely be entertained.

*—Stuart Hampshire*[1]

There is no obstacle to building consciousness into an
intelligent machine.

*—John Pollock*[2]

### CONSCIOUSNESS

The greatest single issue in the current debate over the mind/body problem
is consciousness. Indeed, consciousness has become the focus or rallying point
in the debate. For some theorists, consciousness is the very essence of the mental, so that a full account of any mental state, or activity, or event, of necessity
includes some reference to the phenomenon of consciousness. Thus, failure
to understand, to adequately conceptualize or explain consciousness is *ipso facto*
failure to understand mind as a reality, and as a consequence, the mind/body
problem.[3] Among those who share the view that understanding consciousness

---

[1]Stuart Hampshire, *Thought and Action* (New York: Viking Press, 1967), p. 69.
[2]John Pollock, *How to Build a Person*, (Cambridge, Mass.: MIT Press, 1989), p. 30.
[3]John Searle, *The Rediscovery of Mind* (Cambridge, Mass.: MIT Press, 1992), pp. 111–73.

is crucial to solving the mind/body problem are those who see no possibility of a solution,[4] and those who think a solution, though perhaps possible, is a long way off.[5] Still other theorists understand consciousness in purely functional terms and, for this reason, are entirely sanguine with respect to realizing consciousness artificially, that is, through some suitably designed device.[6] These are, indeed, distinct views even when we allow for some degree of overlap in the accounts of mind which they severally provide. Yet other theorists do not see consciousness as the essence of the mental, hence do not see it as crucial at all to a full account of mind. Consciousness is for them epiphenomenal. We now take a studied look at these positions, though not necessarily in the order in which they have been mentioned above.

### Understanding Consciousness

Of the physical objects we encounter from time to time, some, like ourselves, are conscious, some are unconscious, and some are nonconscious. A filing cabinet, a rock, a stream, a picture are all *non*-conscious, but not *un*-conscious. The term "unconscious" we reserve for the class of things which *has* the capacity for conscious experience. To say that an entity has the capacity for conscious experience is to say that that entity is capable of phenomenal experiences like feeling, sensing, dreaming, and the like. A filing cabinet, however much its drawers may get banged, cannot properly be said to experience the nuisance or thrill of having its drawers banged. This is because an entity of the sort is not so constituted as to be capable of subjective states. Only conscious subjects can experience. The filing cabinet is a mere object in the world. It is not a subject with respect to anything whatsoever, because it cannot be. As Thomas Nagel so very aptly put it, in another context, there is "nothing which it is like" to be a filing cabinet.[7]

But these distinctions do not tell us what consciousness is. True, we have no difficulty recognizing ourselves as conscious. We do not have to pinch ourselves to make the discovery; we never seriously wonder about our being conscious; we never have to peer within ourselves to settle any such issue. But we seem not to know what consciousness is. We merely take our possession of it as an undisputed given. It is one thing to show that something *S* is conscious, quite another to explain what it is in virtue of which *S* is conscious. What exactly,

[4]Colin McGinn, *The Problem of Consciousness* (Cambridge, Mass.: Basis Blackwell, Inc., 1991), pp. 1–22.

[5]Thomas Nagel, "The Mind Wins," in *The New York Review of Books,* XL, no. 5 (March 4, 1993), 40, footnote 6.

[6]Among this fairly large number of theorists are John Pollock—see his *How to Build a Person*— Paul Churchland, and Daniel Dennett. See Paul Churchland, *Matter and Consciousness,* and Daniel Dennett, *Consciousness Explained.*

[7]Thomas Nagel, "What Is It Like to Be a Bat?" *The Philosophical Review (October 1974),* pp. 435–50.

comes the query, is consciousness? How exactly is consciousness related to the brain? These are tough questions.

Once we are committed to physicalism as our metaphysical starting point—the view that whatever exists is physical—then it would seem to follow that if consciousness *is* a member of the class of real things, then it, like everything else there is, is physical, and its true account is a physical one. This conclusion seems inescapable. So far, so good. But what *exactly* does this conclusion amount to? What *exactly* does it mean? It would be a mistake to suppose that theorists agree as to what the conclusion says or entails.

Eliminativists like Rorty and Feyerabend—who hold the so-called "disappearance" version of the identity theory—might be willing to grant that *what* is referred to by the term "consciousness" is a member of the class of what in reality there is but would reject outright the claim that "consciousness" refers to consciousness. Consciousness is, on this view, not a kind of thing and cannot therefore, except elliptically, be referred to. They would consider the position that holds consciousness to be a reality just as mistaken as that which holds that ghosts or mermaids belong to the class of really existing things. So talk about consciousness, for the eliminativist, is really talk about something else, something neurological. Thus the elimination of consciousness leaves the world precisely as it now is, insofar as the kind of its reality contents are concerned. On the eliminativist view, absolutely nothing is lost, since nothing physical is lost. Indeed, what we do gain is a truer ontic inventory.[8]

Very closely related to this view, though in no way the same, is the view that since consciousness is realized in the brain, or through the activity of the brain, it is therefore physically reducible. This view does not deny ontological standing to consciousness; it merely asserts that consciousness can be decomposed or analyzed in terms of other things at a more fundamental level. This view is, therefore, ontically reductive. It maintains that consciousness as a phenomenon answering to a higher, that is, macro, level of description is reducible under analysis to a more fundamental lower, that is, micro, level of description. The procedure is a familiar one. We say that lightning is *nothing but* a sudden electrical discharge due to the ionization of water vapor molecules in the atmosphere, or that sound is *nothing but* the movement of compression waves in the atmosphere. Notice the expression "nothing but" in both reductions. What that expression intimates is that terms standing for the reduced phenomena, such as "lightning" or "sound," can be wholly replaced by terms standing for the referents of the reducing expressions, the expressions following the "nothing but." The corresponding claim with respect to consciousness is that it is *nothing but* neural activity, which is itself decomposable in terms of specific elementary functions.

Before reflecting critically on these two positions, let us consider two other ways of understanding consciousness. Recall that the conclusion above is that

[8]For one version of this view, see Churchland's *Matter and Consciousness*, pp. 58–80.

consciousness is a physical phenomenon. At issue is whether consciousness, because it is physical, is reducible to more fundamental categories—neural processes, events, and the like. This is the crucial question.

We have seen that there are those who answer this question in the affirmative. Let us now consider two views. One says that even if a reduction is in principle a possibility, we humans cannot possibly come up with the theory which will explain the reduction; the other is a denial of the view that consciousness is reducible.

In his essay "Can We Solve the Mind-Body Problem?" Colin McGinn argues that while the nature of consciousness is not inherently mysterious, an understanding of that nature is "cognitively closed" to us. He says:

> A type of mind M is congnitively closed with respect to a property P (or theory T) if and only if the concept-forming procedures at M's disposal cannot extend to a grasp of P (or an understanding of T). Conceiving minds come in different kinds, equipped with varying powers and limitations, biases and blindspots, so that properties (or theories) may be accessible to some minds but not to others.[9]

With respect to consciousness, McGinn says that we do not, as humans, have the cognitive wherewithal to understand how the phenomenon of consciousness, which we come to know by *introspection,* is linked to the brain, which we come to know by *perception.* The problem seems to be that each of these two ways of coming to know is *sui generis*—the one hermetically sealed from the other. What is known by introspection cannot be known by perception, and vice versa. Together these two ways exhaust the means of cognition available to us. We are in an epistemic bind. Consider the musical score on a page of music. The score, in no way mysterious, is cognitively closed to all individuals lacking the capacity to read or understand music. It is cognitively closed to sheep, gnats, monkeys, mosquitoes, and the like—in short, to all but some humans. But humans, too, function within cognitive limits, and those limits are reached with respect to our ability to understand consciousness. As a consequence, not only will we not be able to understand consciousness, we will also not be able to solve the mind/body problem, central to which is the phenomenon of consciousness. The time has come, says McGinn, for us to admit that the solution is constitutionally beyond us. Perhaps some suitably equipped nonhuman individual could produce the explanatory theory; but that theory is cognitively off limits to us.

Let us therefore consider the denial of the view that consciousness is physically reducible. In *The Rediscovery of Mind,* John Searle argues vigorously that the reducibility contention is fundamentally mistaken.

> [C]onsciousness is not reducible in the way that other phenomena are reducible, not because the pattern of facts in the real world involves anything special, but

---

[9]McGinn, *The Problem of Consciousness,* p. 3.

because the reduction of other phenomena depended in part on distinguishing between "objective physical reality," on the one hand, and mere "subjective appearance," on the other; and eliminating the appearance from the phenomena that have been reduced. But in the case of consciousness, its reality is the appearance; hence, the point of the reduction would be lost if we tried to carve off the appearance and simply defined consciousness in terms of the underlying physical reality.[10]

Searle freely grants that consciousness is a biological feature. It is a feature, he emphasizes, which "is caused by neurobiological processes and is as much a part of the natural biological order as any other biological feature such as photosynthesis, digestion or mitosis."[11] So consciousness, according to this view, is a reality. It is as much a feature of the real world as liquidity is, for example. But unlike liquidity, which can be wholly accounted for in terms of the specific behavior of certain molecules or microparticles, consciousness is not similarly reducible to anything more fundamental. The familiar appearance/reality distinction—according to which appearances can be distinguished from their underlying reality—while applicable with respect to liquidity, is wholly inapplicable with respect to consciousness. This is the case, Searle maintains, because the phenomenon of consciousness itself is, after a manner of speaking, all *appearance.*[12] No reduction, at least by present standards, is capable of preserving this, its distinctive feature. The essence of the difficulty facing us with regard to its reduction is that consciousness has a peculiar ontic character which no reduction, at least by present standards, can preserve. Moreover, we are, as living human beings, inextricably involved in consciousness. This means that we cannot, even in principle, escape our own subjective involvement in it in exchange for an objective viewpoint, the better to discover its nature. We cannot view consciousness as, for example, we can view liquidity, as a feature "out there," separable from us, hence amenable to purely objective characterization. We always function from the *inside* of consciousness. We cannot see it in terms *of* something else, or *as* something else; we cannot see it as external to ourselves. It is ontologically distinctive. "The real world," he observes, "the world described by physics, and chemistry and biology, contains an ineliminably subjective element."[13]

This line of reasoning virtually distinguishes two ontological categories. On the one hand are the facts described by physics, chemistry, and biology; on the other hand are facts of consciousness and subjectivity. The former contains ontologically objective facts accessible from the third-person point of view, the latter ontologically subjective facts accessible only from the first-person point

[10]Searle, *The Rediscovery of Mind,* p. 122.

[11]Searle, *The Rediscovery of Mind,* p. 90.

[12][Emphasis mine.] In talking of appearance in this way, Searle has in mind such phenomenal experiences as, for example, what it feels like to be in pain, or what it is like to see red, or taste honey, and the like—that which is, on his view, irreducibly subjective.

[13]Searle, *The Rediscovery of Mind,* p. 95.

of view. Descriptive talk about consciousness and subjectivity from the outside cannot touch the intrinsic, inexorably inner, qualitative nature of either. The subjectivity inherent in consciousness resists reduction to the nonmental. "[T]he ontology of the mental," Searle contends, "is an irreducibly first-person ontology."[14]

There is considerably more, of course, to Searle's position regarding consciousness, but we cannot here give it fuller treatment. We will, however, return shortly to it as we engage it critically. Let us now take a critical look at the positions we have sketched.

### Views of Consciousness

To say, as does the eliminativist, that "consciousness" does not refer to consciousness seems puzzling. Interpreted contentiously, it can be taken to deny that the term "consciousness" is a referring term at all; hence it cannot possibly refer to anything. Or, somewhat neutrally, it can be taken to hold that, even if its status as a referring term were not in dispute, as a matter of fact it fails to refer to its ostensible object since there is no such object. In either case, the result is the same: "Consciousness" does not refer to consciousness.

Universal intuition—if we grant such an animal, or experience, if we do not—is clearly against the first alternative. In the disappearance version of the identity theory, people by and large have no difficulty denying existence to ghosts. In such circumstances the term "ghost" does not refer to a ghost. Such a term has intension—such properties as are depicted by the term—but no extension. The situation is altogether different with respect to consciousness. Though its precise nature remains unexplained, its existence seems an inescapable reality. *We cannot successfully deny that we are conscious.* Moreover, if the term does fail *completely* of reference, is it not mysterious that we manage, one and all to communicate intelligibly something of the phenomenon about which we discriminate when we use the term? Could this consistency of success, so universal, be by chance? It would seem not.

The second alternative seems a more promising one. It in turn has two possibilities. The first of the two, that "consciousness" refers to nothing, we can quickly rule out as logically incoherent. If it refers, it must refer to something, however indistinctly or inaccurately. The second possibility, that the term in reality signals something other than consciousness, is often taken to mean that the real referent is some set of neurophysiological events occurring in the brain or central nervous system. This is the disappearance view of the identity theory all over again.[15]

Let us now move on to the closely related view that consciousness is a real phenomenon but one which, nonetheless, is reducible. One obvious strength of this view is its theoretical consistency. If everything is physical, then there is

---

[14]Searle, *The Rediscovery of Mind*, p. 95.
[15]See pages 67–68 of this book for a criticism of this view.

no room in the universe for nonphysical phenomena. Indeed, the very notion of a nonphysical phenomenon, of an ontologically special case, would on this premise be unintelligible. And once we grant that consciousness is, in some way or other, produced by the brain, recursive decomposition of some sort would, at least in principle, seem as good a route as any to investigating its nature. What is physically realized should in all likelihood be physically explicable. John Pollock, for example, sees no difficulty in effecting the decomposition in strictly functional terms. His self-conscious machine, Oscar, is equipped with a multilevel system of sensors—external perceptual sensors and internal or introspective first- and second-order sensors. Consciousness on his view takes the form of a hierarchical functioning of sensors. Sensors at a higher level make sense of the deliverances of sensors at a lower level. In this way the intelligent machine takes account of itself, qualitative states and all. It acquires self-consciousness.[16]

This way of accounting for consciousness is challenged by both McGinn and Searle. McGinn holds that an understanding of consciousness is congnitively closed to us, and Searle contends that, at least by our present standards of reduction, consciousness is irreducible to anything else.

The notion of cognitive closure is certainly a useful one, although it is transparent. It yields the unalarming observation that what mice cannot possibly understand, men can; what bats can detect, rats are incapable of, and so on. But McGinn has produced no compelling argument to *show* that humans are incapable of understanding consciousness by reason of cognitive limitation. The unbridgeable chasm between the deliverances of perception on the one hand and introspection on the other carries the weight of his pessimism. But while this strategy may have intuitive appeal, it seems to yield its results by begging the question. The argument is something like the following: "We cannot understand phenomenon $X$ because phenomenon $X$ is beyond our capacities to understand." The form of the argument is perfectly valid—"If $p$, then $p$". But the proposition we substitute for $p$ needs to be established as true to make the argument sound, and McGinn does not accomplish this. Indeed, it would be nothing short of amazing if anyone could. He may be right, of course, in saying that consciousness is cognitively closed to us. This thesis, however, even if true, cannot be demonstrated, at least not by anyone limited in the way McGinn thinks we all are. Demonstration by any of us would render the thesis false. To know the limits is to have transcended them.

Searle's view is an intriguing one. It says: Consciousness is irreducibly subjective. Therefore, it belongs to a distinct ontic category. On the face of it, it looks as though this view must entail some form of dualism. We are required to distinguish between the physically reducible and the physically irreducible. This is a distinction between reducible objective features of the brain as a spatiotemporal entity, on the one hand, and, on the other, a subjective feature

---

[16]Pollock, *How to Build a Person*, pp. 1–30.

which, though arising entirely from the neurobiological properties of the brain, is *both physical and irreducible*. It is at once a very bold and difficult position that says of any *X* that it is both physical and irreducible. Such a position runs the risk of being either inconsistent or, worse, contradictory—unless, of course, one of the two predicates is not intended to have its usual semantic import. In that event, one or the other of the two terms must be reinterpreted. From a logical point of view, there is not much we can do with the term "irreducible." And if the term "physical" does not have its standard meaning, it is difficult to see what alternatives are open. To regard the term "physical" as having some nonstandard sense, as some have suggested, renders the irreducibility claim bewilderingly unclear.[17] That strategy may even trivialize the view in question. Searle quite explicitly holds that consciousness is a biological feature of the brain. It would therefore do his position no good to substitute selectively some nonstandard sense for the term "physical" precisely at the point where the irreducibility claim seems to run into conceptual trouble.

Searle himself, it is fair to say, does not provide us much help in settling the metaphysical difficulty implied by the irreducibility claim. He says: "Whether we treat the irreducibility from the materialist or from the dualist point of view, we are still left with a universe that contains an irreducibly subjective physical component as a component of physical reality. . . . [I]ts irreducibility is a trival consequence of our definitional practices."[18] If the purported irreducibility is the trivial consequence of our *definitional* practices, what does this have to do with what presumably is essentially *ontological* irreducibility? Whether or not some *X* is ontologically reducible or irreducible seems to have little to do with our definitional practices. Indeed, in the following passage, the notion of definitional practices is not apparent. Searle writes:

> Now suppose we tried to reduce the subjective, conscious first-person sensation of pain to the objective, third-person patterns of neuron firings. Suppose we tried to say the pain is really "nothing but" the patterns of neuron firings. Well, if we tried such an ontological reduction, the essential features of the pain would be left out. No description of the third-person, objective physiological facts would convey the subjective, first-person character of the pain, simply because the first-person features are different from the third-person features.[19]

If definitional practices are the source of the brain/consciousness problem, then all we need to do is what some eliminativists have long suggested: get rid of those abominable practices. But that will not do, not if subjectivity, as

[17]See Thomas Nagel's, "The Mind Wins," *The New York Review of Books*, p. 40. Searle himself does seem to qualify his use of the term "physical" when he writes as follows: "[O]nce you accept our world view the only obstacle to granting consciousness its status as a biological feature is the dualistic/materialistic assumption that the 'mental' character of consciousness makes it impossible for it to be a 'physical' property." See his *The Rediscovery of Mind*, p. 91.

[18]Searle, *The Rediscovery of Mind*, pp. 123–24.

[19]Searle, *The Rediscovery of Mind*, p. 117.

Searle and others have insisted, is an irreducible reality. The problem is clearly not a linguistic one but an ontological one, as Searle all along maintains.

On the irreducibility view of consciousness, then, are we committed to some form of dualism, perhaps property dualism? Perhaps we can consider physicality as the original ontic category, and the subjectively irreducible and the objectively irreducible as two subcategories, each with its distinctive properties. But in that case, we merely reconceive the physical. Or, alternatively, we can accept physicality as the one and only ontic category and, following Nagel, consider subjectivity (characterized by Nagel's well-put what-it-is-like-to-be-a-bat feature) and objectivity as, in some sense, two *aspects* of this single reality. In either case, the result leaves the mind/body problem virtually unsolved. The problem retains its classic form—one thing not reducible to the other—and we are hopelessly back where we once were a long time ago.

In light of the foregoing, on the irreducibility view of consciousness, we may resist the traditional monist/dualist or materialist/nonmaterialist classifications, but it is hard to avoid some patent form of dualism. Another view might be the thesis that all that exists is physical, and, as a corollary, that whatever is physical is physically reducible. Of course, this must have the qualification that we may not now know how the reduction is to be explained. And if this is at once a monist and a physicalist position, then so be it. Ontological claims do seem to involve some kind of counting.

But we have so far said very little regarding a definition of the phenomenon of consciousness itself. We have pretty much assumed that we know what we are talking about. Let us now turn our attention in that direction.

### In Pursuit of a Definition of Consciousness

The theoretical differences we encountered above are to some extent traceable to the fact that we do not have anything like a *precise definition* of consciousness, no definitive theory.[20] We simply do not know what exactly this phenomenon is.[21] Recall McGinn's contention that understanding consciousness is beyond our cognitive capacities. In his opinion, a definitive theory is beyond human grasp. And Nagel, too, says that our present concepts are incapable of taking us very far in that understanding. By contrast, there is no theory of water. We know that water consists of two parts hydrogen and one part oxygen, and we understand well the behavior of hydrogen and oxygen molecules under given conditions, so there is no need for a theory of water. The same may be said of numerous other objects and phenomena with which we are familiar.

---

[20]By the expression "precise definition" I intend a definition that accurately *describes* what consciousness is. It would be one which expresses the necessary and sufficient conditions for the ascription of consciousness to an entity.

[21]In a bit of an understatement, Francis Crick and Kristof Koch tersely express this in the following way: "The overwhelming question in neurobiology *today* is the relation between the mind and the brain." See Francis Crick and Kristof Koch, "The Problem of Consciousness" in *Scientific American*, 267, no. 3 (September 1992), p. 153. [Emphasis mine.]

Lightning, for example, is nothing but the sudden discharge of electrical energy due to the ionization of water vapor molecules in the atmosphere. We do not need a theory, say, of lead, or of lightning. By and large, once we know the exact nature of the constituent properties of a phenomenon, we are well on our way to explaining it. We do know that consciousness is a natural feature of some biological systems, notably neuronal systems, but we do not know its precise nature. We know a lot about it, but not nearly enough. The way is thus open for a good deal of theorizing, and with it a good deal of controversy.

Let us reflect upon some of what we do know. It is clear that you who are reading this sentence and I who am now engaged in writing it are conscious. We are both conscious *of* something, namely, the sentence. It would be quite unintelligible in this circumstance for either of us to remark that we were indeed conscious but conscious of nothing. Commonly, being conscious is being conscious of something. This feature, its being directed at something or other, is what is sometimes spoken of as its *intentionality,* and that at which it is directed is referred to as its intentional object. A mental state is said to have intentional content. We ask two related questions at this point, one clearly intimated by the use of the term "commonly": (1) Is it not the case that being in a conscious state is *always* being conscious of something? And (2) What difference, if any, is there between being conscious and being aware?

Both questions seem to have more to do with linguistic practice than with the ontology of consciousness or of conscious states *per se.* In the absence of a definitive theory of consciousness, once we determine how we intend to use the terms "conscious," or "consciousness," we have by stipulation set the ontological boundaries. Then the answers are shaped by the particular linguistic practice we adopt. To illustrate, let us suppose consciousness to extend along a continuum so that we can say of it that it underlies all mental states of a system. On one end of the continuum, we suppose the greatest or most intense mental activity—such as attending, noticing, and concentrating. At the other end, we suppose the least active of mental states—a dreamless sleep, for instance. Possessing consciousness *per se* would broadly intimate the occurrence of mental states. In that case a human being, for instance, may be said to be conscious but not conscious *of* anything at all. We can then distinguish between two notions, the broader and inclusive, "being conscious," and the narrower, "being conscious of." The latter, a subset of the former, will, of course, always be intentional. It may also share its congnitive territory with what we would call awareness, the extent to which we know that such and such is going on.

For some, an advantage to this way of conceiving of things would be that the unity of consciousness is thereby preserved. Gone are the scaffoldings of floor after floor or layer after layer of dismal structure; gone the plethora of mental compartments, subsconsciousness and all. In the short run, until a definitive theory emerges, much depends on how we want to talk, which theory we adopt. But talk and reality do not thereby converge.

Let us resume our reflection on what we do know. We do know that consciousness is realized in certain biological systems, for such we are. We may venture to say, as does Searle, that it is a property of such systems; but the term "property" can be problematic. Sometimes the term suggests that what is so picked out is in some sense a part of something, at other times, not. Oxygen is a property of water, but it is clear that there is antecedently no thing which is water and of which oxygen happens to be a property. There is no independently existing thing, namely, water, that may be independent of properties. Water is precisely its constituent properties. So, to say that oxygen is a constituent property of water is to say that without that constituent property there is no such thing as water. It is, in short, a necessary condition for the realization of water.

The same reasoning does not hold when we say that liquidity is a property of water, brittleness a property of glass, or heat or smoke is a property of fire; or when we speak of the property of abstractions like numbers; and so on. "Being a property of" is an inherently ambiguous expression. Except in very clear cases, therefore, we will find it necessary to inquire what exactly its use intends. In holding that consciousness is a property of brains, it is not readily apparent which sense of "being a property of" is in fact applicable to the relationship which consciousness bears to brains. Indeed, if we knew, we would probably not now have a mind/body problem. Crick and Koch would not now be declaring that the overwhelming problem in neuroscience today is the nature of the relationship between the mind and the brain. So in holding that consciousness is a property of brains, we really do not know what that contention amounts to.

So far we can credit ourselves with knowing that we are conscious, and that we are biological systems. And by implication we also know that the systems that we are are alive. Indeed, we do know a bit more: We are self-conscious or self-aware, by virtue, at least, of our ability to reflect on just what we ourselves do know. But along with these acknowledgments is another significant feature about us. It is a feature to which Nagel has given famous expression worth repeating here. "But no matter how the form may vary, the fact that an organism has conscious experience *at all* means, basically, that there is something it is like to *be* that organism . . . fundamentally an organism has conscious states if and only if there is something that it is like to *be* that organism. We may call this the subjective character of experience."[22]

If Nagel is right, for the sorts of things we said we knew of ourselves to be necessary conditions of consciousness, they must be wholly or partially subsumed under the something-it-is-like condition. Or failing this, they must be regarded as not necessary to the ascription of consciousness. The fact that the necessary and sufficient condition for possessing conscious states is expressed with reference to live entities, organisms,[23] presupposes the condition of be-

[22]Nagel, "What Is It Like to Be a Bat?" p. 436.

[23]This is perfectly understandable since the paradigm we start with is none other than ourselves. From there, we work our way outwards.

ing alive. After all, there is nothing it is like to be a bagel, or a bolt of lightning, or a bulldozer. These are not the sorts of entities capable of the kinds of phenomenal experiences we associate with subjectivity. This position raises the familiar question of chauvinism—whether, that is, we can thus exclude fabricated entities answering to some suitable description from the class of conscious entities. Expressed as a challenge, it contends that the issue of consciousness is ill-served by supposing *a priori* that a precondition for its possession is membership in some biological species.

As we note from the title of his book, and from the brief passage quoted at the beginning of this chapter, John Pollock, like numerous others, sees no obstacle to "building consciousness into an intelligent machine." But a question which immediately arises is whether the phenomenon of being intelligent does not already presuppose the phenomenon of being conscious.[24] If that is the case, as indeed it seems to be, an intelligent machine is already conscious, and the real question before us, in all its epistemological fullness, is: *Can* there be an intelligent machine? So, is Pollock's engineering challenge the result of conceptual confusion? Does he assume what he in fact needs to show, that there can be intelligence in the absence of consciousness? This assumption becomes evident if there is talk of an entity's intelligence at the same time as its consciousness is denied. (Incidentally, being self-conscious is not a necessary condition for the ascription of consciousness. Probably also the capacity for self-consciousness requires some sort of conceptual system which only some animal forms are now capable of.)

In sum, we can grant that there is something which it is like to be a bat, but not something which it is like to be a bagel; something which it is like to be me, but not something which it is like to be my hat. Without ruling *a priori* on the biological issue, however, for there to be something which it is like to be an intelligent machine, the machine, like the bat or like me, must be capable of phenomenal experiences. Whatever its particular physico/chemical makeup, it must nonetheless be able to manifest subjectivity by occupying a first-person point of view. Such a machine, while not necessarily possessing a neural system, must be capable of containing the causal powers of neural systems, and in particular, of brains.[25] This requirement brings us to the issue of intentionality, which we merely touched on earlier but which we will now look at closely.

[24]It would seem correct to suppose that the ascription of intelligence to a machine is made because of specific mental operations of which it is capable. If this is so, then ascriptions such as "prefers," "wants to," "is undecided about," "thinks mistakenly that," "believes that," and the like should to some degree apply to such a machine. But these ascriptions all involve conscious mental states. The notion of mental states associated with being intelligent but not with being conscious seems unintelligible.

[25]This seems an altogether natural requirement given that our understanding of consciousness derives entirely from our experiencing it in our own case as neural systems. See also Searle's *The Rediscovery of Mind*, p. 92.

## INTENTIONALITY

The concern of this section is with the notion of intentionality, and with the relation of intentional states to consciousness. To be clear, however, on exactly what we are about in the discussion which follows, we will need, as a preliminary, to distinguish two related senses of the term "intentionality," only one of which will be the present focus of our interest.

The first sense can perhaps best be identified by a simple illustration. Imagine yourself saying to someone, regarding some occurrence for which you take responsibility: "I *did* that." In so claiming, if you wanted to be understood as saying that your action was *deliberate, done on purpose*, we could characterize it as intentional and with that in mind might speak with reference to the *intentionality* of your action. This is an important consideration, of course, since we often want to distinguish between acts that were intended, and those that we did not intend, though we might hold ourselves, or be held, responsible for them. Intentionality in this sense has to do with the special psychological auspices which brought about an act, with the state of mind that motivated the act. This is not, however, the sense of our primary interest in what follows.

The sense of intentionality which is of special interest to us here is the sense that calls attention to a peculiar feature of some mental states: their *being about* or *directed at* something or other, some event or state of affairs. Believing, for instance, is always believing *that* or *in* something; or hoping is always hoping *for* such and such, or *that* so and so; being pleased, always being pleased *with* or *that;* being joyful, always being joyful *over,* or *with respect to,* such and such; and so on. We do not simply believe or hope or become pleased or joyful. In being so directed, a mental state is said to have intentional content, and that at which it is directed is referred to as its intentional object.

That intentionality is a peculiar feature of some mental states—in fact, the large majority of them—is a statement that can be misleading. We must not suppose that it is a constitutive property of such states in the way in which, say, hydrogen is a constitutive property of water, or heat is always a feature of fire. Some mental states, admittedly a relatively small number, are such that, depending on the circumstances, they may or may not be intentional. Some episodes of dread, or of fear, for example, seem to have no discernible intentional object at all. We simply find ourselves in the grip of the particular feeling. So a particular mental state is not always intentional; nor are all conscious states intentional ones. Someone experiencing a certain form of pathological anxiety, for instance, is conscious, but the state in question is not intentional.

Much as we might be tempted to, we do not seriously say of nonstarting motor vehicles or of unyielding door locks that they have a mind of their own. We do not, because they are not the sorts of things that we consider capable of mental states, so we cannot seriously say of them that they possess intentional states. But things get tricky rather rapidly. Just what is the relationship between intentionality and consciousness, and just what sorts of things are capable of intentionality? While the determination with respect to intentionality is clear for things like motor vehicles and door locks, it is not so straightforward with regard to some other things, things like robots or computers or similar devices. Let us look at what a case fitting this latter class might typically be.

Imagine the following. On a tour through an ultramodern hospital, you encounter Max. Max is a device into which is built a set of highly efficient computers and sensors. Max's official designation is floor assistant. Unattended, Max negotiates hallways, waits his turn at the elevators, avoids obstacles, receives and delivers an assortment of items throughout the hospital, makes inquiries, and performs numerous other functions. Now the question with respect to Max is: Does Max have *intentional* states? *Is* Max an intentional system? The question arises solely, of course, in virtue of the characteristics which Max seems to be exhibiting. Presumably one or other of the following might on occasion have been said, and possibly held true, of Max: "Max thinks that . . ."; "Max notices that . . ."; or "Max wants to . . .". How else, we may query, could Max be capable of executing his tasks except by having the relevant intentional states?

The difficulty we encounter in addressing the question derives, at least on the face of it, from the way in which the question is posed—in terms of intentionality rather than in terms of consciousness. Certainly if expressions such as the ones above apply on occasion to Max, then Max must have intentional states, whether or not he is conscious in some standard sense.

Theorists like Dennett, as well as numerous other functionalists, would maintain that Max is clearly an intentional system. Dennett's strategy in support of this view, what he calls the intentional stance, is as follows:

> [T]he intentional strategy consists of treating the object whose behavior you want to predict as a rational agent with beliefs and desires and other mental stages exhibiting what Brentano and others call *intentionality*. . . . I will argue that any object—or as I shall say, any *system*—whose behavior is well predicted by this strategy is in the fullest sense of the word a believer. *What it is* to be a true believer is to be an *intentional system*, . . .[26]

Our floor assistant, Max, successfully negotiates obstacles, waits his turn at the elevator and continues to wait if the elevator is full, does errands, and at times utters relevant questions. Max behaves like a rational agent. From a functionalist point of view, Max is unambiguously an intentional system.

But there is a rather different way of understanding Max's presumed intentionality, indeed, one quite opposed to the view just sketched. According to this view, strongly defended by Searle and others, Max's intentionality is not unambiguously intentional, as the functionalist position would have it, but is best described as an instance of "as-if" intentionality. This form of intentional-

---

[26]Daniel Dennett, *The Intentional Stance* (Cambridge, Mass.: MIT Press, 1987), p. 15. See also his *Brainstorms* (Montgomery, Vt.: Bradford Books, 1978).

ity is to be distinguished from two other forms: the "intrinsic" and the "derived." The former, according to Searle, is a phenomenon possessed by humans and certain other animals as part of their biological nature; the latter is a semantic feature of language, and of certain other kinds of representation.[27]

Since a good deal is made to hang on it, it is important that we clearly understand the nature of Searle's distinction. Consider the following sentences: I am exceedingly thirsty; The wheat fields are exceedingly thirsty; "Ich habe hunger" means "I am hungry." If I utter the first sentence as a statement true of myself, then there actually is in me a conscious feeling of thirst in virtue of which the statement I utter is true. A feeling of thirst is *literally* a feeling *for* something which would assuage that thirst, hence is intentional. Intentionality accounted for in this way is what Searle characterizes as "intrinsic." In contrast, the ascription of thirst in the second sentence made with respect to wheat fields is entirely figurative, since things like wheat fields do not experience feelings of any kind. Wheat-field "thirst" is therefore "as-if" thirst, since it is in reality not an instance of thirst at all. This employment of "thirst" is purely honorific. With respect to the third sentence, the term "means" is an intentional term all right but, as Searle would explain it, its intentionality is derived from the intentionality intrinsic to language users. The conventional marks "Ich habe hunger" translates "I am hungry" precisely because language users make the semantic assignments they do. In sum, only such systems as possess intrinsic intentionality can literally mean, or experience thirst, and the like.

### Is Max an Intentional System?

In light of the foregoing, let us now take a scrutinizing look at Max. The crucial question at issue, of course, is Max's intentionality.

Max, recall, encounters obstacles, duly notes them, and negotiates them by engaging in avoidance maneuvers. Let us suppose, then, that Max encounters a bench in a hallway. Max would work his way around the bench and continue on his way. Now what, if anything, does Max do, or is capable of doing, that is *qualitatively* different from what, say, a flowing river does, or is capable of doing? The river flows *over* some objects, but some it encounters as obstacles—huge rocks, for example, or large masses of earth. In the latter circumstance, the river engages in avoidance maneuvers—it duly flows around the obstacles—and continues on its way. So also, after a manner of speaking, does Max. Objects like bits of paper, posing no particular problem, are passed over; but benches are another matter. Like the river, Max carries out an avoidance maneuver by going around the obstacle and promptly carrying on with his mission. So, with respect to the issue of intentionality, what are we to make of Max's performance vis-à-vis that of the river? And what does either do, if anything, which is *qualitatively* different from what you and I do, or are capable of doing?

[27]Searle, *The Rediscovery of Mind*, pp. 78–82, 156.

On Dennett's account, the difference between Max and the river, or between either of them and either of us, is solely one of degree. There is no *qualitative* difference. All are alike intentional systems and the sense of intentionality which applies to the one applies as well to the other. On Searle's account, the intentionality exhibited by both Max and the river is entirely bereft of beliefs and desires and could not possibly be intentional in the intrinsic sense which he distinguishes. "As-if" intentionality which, for Searle, is the sense instantiated by both these systems, is, in his view, not an instance of intentionality at all.

Common sense or, perhaps better, common belief, seems on the side of Searle. We are inclined to say with respect to the river that in reality it *does* nothing whatsoever. Rivers fall completely outside the class of things to which doings can be literally ascribed. "Doing" is the way we talk about the actions of human or other animal doers. With respect to rivers, there are, we say more seriously, things which happen, events to which the river is causally related. But no belief or other intentional ascription need be made or appealed to in order to explain the relationship between river and event. The plain brute facts of physics are all that are necessary to explain the entire range of river phenomena. And indeed, one reason that we do not go beyond these brute facts is based first and foremost on our own case, on ourselves as experiencing intentional systems. We see no reason to attribute beliefs and desires or any other mental state to things like rivers. For all we know, they are inanimate, that is, nonconscious entities, incapable of having experiences of any kind.

In like vein, Max, while representing an amazing feat of human engineering, does not strike us as the sort of entity capable of making deliberative judgments about states of affairs. Max is not the sort of entity we regard as capable of having a point of view with respect to his activities or to his environment. Intentional ascriptions in everyday life go well beyond the manifest movements or functional output of entities to which the ascriptions might be made. Such movements and outputs may provide strong clues of intentionality but constitute no proof of it. We know exactly how Max does what he does. The brute facts of physics render him and his "gee-whiz" maneuvers practically transparent. Clearly lacking to Max is subjectivity, and with it intentionality in any but a borrowed sense. To be genuinely intentional, Max's "brain," we maintain with Searle, would have to have capabilities identical with those of a biological brain.

This is undoubtedly an extremely conservative view. It essentially holds that the class of intentional systems is *a priori determined,* its membership being closed to any but some animal systems, or to only such systems as can replicate the causal powers of some animal brains. At the same time, however, Dennett's prescriptive intentional stance strikes us as being not only counterintuitive, but excessively liberal. With a little help, practically anything qualifies as an intentional system. On the one hand is what we may term Searle's "apriorism," and on the other is Dennett's *prescriptivism.* The crucial and decisive issue is, once again, the question of the reducibility of subjectivity. It is the issue that lies at the very heart of the mind/body problem. Any viable theory of mind must address it.

In defense of the conservative view, the charge of apriorism need not signal a defect. The conservative views takes seriously the undeniable fact that humans and some other animals are clearly intentional systems. From the vantage point, first and foremost, of our own experience as such systems, we are intimately familiar with the semantic import of intentional ascriptions. To deny this is to make any such ascriptions unintelligible. Talk of the intentional necessarily begins at home, from where and from what we are. Intentionality is a phenomenon inseparable from our status as entities capable of experiencing the world. We accomplish this feat of experiencing the world by our possession of neural mechanisms, in particular, a brain. Perhaps membership in the class of intentional systems to which we clearly belong should require, for each instance, some mechanism capable of duplicating the causal powers of the brain. Entities included in this class would be capable of phenomenal experiences, of experiencing the world from a first-person point of view. Such conservatism seems quite justified. The charge of conservatism or of apriorism does not in itself constitute a nice knockdown argument.

On the other hand, a position that regards thermostats and mousetraps as literally believing this or that turns the very notion of intentionality on its head. In so doing it is entirely compatible with its elimination from serious consideration of the mental. The consistency of this view with the physicalist presupposition, that whatever there is is wholly physical and therefore entirely explicable in terms of the laws of physics, appears to be purchased at too high a price. The *reduction* of intentionality via any stance, intentional or other, seems a metaphysically unlikely prospect. Such a feat requires first the reduction of subjectivity. The *denial* of the reality of either subjectivity or of intentionality seems an especially bold step, indeed one which begs the question: Assuming that they do not exist establishes their nonexistence.

### Are Intentionality and Consciousness Related?

So the question of the relationship between intentionality and consciousness turns out to be a tricky one. There are several ways of understanding the question: First, on the face of it, the question seeks to *discover* a genuine ontological distinction. Second, it inquires no further than the relationships which variously obtain between two terms as they occur in theory after theory. There may well be as many *perceived* relationships between the two as there are theories of mind. The question seeks to discover an enduring relationship between realities picked out by language, and not merely to ascertain how two particular terms in any given theory of mind are related. To this extent, the issue is decidedly and irreducibly ontological. Of course we may also contend that "consciousness" and "intentionality" name nothing at all, so that the question of the relationship between the entities they supposedly stand for is ill-put. But, as we argued above, this eliminativist position is too alarmingly counter-intuitive to be taken seriously.

But once the question of the relationship has taken us to the ontological level, we face once again the larger and persistent issue of attempting to sort out the connection between the mental and the physical. Given physicalism, and given the reality of mental properties like consciousness or intentionality, just what kind of realities are mental realities? Let us take a closer look at an explanatory thesis—call it the thesis of supervenience—which we passed over relatively quickly in Chapter One.

## SUPERVENIENCE

The fundamental thesis of supervenience, with respect to the mind/body problem, is that all mental phenomena are supervenient on physical phenomena. More particularly, all psychological states and properties supervene on or result from neurological states and properties. The notion of supervenience expresses *a relation between two sets of properties at two different levels of description:* the macrolevel and the microlevel. The relation of the macro-properties to the micro-properties is one of total dependence of the former on the latter in the sense that any change whatever on the macrolevel entails a corresponding change on the microlevel. There can be no independent change at the macrolevel. Applied to the mind/body problem, the thesis of supervenience considers psychological or mental phenomena as macro-phenomena which supervene on neural micro-phenomena. Thus any change at the psychological level entails a corresponding change at the neural level. In short, all that is mental is wholly and entirely dependent on the physical. Add to this a thorough-going physicalist premise to the effect that whatever particulars there are are physical. Then it follows as a consequence that all mental particulars are wholly and entirely physical particulars. In light of this, there are, strictly, no psychophysical laws, only physical-physical laws and, by the same token, no psychological laws, only physical laws.

We can now express the relation of supervenience more formally and simply. Necessarily, a set of properties $R$ supervenes on another set of properties $S$, if and only if, for any property $P$ in the set $R$, if anything $x$ has the property $P$, then there is in the set $S$ some property $P^*$ such that $x$ has $P^*$. If we applied this schema to the mind/body problem, any fact at the mental level (any true statement to the effect that such and such is so and so) is totally dependent on facts at the neural level. They alone determine the truth of the statement at the supervening mental level. So on this thesis, any psychological, that is, mental, event whatever can be redescribed entirely in terms of neural microphenomenal states and properties.

The notion of supervenience has its origin in the area of ethics. G. E.

Moore, R. M. Hare, and others considered evaluative properties such as goodness and the like, while not themselves naturalistic properties, to be none the
less supervenient upon the naturalistic or constitutive properties of things.[28]
Two objects possessing the same naturalistic properties down to the last detail
are, of necessity, alike good (or bad); any difference in evaluation entails a difference in their constitutive properties. We may say, therefore, that any object
$O$ is good solely *in virtue of* its possessing just those natural properties $C$ which
as a matter of fact it does possess. So the goodness, $G$, of any object $O$, supervenes on its natural properties.

Note that on this account the natural properties of $O$ do not *cause* $O$ to
be good. $C$ does not stand to $G$ as cause to effect. This is easily seen if we reflect
that there exists no object $O$ apart from just those properties, $C$, which, occurring as they do, constitute $O$. We cannot distinguish ontologically between $O$
and the totality of its properties, for $O$ is nothing over and above its properties,
and $G$ is not in any strict sense the *effect* of $C$. The supervenience relation in the
kind of instance involving moral or ethical predicates is therefore not causal
but *constitutive* in the sense that it is solely *in virtue of the possession of natural properties* that any object $O$ possesses its moral properties.

Another kind of supervenience is causal supervenience, where one set of
properties is the causal consequence of another set of properties. This causal
supervenience relation is the kind presumed by some to hold between mental
states and physical states, more particularly, between psychological states and
neurophysiological states. Searle, for example, says:

> [M]ental states supervene on neurophysiological states in the following way: Type-
> identical neurophysiological causes would have type-identical mentalistic effects.
> . . . if you had two brains that were type-identical down to the last molecule, then
> the causal basis of the mental would guarantee that they would have the same
> mental phenomena. . . . [T]he supervenience of the mental on the physical is
> marked by the fact that physical states are causally sufficient, though not neces-
> sarily causally necessary, for the corresponding mental states.[29]

Kim's causal account is somewhat softer.

> The relationship between a property or an event and its supervenience base itself
> is not *happily* [italics mine] considered as a causal relation, although it is an im-
> portant variety of what may broadly be termed a "determinative relation," and
> there is no causal path from the supervenient event to an effect that is indepen-
> dent of the causal path from the supervenience base to the effect. It is because of
> this second fact that the supervenient event is not a cause *comparable in status* [ital-
> ics mine] to its supervenience base; in effect, it has no causal status apart from its
> supervenience on a base event that has a more direct causal role.[30]

[28]See G. E. Moore, *Principia Ethica* (Cambridge: Cambridge University Press, 1929),
chap. I.

[29]Searle, *The Rediscovery of Mind*, pp. 124–25.

[30]Jaegwon Kim, "Causality, Identity, and Supervenience," in *Midwest Studies in Philosophy,
Vol. IV: Studies in Metaphysics*, eds. Peter French, Theodore E. Uehling, and Howard K. Wettstein
(Minneapolis: University of Minnesota Press, 1979), p. 45.

Supervenience of the mental on the neurophysiological is interpreted by some to entail causal impotence of the mental—one version of epiphenomenalism. For those who hold this view, as we noted earlier, there are in reality no mental causes. Mental phenomena are simply effectless effects of neurophysiological causes. Kim's view, while not expressly denying causal efficacy to the mental, might yet be seen to be, in essence, doing precisely that. While the *reality* of the mental is acknowledged, the passage above accords the mental a greatly diminished causal status. The mental, as macrophenomenal, does not play the robust explanatory role with which we ordinarily associate it. Ordinarily, we decide to do things, we believe we should do things, and we do them, or we refrain from doing them. But for Kim, the correct causal account of any macro-event whatever consists in its micro-explanation. Indeed, as Kim goes on to say, "[M]acro-phenomena in general, . . . are supervenient on micro-processes, and their causal roles must be explicated in terms of the fundamental micro-causal processes."[31]

Even though Kim seems willing to retain talk of the causal role of the mental, we get the strong impression that nothing of significance is added to the microcausal account of an event. "If that is epiphenomenalism," he consoles, "let us make the most of it."[32] We should bear in mind, just the same, that Kim's is an attempt to recognize the reality of the mental. As it emerges in his self-styled "supervenient dualism," the mental is clearly not of the Cartesian variety, and it seems to be somewhat askew of an identity view. Whatever its metaphysical status, its causal role smacks of systematic redundancy, if not of impotence.

On the other hand, Searle's brand of causal supervenience accords with our everyday unexamined ascription of robust mental causation. Deciding to do *X* or not to do *X* is, we freely allow, causally related on occasion to the doing of *X*. We do *X* simply because doing it is what we decide to do, or wish or desire to do; and that is as true an account of *X's* being done as any. On this everyday view, the mental is anything but causally impotent. What better evidence can we have for this than the fact that we *do* things? We act on our beliefs, wishes, desires, and so on.

But, just the same, this optimistic story lends itself to many a challenge. For instance, accounts which purport to ascribe causal efficacy to such mental phenomena as desires or beliefs are fundamentally mistaken in the sense that such accounts fail to identify the real causes involved in the production of action. At best, such accounts are merely shortened versions of the genealogy of the actions they attempt to explain. Accordingly, to explain an action is to do so in terms of its micro-causes. Appeal at the macrolevel of causation, the level of desires and beliefs and so on, is simply appeal at the wrong level. All real causes are microphysical ones. This position calls into question not only the ex-

[31]Kim, "Causality, Identity, and Supervenience," pp. 47–48.
[32]Kim, "Causality, Identity, and Supervenience," p. 45.

planatory utility of such mental notions as beliefs, desires, and a host of other mental phenomena but their ontic standing as well. With particular regard to the initiation of action, the troubling question now is whether mental causation is in reality nothing but "as-if" causation. Are commonsense views with respect to mental causation and sources of action entirely wrong-headed? These are some of the issues we will address in the next chapter.

## IN BRIEF

In this chapter we considered the notions of consciousness and intentionality and the issues surrounding them. With regard to consciousness, we noted that there are those who argue that the nature of consciousness is such that it is cognitively closed to us. While this view holds that consciousness is a feature of humans—and possibly of some other living systems—our cognitive apparatus is limited in much the same way that a rat, say, is incapable of understanding a symphony. Others argue that the notion is nothing but a bit of humbug and should be eliminated from informed discourse about mind. Still there are those who insist that an understanding of consciousness is central in understanding what mind is. We also identified two related senses of the term "intentionality." Of special interest to us was that sense of the term which describes a peculiar feature of some mental states: their being about or their being directed at something. Wishing or desiring, for example, is always *for* something, thinking *of* something, and so on. Thus some mental states are said to have intentional content, and what they are directed at are referred to as their intentional objects.

Supervenience has been proposed as a way of understanding how mental states are related to brain states of an organism. This thesis says that all mental phenomena result from physical phenomena. Some see in this notion a way of preserving talk of consciousness and with it intentionality. But the irreducibility of mental states which are said by some theorists to supervene on the physical poses problems of its own.

## SUGGESTIONS FOR FURTHER READING

FODOR, JERRY A., "Individualism and Supervenience," in *Psychosemantics*, pp. 27–53. Cambridge, Mass.: MIT Press, 1988.

KIM, JAEGWON, "Causality, Identity, and Supervenience," in *Midwest Studies in Philosophy, Vol. IV: Studies in Metaphysics*, pp. 31–49, eds. Peter French, Theodore E. Vehling, and Howard K. Wettstein. Minneapolis: University of Minnesota Press, 1979.

———, "Epiphenomenalism and Supervenient Causation," in *The Nature of Mind*, pp. 257–65, ed. David Rosenthal. New York: Oxford University Press, 1991.

DENNETT, DANIEL, *Consciousness Explained*, pp. 21–98. Boston: Little, Brown and Company, 1991.

McGINN, COLIN, *The Problem of Consciousness*, pp. 1–22. Cambridge, Mass.: Basil Blackwell, Inc., 1991.

SEARLE, JOHN, *Intentionality*, pp. vii–36. Cambridge, England: Cambridge University Press, 1983.

———, *The Rediscovery of Mind*, pp. 83–196. Cambridge, Mass.: MIT Press, 1992.

# 5

## Folk Psychology
## Meets the I

[T]he principled displacement of folk psychology is not only
richly possible, it represents one of the most intriguing
theoretical displacements we can currently imagine.
*—Paul Churchland*[1]

[T]he predictive adequacy of common sense psychology is
beyond rational dispute.
*—Jerry Fodor*[2]

Just as the apparatus of CSP [Common Sense Psychology] is not
rightly seen as a theory, so equally our command of it is not a
command of laws. . . . Or, . . . call them laws if you want to, but
then the notion of laws gets devalued.
*—Kathleen V. Wilkes*[3]


## FOLK TALK

"'Once upon a time,' intones the lecturer, 'a very, very long time ago, there
were beliefs and desires and hopes and imaginings, and thoughts and a lot of
stuff like that. Not, of course, that any such things *really* existed, but people
back there averred that they did. The amazing fact is that for nearly three mil-

---

[1]Paul Churchland, "Eliminative Materialism and the Propositional Attitudes," *Journal of
Philosophy*, LXXVIII, no. 2 (1981), 67.

[2]Jerry Fodor, "The Persistence of the Attitudes," in *Psychosemantics* (Cambridge, Mass.: MIT
Press, 1988), p. 6.

[3]Kathleen V. Wilkes, "The Relationship Between Scientific Psychology and Common Sense
Psychology," *Synthese*, 89 (1991), 21.

111

lennia, people everywhere and in every walk of life would with great serious-
ness say things like 'I *believe* that . . .'; 'I *desire* that . . .'; 'I *hope* that . . .'; 'I *imagine* that . . .'; 'She did thus and so because she *believed* that . . .' . Indeed, the
entire fabric of institutions was made up of those who spread such prescientific
'mentalese.' But then the long overdue occurred. Thanks to the appearance
of several radical, sometimes strident works, an inexorable challenge was
mounted against this monstrously bloated ontology consisting of beliefs, desires, and the entire retinue of propositional attitudes. At long last, the impe-
rious reign of what came then to be called *folk psychology* was nearing its end.' "

This account is, of course, purely imaginary, (by some accounts, impurely)
a bit of futuristic history—reporting an event occurring, say, *circa* 2584. But
suppose now that its account of the fate of notions like beliefs, desires, and the
like were correct. What forms of response is the audience in those circumstances expected to express if responses do not then occur in terms of beliefs
and desires and their variants? Well, we quickly remind ourselves, if the above
account, or something like it, were indeed correct, a scientific alternative would
have already "displaced" (to use Churchland's term) the misguided mentalese
we now indulge in. So the audience in question would have no difficulty responding to the lecture. But the predicament for *us now* is that temporally mired
as we currently are in the mentalese of folk discourse we can form no intelligible conception of what a wholly scientific alternative discourse in those circumstances would be like. In a very real sense, we are at a loss for words to
describe just what individuals in that audience might variously feel. But this already is getting ahead of ourselves. There is a good deal of preparatory ground-
work to complete on the questions we will tackle. So let us address this weighty
issue of folk psychology in measured stages. In what follows, let us try to be as
clear as possible on what constitutes folk psychology, on the character and scope
of the challenges launched against it, and on the positions which can be held
in its defense. Crucial to the foregoing, let us try to be clear on the nature and
import of propositional attitudes, the basic elements of commonsense psychology.

## PROPOSITIONAL ATTITUDES

In the opening paragraph of this chapter, the lecturer referred to the "retinue
of propositional attitudes." But just what are propositional attitudes? To find
out, let us, as a preliminary, consider the following sentences:

1. She **imagined** *that* the door was locked.
2. We **hoped** *that* the train would be on time.
3. They scampered away because they **perceived** *that* they were being watched.
4. We **were certain** *that* it would not rain.
5. She fainted, obviously **believing** *that* the story was true.

Notice that the word "that" is italicized in each of these sentences; and also that the expressions which follow each occurrence of "that" are complete sentences: in the first sentence, for instance, the expression "the door was locked." Now we all know that we can produce sentences willy-nilly without intending to assert anything correspondent. The mere fact that one produces a sentence is not by itself sufficient to show that one has thereby made an assertion. We produce sentences for all sorts of reasons.

But now suppose that someone were to *assert* sentence 1, as opposed to merely mentioning it or talking about it or reciting it. The simple sentence which follows the italicized "that" in sentence 1 would in that circumstance be propositional. And supposing, similarly, that each of the other four sentences, 2–5, were asserted, each expression following the term "that" would be expressing a particular *proposition.*[4] Indeed, we even take the liberty at times of saying that each, in the circumstances described, *is* a proposition. They are regarded as propositions since each affirms or denies that something is, or is thought to be, the case: Each says that something is or is not true. It may help to clarify things a bit if we consider each of the above sentences as being uttered in several different languages. There are then as many sentences as there are languages in which they are uttered. But for each simple sentence so uttered, there is just one proposition expressed. If all five sentences appearing above are appropriately expressed, each simple sentence after the italicized "that" expresses a single proposition.

Accepted idiom lets us say, as we just did, that *sentences* express propositions, but it takes only a moment's reflection to realize that it is *people* who do—in using sentences. *People* affirm, deny, doubt, and so on. Returning now to the five sentences above, notice that certain words (verbs or verb forms) are highlighted—"imagined," "hoped," "perceived," "were certain," and "believing." These all specify in each case a way in which some particular subject is related to something. Let us for the time being identify that something as the proposition expressed after the italicized "that." (We will return a little later on in this section to look more closely at the question of just what it is that is identified.) Thus each verb specifies a *relation* or, as the proponents of the notion of propositional attitudes hold, an *attitude* of a subject with respect to an object. The verbs exemplify or are expressive of propositonal attitudes.

The list of propositional attitudes can be quite long, perhaps infinitely so, depending on how fine-grained our characterization. So far, so good; perhaps. But we are still in the dark regarding the specific character of propositional attitudes. We do not yet know, for instance, *how* they relate to their object, that is, the kind of entity thought to be their object. Indeed, we may concede, from the foregoing discussion, that while we now understand how the term "propositional attitude" is employed in commonsense psychology, we cannot be sure that the term picks out anything real. We may thus challenge our common-

---

[4]There has been a great deal of discussion concerning the ontology of propositions, but that account goes well beyond the scope of the present work.

sense assumption that because we talk the way we do with respect to propositional attitudes, there is something which corresponds to them. What good evidence is there for the ascription of propositional attitudes? In so challenging
our ontology, we imply that we may be radically mistaken when we make ascriptions of the sort we are accustomed to making. This is precisely
Churchland's challenge. We will address that challenge in due course.

As we promised let us now take a closer look at the structure of propositional attitudes, in particular, at their putative object, the sort of thing to which
they are supposed to relate.

As the discussions on the subject indicate, the considerations we need to
take into account in this connection are quite complex and go well beyond
what we can fully engage in here. But because of the significance of propositional attitudes in the issues involved in folk psychology, it is to our advantage
to try to understand something of the way the thesis of propositional attitudes
is structured. One of our best resources in this connection is Fodor. He argues
strongly in support of propositional attitudes from the standpoint of a *representational theory of mind:* "Mind is conceived of as an organ whose function is
the manipulation of representations. . . . "[5] He proposes that "propositional attitudes are relations between organisms and *formulae* [italics mine] in an internal language; between organisms and internal sentences, as it were."[6] He
says further:

> I am taking seriously the idea that the system of internal representations consti-
> tutes a (computational) language. *Qua* language, it presumably has a syntax and
> a semantics; specifying the language involves saying what the properties are in
> virtue of which its formulae are well-formed and what relation(s) obtain between
> the formulae and things in the (non-linguistic) world.[7]

On Fodor's view, in any propositional attitude, at least two basic entities
are involved: (1) the *organism,* the subject of the attitude and (2) the *formulae,*
the internal natural sentence-like structures which represent the content of the
attitude. Let us take, for example, sentence 2 from our list of five above. The
sentence reads, "We **hoped** *that* the train would be on time." The specific attitude is that of hoping, but the mental phenomenon of hoping, we recall is a
*relation.* Exactly what are the elements related in the hope relation? According
to Fodor, one of the entities is picked out by the term "we." The other is a special kind of formula in an internal language (which he sometimes refers to as
the language of thought). This represents the complementary expression following the italicized "that" in our sentence, "the train would be on time."
Formulae, for Fodor, are the *immediate* objects of propositional attitudes.

[5]Fodor, "Propositional Attitudes," in *The Nature of Mind,* ed. David Rosenthal. (New York:
Oxford University Press, 1991), p. 336.

[6]Fodor, "Propositional Attitudes," p. 329.

[7]Fodor, "Propositional Attitudes," p. 335.

Fodor hesitates to refer to the object of a propositional attitude as a proposition partially on the ground that for him propositions are all *content*. As such they can have no syntax. They are purely semantic objects, the sort of things to which language calls attention or refers. Indeed, according to him, formulae mediate between organisms (the subjects of the attitudes) and propositions. In this way propositions are the objects of the attitudes. Elegantly, he says: "Propositions are sheer contents; they neutralize the lexico-syntactic differences between various ways of saying the same thing."[8] This, admittedly, is puzzling, since propositions seem on this view to be some sort of abstract objects, notoriously difficult to pin down. Language seems to point to them as realities in their own right—much like Plato's Forms—but they are not themselves bits of language. At any rate, because of the way in which he conceives of propositions, Fodor would rather consider computational formulae to be the appropriate *immediate* objects of propositional attitudes. His reason is that he does not see how an organism can stand in the requisite relation to a proposition *except* by standing in a relation to some token (roughly, instance) of a formula which expresses the proposition.

We note in passing that in our discussion above, we too ran into the same kind of ontic problem regarding the propositions. We left unspecified what exactly a proposition *is*. Concerning the nature of propositions there is considerable difference of opinion. So Fodor's caution is understandable.

There is an even deeper reason for going cautiously on the view that the objects of propositional attitudes are propositions. Organisms without a natural language—or infants not yet capable of language—may nonetheless be capable of experiencing propositional attitudes. In that circumstance an account in terms of propositions seems altogether too narrow, and therefore unsatisfactory. If this is correct, then the way in which organisms take account of the world must be in terms of some systematic structuring much more fundamental than that of a natural language. Nor can the account be provided exclusively in terms of structures peculiar to human neurophysiology. So it seems that some account along causal/functionalist lines might be correct. But this possibility remains to be examined. To that issue we will turn later in this chapter.

Before leaving this basic discussion of propositional attitudes, let us turn our attention again to the five sentences above. Sentences 3 and 5 not only express propositional attitudes; they also make causal attributions as well. They tell of specific actions or events as occurring in the world and offer as their cause specific propositional attitudes. So in 3, the scampering is because the scamperers perceive something, presumably undesirable. In 5, the fainting is accounted for by someone's believing some particular proposition to be true. In each case,

---

[8]Fodor, "Propositional Attitudes," p. 336. We called attention to this feature of propositions when we pointed out above that one simple sentence uttered in several languages nonetheless expresses one and the same proposition.

a *belief* of some sort is associated with a *desire* of some sort (the desire being only implied) and together they are sufficient in the circumstances to bring about a specific action.

Causal accounts such as the foregoing are nothing new to any of us. Our commonsense ways of explaining events draw very heavily on such connections. We speak of people acting out of conviction, or acting out their beliefs. We praise or blame in proportion as we think it in the power of individual people to do or not to do other than they did. Indeed, propositional attitudes bulk large in a good many of our everyday explanations. They seem so crucial that they fundamentally define the character of a wide range of the institutions that shape our lives. It is now about time we take a close critical look at the pervasive explanatory phenomenon which some, somewhat derisively, have termed "*folk* psychology," and which we have been calling commonsense psychology.

## BELIEF AND DESIRE

In the onslaught against folk psychology, Paul Churchland is the standard bearer. Judging from frequency of mention and from the number of published responses to his ideas on the matter, he is widely regarded as the chief protagonist. His pronouncements are at times as uncompromising as they are radical. Note, for example, the passage appearing at the beginning of this chapter. Elsewhere he says:

> Eliminative materialism is the thesis that our common-sense conception of psychological phenomena constitutes a radically false theory, a theory so fundamentally defective that both the principles and ontology of that theory will eventually be displaced, rather than smoothly reduced, by completed neuroscience. Our mutual understanding and even our introspection may then be reconstituted within the conceptual framework of completed neuroscience, a theory we may expect to be more powerful by far than the common-sense psychology it displaces, and more substantially integrated within physical science generally.[9]

Two closely related questions immediately appear: (1) What exactly is it that constitutes this offending "theory"? and (2) What exactly is so dreadfully wrong with the theory that nothing less than its displacement will suffice?

We will leave the question as to whether commonsense psychology is properly regarded as a theory for later on in this section. For the moment our concern will be to identify its characteristic features. Indeed, if the designation intends anything at all, it at least intimates that what comes under its rubric is no secret to the large majority of people. Most people without much effort seem practiced in its application though they may not be able to say what exactly they are practiced in. So let us proceed by exhibiting a commonsense sample taken from *The New York Times*.

[9]Churchland, "Eliminative Materialism and Propositional Attitudes," p. 42.

The first major study of new efforts to use welfare payments to promote positive behavior has found that a program in Ohio is increasing the school attendance of young mothers. . . . Senator Daniel Patrick Moynihan, . . . who is the leading authority in Congress, is so taken with the results that he is urging the Clinton Administration to offer the same education incentives nationwide. "It's a very powerful thing," Mr. Moynihan said. "We're usually working at the margin, but this was more than a marginal change."[10]

Our commonsense understanding of the release leads us to reason as follows: The welfare policy designers *desired* something *F*, that welfare recipients—specific people—behave in certain ways and not in others; call their desire that *F* occur *C*. Given *C*, they *acted* in a certain way *E*. They issued a policy of a certain sort, *believing D*, that all things being equal, *E* might bring it about that *F*, that is, that welfare recipients behave in the desired ways and not in others. It appears from the narrative above that *C, D,* and *E* figured prominently in the causal chain which actually brought it about that *F*. We are certainly glossing over a number of intervening causal details—many subsidiary beliefs and desires, for example—but, in the habit of everyday commonsense ascription, we would normally say that *C* together with *D* led to *E*, and *E* caused *F*.

Now the policy designers did not develop their new policy in the hope that by so doing hostilities in what used to be Yugoslavia would cease, or that old growth forests would cease to be the subject of bitter disputes. If these unrelated resolutions did come about, the welfare designers could take no credit for them. They *desired* a specific kind of behavior for a specific group of people. They *believed*, moreover, that the string of contingencies they set up by issuing the kind of policy that they did would, all things being equal, bring that desired behavior about. The thing to note about this episode is that the thinking of the designers paid off. The premises and principles to which they appealed served them well. They worked. Indeed, some would claim, the premises and principles have a long history of having worked, over and over again. Their predictive adequacy is thereby established.

In an illustrative nutshell, we have covered all the basic elements of commonsense or folk psychology, aptly characterized by Horgan and Woodward in the following quasi-formal terms.

> Folk psychology is a network of principles which constitutes a sort of commonsense theory about how to explain human behavior. *These principles provide a central role to propositional attitudes, particularly belief and desire.* [Italics mine.] The theory asserts, for example, that if someone desires that p, and this desire is not overridden by other desires, and he believes that an action of kind K will bring it about that p, and he believes that such an action is within his power, and he does not believe that some other action is within his power and is a preferable way to bring it about that p, then *ceteris paribus*, the *desire and the beliefs will cause him to perform an action* [italics mine] of kind K.[11]

[10] *The New York Times,* April 12, 1993, p. A7.

[11] Terence Horgan and James Woodward, "Folk Psychology Is Here to Stay," *The Philosophical Review,* 94 (April 1985), 197.

There are several things we should notice as we consider the causal account from desire and belief to action. In this narrative, as for any narrative of this sort, the causal link between desire and belief, on the one hand, and action, on the other, is not hard and fast. No strict law relates the particular desires and beliefs in the narrative with specific behavioral outcomes. (There is no strict type-type causation.) Such outcomes as occur are ones which on the basis of experience are the ones thought *likely* to occur given certain idealized contingencies. This feature, endemic to causal accounts in which propositional attitudes figure, requires a degree of hedging. This hedging is expressed in the qualifier "all things being equal—*certeris paribus.*" For example, we can say, "All things being equal, if people believe something to be poison, they will not ingest it." It is a feature to which we will return as we come to a critical assessment of folk psychology.

Another thing worth noting is that we commonly repose considerable confidence in the causal efficacy of our beliefs, as well as in our ability to predict behaviors which will result from our believings and associated doings. Whenever we fail, we try to get better at it—we do our homework a bit more carefully. But, except in abnormal circumstances, we carry on as common sense dictates. Except in the company of an ill-tempered behaviorist, we are not the least bit hesitant to offer as *the* reason for our trucking along a raincoat the fact that we believed it was going to rain and that we had no desire to get soaked.

To pursue a question we posed earlier: What is so dreadfully wrong with folk psychology that its passing should be celebrated? Actually, this way of framing the question distorts the nature of the case against folk psychology—henceforth, FP—since not everyone holds this assessment. So we ask the question of those who object to FP. So let us recast it and ask, instead, What is it that those who find serious fault with FP see irremediably wrong?

### Challenges for Folk Psychology

Paul Churchland's diagnosis of what is irremediably wrong with FP specifies three related maladies: (1) FP "suffers explanatory failures on an epic scale," (2) it has remained "stagnant for at least twenty-five centuries," and (3) "its categories appear. . . (so far) to be incommensurable with or orthogonal to the categories of the background physical science whose long-term claim to explain human behavior is undeniable."[12]

Churchland recognizes that he must establish that FP is clearly and undeniably a *theory.* Only so can the above diagnosis make sense. Only so, for instance, does it make sense to speak of FP as suffering "explanatory failures on an epic scale." Only so does its "displacement," its "outright elimination," appear a rational (?) expectation. So Churchland sets out to do precisely that, to establish FP as a theory.

---

[12]Churchland, "Eliminative Materialism and the Propositional Attitudes," p. 74.

He argues that the network of principles and the commonsense conceptual framework of FP render it a theory in the truest sense of this term. We use this body of commonsense wisdom and we characteristically appeal to considerations like beliefs, desires, perceptions, intentions, and so on, to *explain* and *predict* behavior. But explanation and prediction *presuppose* the existence of laws which connect explanatory conditions with the phenomena to be explained—the explananda. Explanation and prediction, and all that these entail, are the necessary and sufficient conditions for theory status—not necessarily good theory but theory nonetheless. FP meets these two conditions; therefore FP is a theory. It follows, therefore, from this conclusion, that the *semantics* of the terms in FP are to be understood in exactly the same manner as the semantics of theoretical terms in the well-established sciences. The meanings, or more exactly, the *references* (the semantic values) of terms in FP must be determined entirely with reference to the network of laws in which those terms occur. This is the way it is (arguably) in the well-established sciences. In those sciences, the references of theoretical terms are not independently fixed. All terms possess their semantic value strictly in virtue of their place in the structure of a unifying theory. Hence Churchland maintains that the theoretical status of FP is beyond dispute.

> FP is nothing more and nothing less than a culturally entrenched theory of how we and the higher animals work. It has no special features that make it empirically invulnerable, no unique functions that make it irreplaceable, no special status of any kind whatsoever.[13]

FP, now established as theory, is weighed in the balance and found severely wanting. It has failed dismally to match the successes of the well-established sciences. Indeed nowhere is its failure more ironically apparent than in its inability to provide a satisfactory account of the way the process of learning takes place in prelinguistic or nonlinguistic organisms—in very young children and the "lower" animals, for instance. The special difficulty here for FP is that if the ability to manipulate and process propositional attitudes is itself learned, then learning cannot logically be defined in terms of the manipulation and processing of propositional attitudes. But learning certainly takes place, and its scope extends well beyond the limits of organisms capable of propositional attitudes. Hence propositional attitudes, themselves learned, cannot constitute the warp and woof of learning. (It follows, too, that knowledge cannot be rendered in terms of propositional attitudes.) The central role FP assigns to beliefs and desires in accounting of behavior is thus called into question. Further, and possibly fatal to FP, its ontological categories and their presumed relations are not reducible in terms of categories peculiar to any of the more basic or lower-level sciences, such, for example, as neuroscience or

---

[13]Churchland, "Eliminative Materialism and the Propositional Attitudes," p. 81.

physics.[14] In short, and to express the situation starkly in Imre Lakatos's apt phrase, FP represents a most "degenerating" research program.[15]

Stephen Stich's concern with FP derives *not* from its being considered a theory but from altogether different considerations. Recall, from above, that for FP, propositional attitudes have content. According to FP, the content of a particular belief state, for example, is that proposition which is its expression. The *content* of the belief that Bill Clinton is the president of the United States is the proposition expressed by the sentence "Bill Clinton is the president of the United States." But it is either true or false that Bill Clinton is the president of the United States. It is true if there is a state of affairs out in the world which corresponds to the proposition expressed, but it is false if there is no such state of affairs. Understood in this way, propositions always have truth conditions. So the belief that $p$ has both content and truth conditions. Indeed, the belief that $p$ has the latter precisely because it has the former—two sides of the very same coin. So the particular content of a belief that $p$, is $p$; and its truth conditions are truth conditions with respect to $p$. Of course, what goes for beliefs goes for a great many other propositional attitudes as well.

What we have just reviewed accords with a *representational* theory of mind. But Stich supposes that the correct theory of mind might not be representational at all, at least, not in the way indicated above. He proposes, instead, what he calls a syntactic theory of mind (STM), according to which mental states are relations of "purely formal or syntactic mental sentences."[16] If it is true that mental states are just relations of essentially *contentless* sentences, FP is shown to be radically false. This is so since the ontology and, derivatively, the functioning of mental states would in that circumstance be altogether different from the central posits of FP. We could not then easily describe mental processes in terms of causal relations of propositional contents or of truth conditions. We could describe them purely in terms of the formal relations of syntactic mental expressions. The upshot? There would be no beliefs; no propositional attitudes; nothing analogous to the mental categories essential to FP. For Stich, this line of attack is tentative but it represents an alternative which poses a serious challenge for FP.

But Stich has a much more telling criticism of FP, which derives its strength largely from a body of experimental literature in social psychology concerning

---

[14]Recall our discussion in Chapter Three of identity theories.

[15]See Imre Lakatos, "Science and Pseudoscience" in *The Methodology of Scientific Research Programmes, Philosophical Papers, Vol. I.* eds. John Worrall and Gregory Currie (Cambridge, England: Cambridge University Press, 1978), pp. 1–7.

[16]Stephen P. Stich, "Will the Concepts of Folk Psychology Find a Place in Cognitive Science," in *From Folk Psychology to Cognitive Science: The Case Against Belief* (Cambridge, Mass.: MIT Press, 1983), p. 209.

dissonance and self-attribution.[17] To help us appreciate the force of this criticism, we need first to recall some of what we noted earlier regarding FP, and also to bear in mind some of what FP ordinarily assumes.

According to FP, we ordinarily *do* thus and so because we *believe* and *desire* so and so. And, likewise, we *say* thus and so because we believe and desire so and so. A given belief, the belief that $p$, say, motivates both the doing and the saying of that which is consistent with the motivating belief. Now suppose we believe that a neighbor of ours is a fraud. If the occasion arises, we *say* that our neighbor is a fraud and we *act* toward our neighbor as befits frauds. Deriving from the same causal source—from the same belief—according to FP our verbal and nonverbal expressions are presumed to be logically consistent the one with the other. We not only attribute our verbal and nonverbal behavior with respect to $p$ to the belief that $p$, but we sincerely assume that belief and behavior *harmonize*. On the one hand are particular beliefs relating causally to their effects, and on the other are behaviors, the causal products of the beliefs. This account, somewhat simplified, gives the commonsense account of the way beliefs relate to behaviors resulting from them.

But experimental studies in social psychology call this tidy story into question. This circumstance provides Stich with what appears to be his strongest reason for questioning the entire account which FP gives of mental states: their ontology, as well as the system of causal relationships which they are commonly presumed to sustain.

As a preliminary, the core of the issue is minimally sketched in the following scenario having to do with self-attribution. Person $P$ is led by an experimenter to make an incorrect inference as to the cause of her, $P$'s, response to a given situation. $P$ is then led—manipulated—to *behave* as though the incorrect response were indeed true.[18] To illustrate, suppose $B^1$ to be the kind of behavior FP associates with correct inference from the belief $F$, and $B^2$ the kind of behavior it associates with incorrect inference from $F$. Suppose, further, that $B^1$ and $B^2$ are incompatible behaviors. Now if we grant, as FP holds, that behavior is directly subserved by corresponding beliefs, then in virtue of $P$'s believing $F$, she should be exhibiting $B^1$, but instead she exhibits $B^2$. The upshot, of course, is dissonance: It is as though one and the same belief is capable of yielding incompatible behavioral outputs. Alternatively, instead of one belief, $P$ in fact holds at one and the same time two incompatible beliefs.

---

[17]For details on a classic example of self-attribution and dissonance, see Michael Storms and Richard E. Nisbett, "Insomnia and the Attribution Process," *Journal of Personality and Social Psychology*, 16, no. 2 (October 1970), 319–28. See also Richard E. Nisbett and D. D. Wilson, "Telling More Than We Can Know: Verbal Reports on Mental Processes," *Psychological Review*, 84 (1977), 231–59.

[18]Stich, "The Future of Folk Psychology," p. 232.

In one of the several self-attribution and dissonance experiments which provide the grounding for Stich's skepticism with respect to FP, insomniacs were the responding subjects. A number of insomniacs were asked by the experimenters Storms and Nisbett to keep a record of the exact times they fell asleep. Having done so for several days they were divided into two groups, an arousal group and a relaxation group, and a supply of placebo pills was prescribed to be taken by each subject fifteen minutes before retiring. But whereas the arousal group was told that the pills would produce rapid heart rate, breathing irregularities, and other symptoms characteristic of insomnia, the other group was told the exact opposite. Attribution theory predicted that subjects in the arousal group would fall asleep sooner after having taken the pill because they would have attributed their symptoms to the pill rather than to their ongoing insomniacal baggage. On the other hand, the relaxation group would take longer, for since their symptoms persisted in spite of their having taken the pill, they would infer that their ongoing complaint must really be severe and this would further disturb them. The predictions were sustained for both groups. Of particular interest is that the subjects in the latter group denied that they engaged in anything like the reasoning which attribution theory predicted would occur to account for their taking longer to fall asleep. Instead, they produced a number of fantastic reasons.

This experiment provides Stich with just a part of what he needs to develop his view that verbal and nonverbal behavior may be served by different "belief-like" cognitive systems. To accomplish this he considers the foregoing experiment along with other experimental work done by Nisbett and Wilson.[19]

> These investigators noted that the experimentally manipulated effect . . . in attribution and dissonance studies was generally some non-verbal indicator belief or attitude. However, when the non-verbal behavior of subjects under different experimental conditions seemed clearly to indicate that they differed in belief or attitude, their verbal behavior often did not indicate any difference in belief or attitude. Moreover, when subjects' attention was drawn to the fact their behavior indicated some change had taken place, they denied that the experimentally manipulated cause . . . had been at all relevant to the change. Rather, they constructed some explanation of the change in their behavior in line with socially shared views about what sorts of causes are likely to produce the behavior in question. The picture this suggests is that subjects' verbal reporting systems have no access to the processes actually underlying their nonverbal behavior changes.[20]

From this state of affairs, Stich reasons that the cognitive states underlying verbal behavior may be distinct from those which underlie nonverbal behavior. Ours, he speculates, may be a cognitive system which "keeps two sets of

[19]For full details of these experiments as well as of the preceding one, see Richard E. Nisbett and D. D. Wilson, "Telling More Than We Can Know: Verbal Reports on Mental Processes," pp. 231–59. See also Michael Storms and Richard E. Nisbett, "Insomnia and the Attribution Process," pp. 319–28.

[20] Stich, "The Future of Folk Psychology," p. 233.

books": one set for verbal behavior and another set for nonverbal behavior. The same mental state does not causally motivate the sincere assertion that *p,* nor is it responsible for the nonverbal behaviors logically consistent with the assertion, as FP contends. Rather, studies on self-attribution and dissonance strongly suggest that distinct subsystems are at work. This would account for the dissonance with respect to behaviors. And if this is true, Stich maintains, it would constitute "a finding for which folk psychology is radically unprepared. . . . [S]tates similar to the one underlying our own ordinary utterance of 'p' do *not* also participate in the production of our nonverbal behavior.[21] FP's view of the role of propositional attitudes is severely, perhaps irreparably, undermined, for commonsense self-attributions are shown to be fundamentally wrong. In making self-attributions, we may, in the words of Nisbett and Wilson, be "telling more than we can know."[22]

Moreover, the simple structural relationship presumed by FP to hold between isolable beliefs and correspondingly isolable bits of behavior might likewise be questioned. Stich contends:

> There is no a priori guarantee that our belief store is organized in this way. It might be the case that there is no natural or segregable part of the belief store which *can* be isolated as playing a special role in the production of individual speech acts. *If this turns out to be the case, however, typical belief attributions will misfire in a quite radical way.* They assume that there is some isolable belief state which plays a central role in the production of speech acts, and they assert that the subject has a state similar to the one which would play this role were the content sentence uttered in earnest. *If this assumption turns out to be false, belief ascriptions will typically lack a truth value.*[23]

Rather than isolable beliefs, each with a particular content, an intricate network of mental formulae devoid of intentional content becomes, for Stich, the more plausible model of mind and its operations. While Stich sees no possibility of reconciling the theoretical claims of FP with those of cognitive science, he is guarded about the future of FP. The jury is still out, he observes, but the prospects for commonsense psychology look extremely unpromising.

Churchland and Stich have approached the criticism of commonsense psychology from different positions. Churchland considers commonsense psychology to be a *theory* that has long overstayed its welcome. It constitutes, he stridently declaims, a degenerating research program whose ontology is at one with caloric fluid, ghosts, witches, and the entire prescientific, hoary-haired rabble. For him FP is radically and irremediably "bad stuff" and should be eliminated. It must now give way to neuroscientific theory. Of a similar opinion, less passionately, but perhaps no less firmly, Stich inveighs against FP on the basis

[21]Stich, "The Future of Folk Psychology," p. 231.

[22]Nisbett and Wilson, "Telling More Than We Can Know: Verbal Reports on Mental Processes," p. 231.

[23]Stich, "The Future of Folk Psychology," p. 238. [Italics mine.]

of experiments done in social psychology and research in cognitive science. The entire corpus of FP's propositional attitudes, notably its account of beliefs, is called into serious question. It is time we turned to an examination of those criticisms.

## A Critique of the Criticisms

The weight of Churchland's criticism of FP rests crucially on his contention that FP is a theory, and a degenerating one. As a cautionary note, before examining the purported irreducibility in materialist terms of "the realm of the intentional, the realm of the propositional attitude," Churchland warns: "[S]uch an examination will not make sense, however, *unless it is first appreciated that the relevant network of common-sense concepts does indeed constitute an empirical theory* [italics mine] with all the functions, virtues, *and perils* entailed by that status." Note also the following passages. "*Seeing* our common-sense conceptual framework for mental phenomena *as* [italics mine] a theory brings a simple and unifying organization to most of the major topics in the philosophy of mind, including the explanation and prediction of behavior, . . ." "[T]he recognition that folk psychology *is* a theory provides a simple and decisive solution to an old skeptical problem of other minds." "Not only is folk psychology a theory, it is so *obviously* a theory that it must be held a major mystery why it has taken until the last half of the twentieth century for philosophers to realize it. The structural features of folk psychology parallel perfectly those of mathematical physics; . . ." And finally, "*Given that* [italics mine] folk psychology is an empirical theory, it is at least an abstract possibility that its principles are radically false and that its ontology is an illusion."[24] That commonsense psychology constitutes an empirical theory runs vitally through Churchland's arguments against FP.

But what if FP is not properly regarded as a theory, as some maintain?[25] It is a long, logical step from the permissive "*seeing . . . as*" to the established "*given that.*" For all sorts of reasons—convenience of treatment, for example— we may want to see something *A* as being of kind *B;* but by so seeing, *A* does not become a member of kind *B*. It yet remains to be shown on independent grounds that *A* indeed is, or has all along been, a member of kind *B*. Although Churchland tells us that seeing FP as a theory has the advantage of bringing unity to the wide variety of topics addressed in the philosophy of mind, the permissiveness of this move, that is, its heuristic life, is only apparent. His real concern is to establish that FP is indeed a theory—whatever the advantages or

---

[24]For all the passages cited in this paragraph, see Churchland's "Eliminative Materialism and the Propositional Attitudes," pp. 42–47.

[25]See John Haldane, "Understanding Folk," and Kathleen V. Wilkes, "The Relationship Between Scientific Psychology and Common Sense Psychology," in *Folk Psychology and the Philosophy of Mind,* eds. Scott M. Christensen and Dale R. Turner, (Hillsdale, N.J.: Lawrence Erlbaum Associates, Publishers, 1993) pp. 263–87, 167–87.

disadvantages of so regarding it. So the question before us is: Is it, or is it not, a theory?

Perhaps the real question is not whether or not FP is a theory, for posed in that way, the question can be answered quite trivially in the affirmative. Rather the question should be whether or not FP is a theory in exactly the same strict sense as any theory in the physical sciences is. We need to be clear on exactly how we understand the term "theory." In everyday discourse, the term occurs along a continuum of senses ranging from the loose to the strict and scientific, from theory of housing and urban development on one end of the continuum to theory of atoms on the other. But Churchland makes it clear that the sense he intends is the strict and scientific. So to that we should turn.

It is a characteristic of theories, in the strict and scientific use of the term, that they are subsumed by a network of strict laws or law-like generalizations expressive of regularities, of invariant relationships. Phenomena encompassed by these laws can be exactly specified, and as a consequence, theories which embody these laws can be formulated with mathematical exactness. Theories developed from these laws explain and predict events without the need for their being "hedged" by contingency qualifications. A central issue is the character of its generalizations, in particular, whether they are expressive of laws analogous to those found in the physical sciences.

Using the propositional attitude "desire" as an example, we might express a typical generalization in FP as follows: For any $p$, and for any $q$, if $p$ desires that $q$, and if $p$ believes that some action of the sort $r$ can bring it about that $q$, and if the desire that $q$ is not successfully overridden by some countervailing desire, then, all things being equal, $p$ will engage in $r$ so as to bring it about that $q$. We are able to derive this schema, and attest to its correctness, not on the basis of our knowledge of invariant relationships we have noted in the operations of nature but solely through our acquaintance with the way people, notably ourselves, tend to behave. The terms in the schema are, for all practical purposes, indeterminate and vague: Boundary conditions cannot be finely specified. As such, they are resistant to strict law-like generalization. Whatever the real-life substitutions we make in the above schema, we would have no idea of how to fill out all the requisite conditions for $p$'s engaging in action $r$. As Haldane put it in a similar illustration, "we know how one might continue the list" of provisos with respect to $p$'s coming to do $r$, but "the trouble is that we also know we cannot complete it."[26] We might conclude, as he did, that the kind of generalization instantiated in our FP schema is not a law at all.

But this sort of generalization is indeed typical of those encountered in commonsense psychology and as such is not at all analogous to the generalizations characteristic of the physical sciences, in particular, of those found in physics. If this is the extent of what FP has to show, then there does not seem

---

[26]Haldane, "Understanding Folk," p. 274.

to exist a sufficiently secure nomological footing for Churchland's assertion
that FP is a theory. This is true since such an assignment presupposes the existence of laws of a very different character. Again, as Haldane aptly expresses
it: "The point is that the indeterminacy of our inherited ways of describing and
understanding one another is such that no genuine, universally quantified,
psycho-behavioral conditionals are specifiable."[27]

The moral of the preceding might be: "No law, no theory." But perhaps
we approached the question of the theoretical status of FP from the wrong direction. We might object that the nomological character of FP is clearly implied
from the fact that FP purports to explain and predict psychobehavioral phenomena, and for certain sorts of cases, does so with great success. So the ironic
rejoinder to the above moral might be "No theory, no explanation, and no
prediction." But clearly there *is* explanation and prediction going on in FP.

The matter becomes a bit involved at this stage. The irony in the rejoinder can be successfully met, however, in at least one of two ways. First, *if* the rejoinder shows that the logical relationship between theory, on the one hand,
and explanation and prediction, on the other, is essentially definitional, and
so can appropriately be rendered by a biconditional expression,[28] then that
strategy begs the question. The relationship between the terms becomes *stipu-
latively analytic.* Biconditionality is purchased at the price of stipulation. *We may
therefore simply reject the stipulation.* Second we may hold that generally the logical relationship between the two terms is contingent, and that it is properly
captured by a simple conditional (of the form, if *p* then *q*). In this case, the
absence of theory need not logically imply the absence of explanation and prediction. It also permits us to admit to the presence of explanation and prediction without, fallaciously, admitting to the presence of theory. This move,
however, still leaves us with the onus of specifying just how, in those circumstances, to understand the notions in the simple conditional relation, especially
those of explanation and prediction.

At this stage, several possibilities are open. We may admit that predicted
action is caused without thereby implying appeal to strict law-like elements in
what causes the action. We have already argued above that we may find good
grounds for denying that the generalizations which characterize FP are subsumed by laws at all. Certainly there is nothing analogous to such laws as occur
in a science like physics. We may maintain that the causes of rationalized action are not reducible in any strict sense to law-like regularities. Instead, we may
invoke here a view owed to Davidson, that a strict *causal* account of action does
not tell the story of actions *qua* actions. Reasons are not strictly reducible to
causes.

---

[27]Haldane, "Understanding Folk," p. 274.

[28]A biconditional expression has the form {(If *p* then *q*) and (if *q* then *p*)}; sometimes telescoped as: (*p* ≡ *q*). Substituting *T* for *p*, to stand for theory, and *E* for *q*, to stand for both explanation and prediction, the second alternative, discussed later in the paragraph, would be formally
expressed merely as (*T* ⊃ *E*).

Or, as Haldane proposes (drawing upon a typical child/adult exchange in answering *why*-questions in which every succeeding answer moves to a new level), we may explore the possibility of developing a model which permits a more pluralistic ontology. This would permit *rational causes.* "On this view," he says, "there is no reason to suppose that the explanation of action has a single form, or that it logically requires generality or the distinct existence of terms of the relations involved."[29] Indeed, this maneuver captures and preserves much of what now seems to make FP appealing because it explains and predicts. It is not at all established that an ontology that countenances desires, wishes, hopes, fears, weakness of will, or strength of conviction is indistinguishable from one that accepts witches, ghosts, gremlins, or caloric fluid. (The challenge is to distinguish between real and apparent ontological inflation.) And it is not evident that generalizations which include notions such as wishes and the like are for that reason alone hopelessly flawed. The level at which the *why*-question is posed makes a substantial difference as to what sort of dictionary of terms we consult in response. At least, common sense seems to see it that way. *To suppose, a priori, that explanation is always of a single type is to assume the responsibility of explaining without circularity or prescription just why this is so.*

So we may concede on logical grounds that indeed FP explains and predicts, but without thereby granting that FP is a theory, as the argument in the preceding paragraph was intended to show. The terms it characteristically employs are imprecise and richly vague. Its generalizations are *homespun* and therefore lack the systematic and nomological specificity typical of generalizations in the physical sciences. It should therefore come as no surprise that its generalizations must be hedged by the all-obliging *ceteris paribus* fences—other things being equal. FP is not a theory ripe for displacement because of failing to account for certain phenomena, such as depression and so on. It could not possibly have failed as a theory since it never was a theory in the first place. Its explanations and predictions never aspire to being scientific in any deliberate sense. Moreover, as Wilkes reminds us, commonsense psychology does considerably more than explain and predict.[30] It warns, cajoles, conjectures, jokes, encourages, finds guilty, pleads innocent, compromises, curses, swears, loves, hates, values, encourages, scolds, conceives, condemns, and the like, *ad nauseam.*[31]

There seems little gained in making woodpiles out to be so many ammunition dumps on the grounds that they represent so much firepower. Quite conceivably, the danger lies elsewhere. Perhaps FP, commonsense psychology,

[29]Haldane, "Understanding Folk," p. 277.

[30]Kathleen Wilkes, "The Relationship Between Scientific Psychology and Common Sense Psychology," p. 176.

[31]For a discussion of the multiple uses of language, see Ludwig Wittgenstein, *Philosophical Investigations,* trans. G. E. M. Anscombe (New York: Macmillan Company, 1953), secs. 23–24.

call it what you will, is wrongly classified and, for all practical purposes, quixotically targeted.

Let us now return to Stich's unease with the ontology of FP, in particular with his concern that there may in fact be no such things as beliefs. Inspired by research in social psychology on attribution theory and dissonance theory (recall the Storms/Nisbett research involving insomniacs), Stich concludes: "If we really do have separate verbal and nonverbal cognitive storage systems, then the functional economy of the mind postulated by folk theory is quite radically mistaken. And under those circumstances I am strongly inclined to think that the right thing to say is that *there are no such things as beliefs.*"[32] But there is another obvious and plausible way of interpreting the data, one which, if correct, yields an altogether different conclusion and leaves the ontology of FP largely unaffected. In accounting for the apparent independence of the causal cognitive mechanisms which control verbal and nonverbal behaviors, we might appeal to the notion of latent or unconscious beliefs and the causal efficacy of such beliefs. In that case there is no need to postulate different and independent causal mechanisms for the two kinds of behavioral effects.

Ordinarily, we expect that the verbal and nonverbal behavioral effects of a given belief would be consistent, the one sort with the other. If person $P$ believes that $Q$, all things being equal, we take it that $P$'s verbal utterances with respect to $Q$ would be of a certain sort, and also that $P$'s nonverbal behavior would fit or be consistent with those utterances. However, as we noted above, research in social psychology seems to contradict this account. But the consistency account we just gave with respect to verbal and nonverbal behaviors is perhaps a bit too tidy. It does not allow for the possibility of nonverbal behavior due largely to latent and unconscious beliefs whose manifestation may appear to contradict our conscious verbal behavior. The belief that $Q$—like all of our other beliefs—is cognitively nested in the sense that it presupposes as well as entails numerous other beliefs which themselves are also cognitively nested. A belief which has no presuppositions whatever and no entailments is scarcely thinkable. Obviously, the belief that $Q$, with its entourage of presuppositions and entailments—most of which are unconsciously held—is not the only belief set that one has. People believe all sorts of different things. So if beliefs do dispose one to behave, it seems reasonable to suppose that the dissonance or slippage between our verbal and nonverbal behavior may not derive from the absence of beliefs. On the contrary, it may come from the influence of numerous unconscious beliefs on our nonverbal behavior—arguably the more primitive of the two types. The idealized consistency account we gave above would seem to fit best in connection with beliefs consciously and actively held. The differences which the research calls attention to may have more to do with different levels of belief than with the absence of beliefs. The foregoing deals with only one of Stich's central arguments for questioning the viability of FP.[33]

---

[32]Stich, "The Future of Folk Psychology," p. 231.

[33]For a critical discussion of Stich's view on the viability of FP's ontology, see Terence Horgan and James Woodward's "Folk Psychology Is Here to Stay," pp. 204–23.

## Reducibility

Let us suppose, as does Churchland, that FP can be considered a theory. Now Churchland contends that FP stands hopelessly condemned on the grounds that it fails the crucial litmus test of scientific reducibility. "Its intentional categories," he observes, "stand magnificently alone, without visible prospect of reduction. . . ." And commenting on its theoretical virtues, or lack of them, he says, "FP suffers explanatory failures on an epic scale." The explanatory failures are due quite largely to the fact that the categories of FP, hence its law-like generalizations, are dismally irreducible.

Reductionism— reducibility—is one of those notions which it is easy to oversimplify. At its simplest, it is the claim that "some object, state, process, event, or property 'is just' or 'is nothing more than' the physical ingredients that compose it."[34] This, however, obscures the fact that there have been distinct ways of understanding the notion of reduction itself. Any simple formulation is thus apt to be misleading. Carnap's conception of reduction, for example, sought to eliminate any shade of metaphysics, so reduction was conceived as the formal reduction of certain kinds of linguistic expression to others. Others, unlike Carnap—Putnam, for example—have viewed reduction as concerned with ontologies—one ontology being reduced in terms of another. Then, too, we may distinguish, as does Trout, between what he calls "predicate reductionism" and "law reductionism." According to the former, "the central terms of 'higher-level' theories, from biology to sociology, will ultimately be defined in terms of, and thus eliminated in favor of, the more basic vocabulary of physics or chemistry." According to the latter, "the laws of higher-level theories such as those of economics and sociology can be explained in terms of, and thus replaced by, those of some lower-level theory like individual psychology, biology, chemistry, or physics. In other words, economic laws about market segmentation can be replaced by complicated psychological laws . . . which in turn can be replaced by still more complicated biological laws . . . in which individual physiologies ultimately produce the behavior in question, and so on."[35]

There is also inter-theoretic reduction. With the application of what are suggestively referred to as "bridge-laws" and rules of correspondence, theory $T_1$ is reduced in favor of theory $T_2$. The function of bridge-laws is to link ontologies, the ontologies, say, of $T_1$ and $T_2$. In this role bridge-laws indicate identities, since they are supposed to manifest exactly which entity in the theory to be reduced is to be linked with exactly which entity in the reducing theory. But identity is a symmetric relation—if $A$ is identical with $B$, then $B$ is identical with $A$. Nevertheless, an often important reason for reducing one theory in favor of another is the elimination of the ontology of the theory being reduced in fa-

[34]J. D. Trout, "Reductionism and Unity of Science," in *The Philosophy of Science,* eds. Richard Boyd, Philip Casper, and J. D. Trout (Cambridge, Mass.: MIT Press, 1991), p. 387.
[35]Trout, "Reductionism and the Unity of Science," p. 387.

vor of the ontology of the reducing theory, that of $T_1$ by that of $T_2$. As often happens, however, the reduction cannot easily proceed. For instance, notions in the theory being reduced may resist straightforward expression in terms of the identity relation expressed by bridge-laws. In such circumstances, we might resort to the unsatisfactory expedient of expressing the reduction in the form of a disjunction. For example, $E$ in $T_1$ is identical with $a$, or $b$, or $c$, or $d$, and so on *ad infinitum*, in $T_2$. But in so doing the identity relation, hence the reduction, becomes hamstrung. Trout gives us an excellent example of this kind of difficulty and provides a salutary comment.

> On the traditional account of reduction, the predicates of a special science are linked biconditionally to predicates of physics, via "bridge-laws." The unity of science version of physicalism requires that the natural kinds expressed by predicates in an ideally completed special science each correspond to a natural kind expressed by a predicate in an ideally completed physics. But when we consider a representative bridge law, it appears that no such reduction is forthcoming. *For example, the event predicate, "monetary exchange" is routinely implicated in economic generalizations, but the money exchanged can be in the form of copper, gold, wampam, shells, etc., making the set of biconditionally related physical predicates enormously disjunctive.* [Italics mine.][36]

He also notes:

> This example serves two important functions. First, it shows that we can be good physicalists without being reductionists, because we can claim that each token higher-level state is identical to a token physical state without claiming that there are smooth identities. Second, it represents a pervasive and representative counterexample to the common view that reductionism is a trend within science, because it involves an important higher-level kind that is rendered explanatorily impotent once defined in physical terms.[37]

On the assumption that commonsense psychology is indeed a theory, Churchland focuses on the irreducibility of its categories and of its law-like generalizations. But we might now defensibly argue that such ontic categories in FP as resist reduction in terms of the categories of neuroscience need not, for that reason alone, be considered bogus. They may be largely akin in ontic import to notions like "monetary exchange," only much more vague. Perhaps, like "monetary exchange," they are ontically significant, though not reducible in any straightforward way to the categories of a reducing theory. Perhaps notions like beliefs, hopes, fears, joys, loves, expectations—in short, the bulk of the propositional attitudes—are ontically irreducible but not ontically insignificant. They are certainly not semantically empty. We know perfectly well what it is to believe with all our heart, or to be beside ourselves with burning desire but what we mean when we say such things is not the least bit amenable

---

[36]Trout, "Reductionism and the Unity of Science," p. 390.
[37]Trout, "Reductionism and the Unity of Science," p. 390.

to reduction as in the categories of neuroscience. And it does not follow that whoever utters such expressions utters wholesale ontic nonsense on the grounds that the categories ostensibly appealed to simply fail to exist.

But we may also wonder, as some have done, whether the demand for reducibility has not been excessive. Perhaps its limits have been reached on some occasions when we find some notions stubbornly resistant to it. The fault may not always lie with the recalcitrant notions but, possibly, with the reductionist's two-pronged fork—reduce or be eliminated. There seems room for another prong, somewhere in the middle. The fork as now featured smacks of physicalism gone wild, systematically bullying its way along, armed with a fistful of begged questions among which is the justification of pervasive reductionism.

### Folk Psychology as Theory

For reasons of space limitations, the matter of the epic failure of FP as theory must be handled more briefly here than it deserves. Recall that generalizations are of two kinds: *universal* and *existential*. Churchland's charge of theoretical failure has to do more with the latter kind than with the former. The reason is quite simple. Universal generalizations are not ordinarily regarded as having existential import, but existential generalizations, as the term suggests, do have existential import, for they indicate that at least one thing exists. So, for example, if there exist *no* witches, then for the following propositions, the attached truth values would hold: "All witches are toothless brutes" (true); "No witches are toothless brutes" (true);[38] "Some witches are toothless brutes" (false); "Some witches are not toothless brutes" (false). The two universal propositions are said to be *vacuously* true. This being so, it is hardly worth haggling over the explanatory or predictive power of universal generalizations. The real issue in the Churchland charge lies with the explanations provided for particular instances of behavior: for those particular times when the explanatory claims one makes cannot properly be said to be vacuously true.

So let us look at the following account: "Believing that it would rain, I decided to take along my umbrella. My neighbor must have thought much the same thing, for I noticed that she, too, was carrying along an umbrella." This account neither explicitly nor implicitly says anything about the behavior of people generally with respect to rain. It provides a reasonable and perfectly good explanation of the umbrella-carrying behavior of both the speaker and her neighbor for the particular time under consideration. Past experience must have provided the pragmatic justification for the behavior in question. For each, the carrying of the umbrella in just those circumstances was an example of a belief in action, and that fact would be obvious to anyone who knew anything

---

[38]Both these universal propositions are true in virtue of the fact that they express conditionals whose antecedents are false, and a false statement materially implies any statement whatever, just as a true statement is implied by any statement whatever. This somewhat surprising result can be readily exhibited on a truth table.

about rain and umbrellas. No further explanation seems necessary. That it did not as a matter of fact rain, or that we now have no idea of what either person would be disposed to do if faced in the future with a similar threat of rain, in no way vitiates the explanation which this particular account provides. The explanatory account given for particular actions on particular occasions provides no basis whatever for predicting future behavior in like circumstances. This in no way faults the epistemic quality of the explanation. There seems no justifiably good reason why, to have explanatory power, commonsense belief ascriptions need to be universalizable and reliably predictive as a consequence. To ask that much of FP is to ask considerably more than is ordinarily of interest or concern to those who use the language of propositional attitudes, to require what FP has never aspired to becoming, a theory in the strictest scientific sense. Perhaps the best argument in defense of FP is that explanations of the type have worked enormously well for a considerably long time, for most people, and for most of the time.

Churchland's verdict that FP's *explanatory* failures are of epic proportions therefore seems unmerited or, at the very least, much exaggerated. It can be defensibly regarded as a finding based on a dubious minor premise. For the status of FP as an empirical theory, on which the verdict of explanatory impotence rests, is still very much at issue.

### Further Views: To Eliminate or Not to Eliminate?

As might to be expected, noneliminativists are not all of the same stripe with respect to FP. The extensive roster includes people such as Fodor, Dennett, and Davidson—to name just a few holding widely dissimilar views.

Davidson recognizes the legitimacy of folk-psychological discourse but, by the same token, sees no possibility of its ever becoming scientific. For Davidson, recall, the categories of FP are not physically reducible. Every mental event-token in FP is identical with some physical (neurological) event-token but is not reducible to it. In other words, there is psychophysical identity of a sort, but the odd thing about this kind of identity is that there are no bridge-laws connecting mental event-types with neurophysiological event-types. "Funny monism," you muse. Davidson calls it *anomalous monism*. But, and extremely important, this fact does not of itself constitute a flaw in FP, certainly no reason (with due respect to Paul Churchland) for its elimination. It does not render FP a degenerating research program. Indeed for Davidson, FP represents no research program, degenerating or otherwise. Its nonreducibility is a fact that simply has to be taken into account in understanding FP. Of course the good news about this way of understanding things is that FP's integrity, its dictionary of platitudes, as a way of discoursing about the mental, remains intact. The bad news is that it can never grow up: Psychology can never *become* a science. Davidson's view stands in bold contrast to Churchland's calls for summary execution of FP on the grounds that irreducibility is a nonreprievable capital offense.

But perhaps more important than its merely contrasting with Churchland's view is the fact that Davidson's view constitutes a clear and appealing alternative to elimination. Indeed, the mere existence of Davidson's view makes just as clear that the case for elimination cannot be made solely on grounds of nonreducibility. This premise by itself cannot yield the desired conclusion. The syllogism for elimination may be something like the following: "Theories that are nonreducible to the categories of a more fundamental science are theories that should be eliminated; FP is a nonreducible theory in this sense; therefore FP is a theory that should be eliminated." In this case Davidson's view with respect to the nonreducibility of the mental would render the major premise very doubtful. In consequence, the soundness of the argument remains in doubt. We also wonder at the justification of the major premise. It is not a tautology; its truth is not obvious. Understood as an empirical claim, what kind of evidence will establish it as true? But then, again, it also assumes the form of a doctrine and not a claim. This further complicates things.

Dennett, too, accepts FP discourse but with very definite qualifications. On his view, notions such as beliefs and desires derive entirely from, and are fully parasitic on, the myth according to which we conceive of ourselves as rational agents. Absent the myth, absent the belief/desire attributions. So for him, beliefs and desires are not real internal states which stand to external behavior in the way in which internal, mechanical structures like cogs and levers stand to the observable consequences of their operations. Belief and desire ascriptions are fitting, but solely in an *instrumentalistic* sense. "The role of the concept of belief," he says, "is like the role of the concept of a center of gravity, . . . people really have beliefs and desires . . . just the way they really have centers of gravity and the earth has an Equator."[39] Hence the referents of these terms, on Dennett's version of FP, are not such entities as can be inferred on the basis of some scientific theory. On the contrary, they are best identified as abstractions. The referents are essentially logical constructs, useful fictions. Here again, the mental categories of FP are not due for elimination. The good news about this way of conceiving of FP is that we can live with its categories, at least the ones that are entirely resistant to all scientific overtures. The bad news is that by dint of its fictional standing, FP obviously becomes compatible with virtually any and every viable scientific theory of cognition. This is because its claims could not possibly contradict the claims of any such theory. Mythical or fictitious entities are at best *as-if-* or *pseudo*entities and as such cannot be said to represent any serious conflict with the scientifically real. So FP survives, but as a useful fiction.

This account of the ontic status of belief and desire also stands in marked contrast to that view provided by Fodor. For him propositional attitudes are

[39]See Daniel Dennett, "Three Kinds of Intentional Psychology," in *Folk Psychology, and the Philosophy of Mind*, eds. Scott M. Christensen and Dale R. Turner (Riverside: University of California Press, 1993), pp. 129–33.

real in the sense discussed earlier in this chapter and "the predictive adequacy of common sense psychology is beyond rational dispute."[40] Indeed, on his account, if FP is indicted because of its need to immunize its generalizations by resorting to ceteris paribus vaccine, "equal treatment based on equal justice requires that the same verdict be pronounced on all the special sciences—all, that is, with the sole exception of physics."

In essence, Fodor's response to the criticism that the inability of FP to explain and predict is clearly exhibited in its characteristic need to resort to the ever handy *ceteris paribus* hedge is a valid *tu quoque* (you also) argument: indeed, a *sound tu quoque* argument. Singling out geology, Fodor reminds the critic that a simple generalization like "rivers erode their outer banks," which passes almost as a truism, is nevertheless one which holds true by virtue of the idealized counterfactual conditionals which it subsumes. This generalization is true, but it implies certain provisos: that the outer banks are not sealed or otherwise protected against erosion, that the world does not come to an end, and others such, ad indefinitum; in short, that no countervailing state of affairs makes erosion impossible. This amounts to the admission that the all-things-being-equal proviso—the offending *ceteris paribus* hedge—is implicitly appealed to. What holds true for geology, as a special science, holds just as well for all the other special sciences, as distinct from physics, considered *the* basic science. It would hold just as well for neuroscience as it would for biology, and so on. The issue is best appreciated not in terms of the *degree* to which the hedge is employed in these special sciences, but in the very *nature* of these areas of study *qua* special sciences. The hedge is not peculiar to FP. Furthermore, its presumed greater visibility in FP is of no special significance. Its presence is what matters and in this FP shares shop with all the special sciences.

Of course sharing shop with others is one thing; justifying the use of shop space is quite a different thing. Merely showing how FP is like other disciplines does not establish its viability as a colleague. But exactly what form justification should take is hardly ever straightforwardly clear. That case has to be independently made. With respect to FP, everything hangs on just what FP is made out to be, and what, as a consequence, it should reasonably be capable of. On this front there is wide difference of opinion. On the one extreme are those who give FP an almost clean bill of health; on the other are those who see its ailment as terminal and its passing long overdue. Located somewhere between are some very important points of view—Davidson's, for example. So, the crucial question remains: Exactly what, if anything, needs justification, and on what grounds? As John Searle might well enquire, "What's the problem?" It is not a part of the notion of justification that it is to determine what needs justification. That task is largely a perceptual one.

On the conviction that FP may be compatible with a developed cognitive science, indeed that it is indispensable to it, Fodor presents what he calls a rep-

---

[40]See Fodor's "The Persistence of the Propositional Attitudes," pp. 222–26.

resentative theory of mind (RTM), which incorporates the propositional attitudes of FP. (Earlier in this chapter[41] we discussed his view of propositional attitudes.)[42] Stich remains pessimistic regarding the possibility of any absorption of FP in a mature cognitive science. However, the self-attribution and dissonance experiments to which he appeals to support his position on FP were themselves carried out in terms of belief/desire categories, the fundamental stuff of FP. A similar story holds for research done in cognitive science. We assume for the time being that FP's categories are suspended.

But the question arises as to how cognitive experimentation would proceed if not in any way correlated with or monitored by categories like belief and desire, which make up the propositional attitudes characteristic of FP. In their complete absence, what will we find out about ourselves as human beings, indeed, as persons? What can neuroscience alone say about humans as persons? Or will person-talk and all that goes with it—practically everything not physically reducible, friendship, for example—disappear from the way we think? What becomes of notions like self and self-referential terms, for example? What would be the ontology which, without *real* ontological loss, would replace the familiar ontology of FP? We must avoid bleeding heart arguments whose only merit is the supposed goodness of the good old days. But there nevertheless is considerable truth to Fodor's contention that "we have no idea of how to explain ourselves to ourselves except in a vocabulary which is *saturated* with belief/desire psychology. . . . What Kant said to Hume about physical objects holds, *mutatis mutandis,* for the propositional attitudes; we can't give them up *because we don't know how to.* "[43]

The fact is that with propositional attitudes out, out too must go the entire gamut of studies which utilize them: all the social or special sciences, history, art, ethics, religion, and so on. So, too, must notions like "I" and "my" and "mine" and "you" and "yours" and all the rest in this class. *And with FP gone, there is not much provision left for conversation.* An ineffable silence seems to take over. Atoms and the void have the last say, but they have no will to exercise the option.

## IN BRIEF

Let us conclude this chapter with a quick backward glance. In order to grasp the controversial issues of commonsense psychology or, perhaps less felicitiously, folk psychology, we commenced the chapter with a discussion of the nature of propositional attitudes. That done, our ensuing discussion high-

---

[41]See page 114 above.

[42]For an account of how Fodor develops his RTM, see his "The Persistence of the Attitudes," pp. 227–45.

[43]Fodor, "The Persistence of the Attitudes," p. 229.

lighted belief and desire since these are the attitudes commonly thought to be at the very core of FP. They are exactly the ones which parties to the issue of FP characteristically address, for the fate of these becomes the fate of all the other attitudes. We paid special attention to (1) the eliminativist views of Churchland and Stich; (2) the noneliminativist "anomalous monism" of Davidson, whose version of the identity theory admits mental-event tokens; (3) Dennett's instrumentalism; and (4) Fodor's account of propositional attitudes, their practical indispensability, and their place in a fully developed cognitive science—his representative theory of mind (RTM). We looked critically at the arguments for and against FP.

If we distinguish between a soft sense of theory, constituted by equally soft laws, and a hard or strict sense of theory, similarly constituted by strict laws, then we may conclude with the pronouncement that folk psychology is both bad and good theory. It is bad in the latter sense only; good, indeed very good, but in the former sense only. As we noted above, contrary to Churchland's insistence, an insistence critical to his eliminativism, it is not all obvious that FP is a theory in the same sense in which physics is. It was never the object of deliberate formulation. Its generalizations are anything but nomic: They represent no invariant relationships. And it is not at all obvious that it is a failed theory because its explanations and predictions do not pass strict scientific muster. This assessment holds only if it can be shown without question-begging or prescription that FP is a theory in the strict sense, or that all theories die in this manner. A more modest claim, and one which more economically fits the facts, is that FP, while roughly functioning like strict theory, is something significantly less. It is, by and large, good folk-theoretical wisdom rooted in the dynamics of folk experience—witness its universal, everyday success. This alone seems to assure its longevity.

But its successes and failures aside, at the very heart of FP is our conception of ourselves as persons, as agents who not only do, but who also value; who joke, conjecture, cajole, and reprimand. The language of FP is the language characteristic of persons—"I," "my," "mine," "you," "yours," "community," "society," and so on, and so on, and so on. The entire corpus of our social vocabulary is so integrally a part of how we manage to conceive of our selves as selves that it seems unlikely that its place can be taken by tidier terms expressive of a more apt ontology. In the final analysis, perhaps Horgan and Woodward got it right: FP is here to stay!

## SUGGESTIONS FOR FURTHER READING

The anthology *Folk Psychology and the Philosophy of Mind,* edited by Scott M. Christensen and Dale R. Turner, brings together a collection of papers on folk psychology. The suggested readings immediately following are found in that volume:

BECHTEL, WILLIAM, AND A. A. ABRAHAMSEN, "Connectionism and the Future of Folk Psychology,"
pp. 340–67; PAUL M. CHURCHLAND, "Eliminative Materialism and the Propositional
Attitudes," pp. 42–62; JOHN HALDANE, "Understanding Folk," pp. 263–87; TERENCE
HORGAN and JAMES WOODWARD, "Folk Psychology Is Here to Stay," pp. 144–63; GERARD J.
O'BRIEN, "The Connectionist Vindication of Folk Psychology," pp. 368–84; STEPHEN P.
STICH, "The Future of Folk Psychology," pp. 93–116; KATHLEEN V. WILKES, "The
Relationship between Scientific Psychology and Common Sense Psychology," pp. 167–86.
COPI, IRVING M., AND CARL COHEN, *Introduction to Logic* (8th ed.), pp. 5–7, 327–35. New York:
Macmillan Publishing Company, 1986.
DAVIDSON, DONALD, "*Mental* Events," in *Experience and Theory*, pp. 79–101, eds. L. Foster and
J. W. Swanson. Amherst: University of Massachusetts Press, 1970.
SMART, J. J. C., "Davidson's Minimal Materialism," in *Essays on Davidson: Actions and Events*, pp.
173–82, eds. Bruce Vermazen and Merrill B. Hintikka. Oxford, England: Clarendon
Press, 1985.
SUPPES, PATRICK, "Davidson's Views on Psychology as a Science," in *Essays on Davidson: Actions and
Events*, pp. 183–89, eds. Bruce Vermazen and Merrill B. Hintikka. Oxford, England:
Clarendon Press, 1985.

# 6

# Do I: Really?

[N]omological slack between the mental and the physical is
essential as long as we conceive of man as a rational animal.
　　　　　　　　　　　　　　　　　　　　*—Donald Davidson*[1]

Let us not forget this: when 'I raise my arm,' my arm goes up.
And the problem arises: what is left over if I subtract the fact
that my arm goes up from the fact that I raise my arm?
　　　　　　　　　　　　　　　　　　　　*—Ludwig Wittgenstein*[2]

It is very fitting in this final chapter, given the ground we have now covered, to consider the issue of human agency. In particular, we should discuss the widely accepted view that persons, as rational agents, do at times *initiate* events. However, since the subject of human agency itself constitutes the core of a complex area of inquiry, space constraints necessitate that our consideration here be introductory only.

## WAS THE I EVER RESPONSIBLE?

Let us consider the following question: Is it possible to *do* anything in a world in which all that happens is causally necessitated? We cannot provide a definitive answer to this question until we are clear as to what exactly is being asked. Among the things we need to know are (1) what sorts of referents are intended

[1] Donald Davidson, *Essays on Actions and Events* (Oxford, England: Clarendon Press, 1980), p. 223.

[2] Ludwig Wittgenstein, *Philosophical Investigations*, trans. G. E. M. Anscombe (New York: Macmillan Publishing Company, 1953).

by the expression "all that happens," and (2) how the term "do" is to be interpreted. We assume that the thesis of causal necessitation (CN) holds that for any event *e*, there is another event or set of events *c* which is so related to *e* that given *c*, *e* necessarily follows; that is, *c* causally necessitates *e*.[3] CN thus expresses a strict nomological relationship between *c* and *e*. Given various background conditions, the explanation for the occurrence of any event *e* is invariably and wholly provided in terms of some other event or set of events *c* which has *e* as its effect.

What are we to make of the expression "all that happens"? It includes both what we ordinarily refer to as mere occurrences—mindless events like the falling of leaves in autumn, lightning flashes, digestion, and solar eclipses—and such minded occurrences as thinking of Naples, composing a symphony, and doing algebra. It does not distinguish between occurrences for which a description in a purely physical vocabulary suffices, and those which include something vitally more, something decidedly mental. Mindless as well as minded events are lumped together to constitute "all that happens" and therefore are subject indifferently to causal necessitation. On this understanding, there is no event whatever which is not a causally necessitated happening.

Let us now consider the notion of doing something. Recall Wittgenstein's query at the beginning of this chapter: "What is left over if I subtract the fact that my arm goes up from the fact that I raise my arm?" There is the obvious fact, when I raise my arm, that my arm goes up. But there is also the undeniable fact that *I* am causally involved in its going up. Assuming that its going up is directly intentional, not only am I aware of what is going on, but *I* bring it about that my arm goes up just when it does. I *do* something here and now: The upward movement of my arm is *my* action.[4] I am neither a passive nor surprised spectator at my arm's going up. Had I different intentions, I would have directed my arm appropriately—in my pocket, or stiff along my side. So my intentions in this case determine what I do with my arm. Of course we should bear in mind as we proceed that the sorts of occurrences which count as doings differ considerably. We do rather simple things like place periods at the ends of sentences; and we do other more complex things like build houses, buy and sell, bargain, make promises, and authorize. But we also do things like befriend, refrain from speaking, and fret. Some intentional doings, building a house, for example, involve a complex of other intentional doings. There is no one thing we do which by itself constitutes building a house. So there is no simple account of what constitutes doing something. Some things we do require our presence in particular places and in particular circumstances; others do not. Some, interestingly, we may do by doing nothing in particular—showing contempt, for example.

---

[3]See Brand Blanshard, "The Case for Determinism," in *Determinism and Freedom in the Age of Modern Science,* ed. Sidney Hook (New York: New York University Press, 1958), pp. 19–30.

[4]Doings and actions are sometimes distinguished, but for our present purposes we will regard them as interchangeable.

With that in mind, let us provisionally concur with the usual view that intentional doings or actions are distinguished by the fact that they are occurrences which only rational agents can bring off. These agents are characteristically, though not exclusively, persons. On this commonsense view, to say that my arm goes up is not to say that my arm does anything but that my doing involves the movement of my arm. And closely related, while it is true that the raising of my arm requires muscular contractions of a specific sort, displacement of air, and so on, I cannot without some obvious oddity be said to have intentionally done all those things. So we should ideally distinguish between intentional and unintentional action, as well as between conscious and unconscious action. Certainly, not everything I do is intentionally done, or consciously done. Driving a car competently provides a good example. A good deal of what counts as good driving is performed unconsciously. Much of it has become second nature—applying the brakes, shifting gears, indicating turns, and so on. As a rule, we intend only a few of the events associated with, or occurring as a consequence of, the things we intentionally do.

But the question has less to do with these finer distinctions and more with intentional action as the primary concern. It is precisely this kind of action which appears to be in sharpest conflict with causal necessitation. The notion of intentional action seems ordinarily to presuppose the possibility of freedom of action, indeed to be defined in terms of it. Hence if freedom of action is an illusion, there are in reality no doings after all, only happenings. So the question we have been exploring can be justifiably taken as inquiring whether freedom of action and causal necessitation are in reality contradictory notions. Can they possibly coexist in the same world?

### Is the I Rational?

It is common practice to distinguish sharply between the *bona fide* doings of rational human agents and the *apparent-only* doings of such entities as fall outside of that class. Of the latter, but not of the former, we typically say that the phenomena they exhibit are fully accounted for by the operations of the laws of physics. We can fully explain the motions of branches waving in the breeze with reference to principles of atomic physics, aerodynamics, thermodynamics, and so on. But not so for the motions of an arm waving good-bye, or gesturing, or voting in favor of a bill, or signaling; for rational agents, by contrast, possess capacities which place them in a unique class. Rational agents characteristically deliberate, desire, intend, purpose, believe, establish goals, and so on.

But, we may object, this is all wishful thinking. In the first place, all physically identifiable events or states are sufficiently accounted for by the laws of physics. These laws apply indifferently to *all* spatiotemporal objects. There are no special cases where physical law is concerned. The upward movement of an arm is an identifiably physical event, hence wholly explicable in terms of those laws. Further, there are no *distinctively* mental events. There is therefore virtually no qualitative difference between what goes on when an arm goes up and when, as ordinary folk talk allows, it makes the trip deliberately. Further, talk about human agents voluntarily or freely acting or initiating this or that process, as if independent of antecedent causes, seems hardly intelligible. Such talk appears to credit agents with pulling off an incredible act: stepping outside the universal stream of causes to become themselves initiating causes. In sum, the agent story suffers from at least three weaknesses: (1) it allows for distinctively mental events; (2) it credits mental events with effecting physical change, and (3) it requires, as a metaphysical presupposition, that agents be sometimes nomologically free.

The crucial question here, at least with respect to human agency, is whether the experience we all share of being active rational agents in the world we inhabit is entirely illusory. Are we all deluded in supposing that our deliberations and purposes are causally efficacious in bringing about the changes we desire? What, at any rate, is the metaphysical status of our intentions, our deliberations, our purposes, and so on? And where do *I* or *you*, as agent, come in?

These questions are not altogether new to us. They were at least intimated by several of our discussions above, especially of intentionality and of propositional attitudes. They are the sorts of question that go to the very heart of what we think we are. We all consider ourselves persons whose very existence in communities is made possible by the fact that we can voluntarily effect significant physical changes in our circumstances. We act in all sorts of ways in keeping with our purposes. We have reasons for doing things and these explain their being done. We see ourselves as actively shaping some of the conditions that affect the sort of life we think desirable, and with that understanding have developed institutions and technologies. We choose to build bridges, or not to build them; to compose symphonies, or not to compose them; to go for walks, or not go for walks. Can it be, however, that *we* do none of the things we credit ourselves with doing, that in fact these "doings" are in no real sense the products of *our* intentions in action? In the final analysis, what becomes of the purposive mind? Is mind in reality epiphenomenal? Were the epiphenomenalists right all along?

## Is The I Free to Act?

Let us reflect for a moment on the principle of causal necessity. Recall that for any event *e*, there is another event or set of events *c* so related to *e*, that given *c*, *e* necessarily follows. This principle holds for any and all physical events, that is, for any and all events which can be fully described in a vocabulary consisting of only physical terms. Often coupled with this principle is the strict materialist claim, that *all* events are without exception *entirely* physical and fully describable in physical terms. If that is the case, then if there are mental events, it follows that they are in reality physical, hence subject to causal necessity. This represents one version of identity theory. But, there is another and quite influential identity view, owed to Davidson and called by him *anomalous monism*. On this view, each mental event-token is identical with some physical event-token but is not nomologically reducible to it. As Davidson puts it: "Mental events such as perceivings, rememberings, decisions, and *actions* resist capture in the nomological net of physical theory."[5] [Italics mine]. Of course, Davidson accepts the materialist claim that all events are physical, but he rejects the view that mental phenomena are fully describable in purely physical terms.

So it is possible, at least on this version of identity, to accept the claim that all events are physical and subject to causal necessity. At the same time, we can reject the contention that causal necessity extends to mental phenomena as described in a mentalistic vocabulary. If Davidson's anomalous monism is correct, in particular if "there are no strict deterministic laws on the basis of which mental events can be predicted or explained,"[6] we must, as does Davidson, acknowledge the *autonomy* of the mental. This would be one way of meeting the charge that all our intendings and believings, and desirings, and purposings, and the like are in actuality illusory. For if the mental is not in some sense nonreducible and autonomous, freedom of action is indeed an illusion. All our supposed doings are nothing but happenings. But freedom of action is for us a fundamental and defining feature of what we consider ourselves to be. Kant expresses the problem as follows:

> As a rational being and hence as belonging to the intelligible world, man can never think of the causality of his own will except under the idea of freedom; for independence from the determining causes of the world of sense (an independence which reason must always attribute to itself) is freedom. Now the idea of freedom is inseparably connected with the concept of autonomy, . . .[7]

Note also, Kant says:

> [E]ven though . . . reason for speculative purposes finds the road of natural necessity much better worn and more serviceable than that of freedom, yet for practical purposes the footpath of freedom is the only one upon which it is possible to make use of reason in our conduct. Therefore, it is just as impossible for the most subtle philosophy as for the most ordinary human reason to argue away freedom. Hence philosophy must assume that no real contradiction will be found between freedom and natural necessity in the same human actions, for it cannot give up the concept of nature any more than that of freedom.[8]

With reference to the question of whether it is possible to do anything in a world in which all that happens is causally necessitated, anomalous monism has considerable appeal. It describes, precisely the kind of world with which we

---

[5]Davidson, *Essays on Actions and Events*, p. 207.

[6]Davidson, *Essays on Actions and Events*, p. 208.

[7]Immanuel Kant, *Grounding for the Metaphysics of Morals*, trans. James W. Ellington (Indianapolis, Ind.: Hackett Publishing Company, 1981), pp. 53–54. The reading "can man" in the translation has been corrected to read "man can."

[8]Kant, *Grounding for the Metaphysics of Morals, "*p. 56.

are familiar, the world in which we see ourselves as agents who deliberate and do things in keeping with our intentions and purposes. True, this view holds that the mental supervenes on the physical, hence is causally dependent on it; but the mental is not at all subject to causal necessity. It is nomologically independent. Indeed Davidson contends:

> Two features of mental events in their relation to the physical—causal dependence and nomological independence—combine, then, to dissolve what has seemed a paradox, the efficacy of thought and purpose in the material world, and their freedom from law. When we portray events as perceivings, rememberings, decisions and actions, we necessarily locate them amid physical happenings through the relation of cause and effect; but as long as we do not change the idiom that same mode of portrayal insulates mental events from the strict laws that can in principle be called upon to explain and predict physical phenomena.[9]

So on Davidson's anomalous monism, propositional attitudes retain the place they have always assumed in our ordinary discourse. We still intend, we still devise means to ends, and we still act on our designs.

Anomalous monism, however, leaves us with a vexing metaphysical puzzle. For as Davidson pointed out, its strength resides in the fact that we have adopted two sorts of language to talk about the world: (1) the language characteristic of propositional attitudes—perceivings, rememberings, and so on—essentially, the language of agency and (2) the language whose terms refer to only physical entities and events. Granted that this is so, we still do not know a great deal about mental events, other than that they are supervenient on the physical. (Davidson understands supervenience to mean that if two events are exactly physically alike, they cannot differ in some mental respect, "that an object cannot alter in some mental respect without thereby altering in some physical respect.")[10] Further, if the metaphysical anomaly is preserved by language, by the way we standardly portray events, then one way of ridding ourselves of it may be to change the way we standardly talk. The real particulars of the world are unaffected by change in our discourse about the world. If linguistic habits are at fault, as eliminativists believe, then metaphysical housecleaning requires a radical departure from those habits. If there are no supervenient mental events, we lose nothing at all by making no mention of them. Of course, with mental events gone, gone are intentions, beliefs, desires, and so on—the entire roster of propositional attitudes. And by the same token, reference to agents and actions seems out of place.

### The I as Cause

It may now appear that we have not made a great deal of headway with our question of causal necessity. But is this really the case? Perhaps the posi-

---

[9]Davidson, *Essays on Actions and Events*, pp. 224–25.
[10]Davidson, *Essays on Actions and Events*, p. 214.

tion represented by anomalous monism deserves a second look. Perhaps it is not as implausible as it might at first have appeared. Perhaps it does have substantial metaphysical merit after all. In particular, maybe mental phenomena cannot possibly be described in a language which employs only physical terms. Perhaps it is impossible to characterize relationships between physical and mental phenomena in strict law-like terms—that indeed there are no psychophysical laws to relate the two types. Moreover, with dualism ruled out, anomalous monism seems an attractive alternative. It comes rather close to matching the way we conceive of ourselves as rational agents in the world. We experience ourselves as perceiving, believing, desiring, deliberating, and so on, and as acting at times in keeping with our judgments. Our intentions are real to us. It seems that anomalous monism leaves all this intact.

Imagine the following scenario. You had a very short lunch break last Tuesday, so you walked to the nearby grocery store and purchased yourself a single ripe banana. That, you said to yourself, should do it until dinner time at six. Let us now attempt a close look at some crucial events. It is clear that you did not see yourself in the role of a curious spectator wondering where in the world you were headed and what you were up to. And you were not the least bit surprised when you left the store with the banana. To bring off the whole affair, you intended to do several things: to go to the grocery store; to walk rather than employ some other means of getting there; to buy a single ripe banana, rather than steal it or beg for it; to have something to eat at lunchtime rather than to go hungry; to report to work in the afternoon on time rather than late. There were decidings, and desirings, and believings, and the like— all mental events. But there were also numerous physical events: walking to and from the store, taking up the banana, paying money for it, and so on. Somewhere in all this there were *psychophysical linkages* such as, for example, between the way your intentions and desires were carried out and the way in which *you* conceived them. You were in effective control of the events. But how?

If all the mental events associated with the affair—your intentions, your reasons, your desires—were necessitated, or caused entirely by antecedent mental events or states, then *you* had nothing to do with your getting the banana. Perhaps mental events are incapable of effecting physical states, either by being causally impotent— if epiphenomenalism is true—or by following a career all their own, though perfectly synchronized with particular physical events and processes—if psychophysical parallelism is true. Then in either circumstance *you* would have had nothing to do with your acquiring the banana. You might speculate, no doubt, that if that were true, you might well have been surprised at the orderly sequence of events. But you were not surprised. On the contrary, you considered yourself the person responsible for the events having gone the way they did. You were the controlling, purposive force. You determined the structure of the affair. Presumably, you would have done differently had you chosen to do otherwise. But how did *you* come in? How did you become *the* causal agent?

You evidently had reasons for doing what you did. But those reasons, you must concede, were not created then and there out of nothing. They were occasioned. Assuming that you acted rationally, there must have been some plausible account for your having just those reasons and not others, and for your doing just those things you did and not others. Let us suppose, for instance, that you were hungry. Now you either are or are not hungry. And whether you are or are not hungry is not a matter of your choosing or willing. But with this unwilled state insistently present, as a consequence you intend to do something by way of response. This is, for us, a critical juncture: It is a juncture where cause, *not* of your making, and *your* intention meet.

But intentions, too, are not spontaneous, or random, or uncaused occurrences. They, too, like states of hunger, owe their existence partly to the circumstances which give rise to them. Hence intentions must take their place somewhere in the complex web of causes. So the intention is yours, but *you* did not cause it. You did not originate it. So, too, in all probability, for your other mental states. But if this is the genealogy of action, then you did nothing: really. *Your mental states had no need of you.* There is nothing for you to contribute, nothing for which you may take credit or accept blame.

But something seems quite wrong here. The central issue, of course, is whether what we consider our doings, particularly our direct intentional actions, can be decomposed and dismissed in strictly causal terms. There are those persons who argue that a plausible account of rational action must exhibit compatibility between causal necessity and freedom of action. Indeed, they maintain that freedom of action has to be understood within the framework of overall causal necessity. Then there are those who view freedom of action and causal necessity as fundamentally incompatible notions, so that any attempt to reconcile the two must be seriously mistaken. For such persons, the correct account of rational action must escape the causal net. The former position maintains that there is no escape from causal necessity; the latter rejects this view and holds that some events are not necessitated, in particular those constitutive of rational action.[11] We cannot here go into the relative merits of those opposing positions; that will take us well beyond the scope of the present work. Suffice it here to call attention to the fact that we often think of ourselves as being quite free to act on alternatives, to do this, or just as freely, to do that. We sometimes consider ourselves as agents free to bring about this or that action, to raise an arm or not to raise it, to see such occurrences as our doing. And while experience is hardly a sure metaphysical guide, there does seem to be something about the mental that resists causal reduction, something about *seeing ourselves as agents* that stubbornly resists physical reduction and nomo-

[11]For discussions of these and other positions, see John Hospers, "Meaning and Free Will," *Philosophy and Phenomenological Research*, X, no. 3 (March 1950), 307–30; Brand Blanshard, "The Case for Determinism," pp. 19–30; William James, "The Dilemma of Determinism," in *Essays on Faith and Morals*, selected by Ralph Barton Perry (New York: Longmans, Green and Co., 1947), pp. 145–83; C. A. Campbell, "Is 'Freewill' a Pseudo-Problem?" *Mind*, LX, no. 240 (October 1951), 441–65.

logical explication. As Davidson observes, "the nomological slack between the mental and the physical is essential as long as we conceive of man as a rational animal." And to continue seeing ourselves as rational virtually guarantees recognition of some propositional attitudes. Following Fodor, we may maintain that we would not know how to do without them.

The contention that "all that happens" is causally necessitated is neither intuitively obvious nor demonstrably certain. This, of course, holds as well for its denial. At best, both views are posits. However, it is difficult to conceive of any event which owes its existence to none other than itself, in short, that is its own explanation. But to hold that we can always explain any event *e* with reference to some antecedent event *c* does not amount to the claim that the relation of *c* to *e* is one of causal necessitation. So, for example, while we explain your walking to the store to get yourself a banana with reference to your hunger, we cannot conclude that your actions were necessitated by your hunger. It is conceivable that you might freely have done other than you did. You might not have decided to go to the store, or you might have gone and not chosen a banana, and so on. So there may be a class of events, those characterized by propositional attitudes, which, while not immune to causal explanation of some sort, is nevertheless not amenable to strict law-like explanation. Such events are, in Davidson's terms, causally dependent but nomologically independent. And indeed there is considerable merit to Davidson's view that these two features combine "to dissolve what has seemed a paradox, the efficacy of thought and purpose in the material world and their freedom from law."

On this view, there is the possibility of *bona fide* doings since not all that happens is causally necessitated. And on this view, too, the *I* of self-reference is not a theater where mental events are enacted. Instead it is a person that on occasion is the agent responsible for the occurrence of certain mental events— events such as deciding, intending, choosing, and so on. I, or you, the person, decides, intends, chooses, and so on.

But an eliminativist is in no way persuaded by all this. She may counter with the plausible contention that far from removing the presumed paradox of the efficacy of thought in a material world, this view merely glosses over it. The problem of agency remains unresolved. She may contend that there is no *I*, nor *you*, nor *person* over and above the causal stream of events. So the *you* and *I* of agency are dummy entities which contribute nothing whatever to the explanation of events. Terms like "I" and "you" do not refer to effective agents, or for that matter to real entities. They are essentially place holders. At best, they serve merely to group events.

It is perhaps, finally, our *experience* as active agents in the world which will prove decisive. But, as we observed above, the experience of seeing ourselves as effecting this or that change may make no contribution to settling metaphysical problems. Any argument for agency based solely on experience may accomplish little more than beg the question, assume just what it presumes to prove. What we experience and what science tells us may be quite substantially different. For the time being, however, experience appears to have the last (though very controversial) word.[12] But this uneasy resolution in favor of experience, understood as an inner, that is, subjective, phenomenon raises afresh what some regard as the most persistent issue of all, the issue of qualia. To that we now briefly return.

## QUALIA AGAIN

Any successful analysis of the mental must address the issue of qualia: the question of whether or not there are such things as qualia and, if there are, what their significance is in an organism's mental life. Recall that the term "qualia" refers to what some have called the subjective or phenomenal character of experience. Put differently, it captures the phenomenon expressed in saying that there is something it is like to be an entity possessing conscious mental states— a person, a bat, an owl, for example. As Nagel put it, "[T]he fact that an organism has conscious experience *at all* means, basically, that there is something it is like to *be* that organism. . . . [F]undamentally, an organism has conscious mental states if and only if there is something it is like to *be* that organism— something it is like *for* the organism."[13] It follows from this way of understanding the relationship between conscious mental states and qualia that if conscious mental states are *fully* reducible, so too, in virtue of this possibility, are qualia.

Eliminativists see no special difficulty here. Assuming physicalism, they maintain that the mental is physically reducible without residue. This would mean that if qualia exist at all, they exist as mental states or properties and are accordingly fully reducible. The difficulty of course with this position is in deciding under what circumstances a successful reduction of qualia has been achieved. For if qualia exist as mental states or properties, the uniquely *subjective* features of experience, they are resistant to *objective* identification. So no reductive analysis can succeed, since any such analysis has of necessity to be expressed in objective categories and omits precisely what the analysis is supposed to be an analysis of. The essential subjectivity of qualia renders obtuse any attempt to make them objectively describable. Indeed Nagel remarks:

> It is not captured by any of the familiar, recently devised reductive analyses of the mental, for all of them are logically compatible with its absence. It is not analyzable in terms of any explanatory system of functional states, or intentional states, since these could be ascribed to robots or automata that behaved like people though they experienced nothing.[14]

[12]For a discussion of the problem of agency, see J. David Velleman, "What Happens When Someone Acts," *Mind,* 101 (July 1992), 461–81.

[13]Thomas Nagel, "What Is It Like to Be a Bat?" *The Philosophical Review* (October 1974), p. 436.

[14]Nagel, "What Is It Like to Be a Bat?" p. 436.

And as we noted in Chapter Three, other believers in qualia have developed arguments based on inverted qualia and absent qualia to show that qualia cannot be reduced.

But there is also a "compatibilist" view proposed by yet other believers in qualia, notably by Shoemaker, according to which "a functionalist account *can* be given for what it is for a property to be a quale, . . . and of what it is for mental states to be in greater or lesser degrees similar in qualitative character."[15] Shoemaker accepts the contention made by some incompatibilists, notably Block and Fodor, that an individual quale cannot be functionally reduced. This contention is borne out by the possibility of inverted qualia. But he rejects the view that qualia as types are irreducible. His argument is quite simple.

> A creature functionally just like a creature having qualitative states would itself have to have qualitative states, for it would have to have states standing in relations of qualitative similarity and difference to one another that are isomorphic with the relations of qualitative similarity and difference holding between the states of the creature which is its functional duplicate.[16]

Schematically, the argument is as follows: If *A* is a functional duplicate of *B*, and if *B* possesses qualitative states, then so too does *A*, since *A* is isomorphic with *B*, and the same relations which hold between qualitative states *Q* with respect to *B* would also hold between qualitative states *Q* with respect to *A*. Once we grant functional isomorphism, the argument is straightforward enough and valid. But its soundness remains an open question, for the argument rests on an acceptance of a functionalist theory of mind. Whatever merit it possesses is derived from that possessed by functionalism. If functionalism represents the correct view of mind, the reducibility of qualia is scarcely an issue. But we do not know that it does. And it is precisely this larger question that we need to resolve. In the circumstances, we do not know that qualia are functionally reducible. We know only that *if functionalism is true*, then qualia are presumably *ipso facto* in principle reducible. But we cannot properly assume the truth value of that conditional.

Our special interest in returning now to the issue of qualia is in its intimate connection with issues of consciousness and, somewhat more broadly, in the place of qualia in the folk-psychological economy. For some, Nagel, for example, there is an inseparable connection between consciousness and qualia. For them, all conscious organisms have qualitative states. There is something it is like to be this or that conscious organism, but nothing it is like to be this or that cloud or broomstick. So what distinguishes between entities which functionally simulate conscious mental states and genuine possessors of conscious mental states is that the former, unlike the latter, are not capable of phenomenal experience. They are incapable of occupying a distinctively subjective point

---

[15]Sydney Shoemaker, "Qualia and Consciousness," *Mind*, C, no. 4 (October 1991), 507. [Italics mine.]

[16]Shoemaker, "Qualia and Consciousness," p. 507.

of view. Hence the notion of qualia is an essential part of the complex of notions that make up folk psychology. And once folk-psychological description persists, talk of qualia of necessity persists with it.

It is perhaps not crucially necessary to distinguish, as does Shoemaker, between what he calls *quasi*-qualia and qualia. We do not need to distinguish between phenomenal states present in conscious organisms lacking the capacity for introspective awareness and those states in humans which, through the mediation of language, are introspectively accessible. It is, of course, a very useful distinction, especially if, for example, we are convinced that qualia play a fundamental role in the acquisition of beliefs.[17] But that is a view which nonfunctionalists are very likely to reject. At any rate, if the capacity for introspective awareness entails the capacity for phenomenal awareness, and if the notion of being phenomenally aware is a crucial one in the repertoire of folk psychology, we are again faced with the issue of assessing the merits of folk psychology as a way of understanding ourselves. This, as we have seen, is a difficult undertaking.

But if, as Shoemaker and many others hold, folk-psychological states, and the ability expressed through language to make self-ascriptions about those states, are part and parcel of the same evolutionary process, the task of their assessment becomes difficult perhaps impossible.[18] We are faced, however, with a phenomenon which, whatever else may be said of it, has had obvious survival value. Whatever form a developed science of mind takes, we will no doubt have to reckon with this fact.

## IN BRIEF

In this final chapter the central issue has been that of human agency. The issue as we considered it is perhaps best expressed here in a troublesome question posed by Wittgenstein. He observes as follows: "Let us not forget this: when 'I raise my arm,' my arm goes up. And the question arises: what is left over if I subtract the fact that my arm goes up from the fact that I raise my arm?"[19]

## SUGGESTIONS FOR FURTHER READING

### Classical Texts

DAVIDSON, DONALD, *Essays on Action and Events*, pp. 207–25, 245–59, Oxford, England: Clarendon Press, 1980.
KANT, IMMANUEL, *Grounding for the Metaphysics of Morals*, pp. 49–55, trans. James W. Ellington. Indianapolis, Ind.: Hackett Publishing Company, 1981.

[17]On this possibility, see Shoemaker, "Qualia and Consciousness," p. 510.
[18]Shoemaker, "Qualia and Consciousness," pp. 513–14.
[19]Wittgenstein, *Philosophical Investigations*, sec. 621.

McCann, Hugh, "Volition and Action," *The Philosophical Review* (October 1974), pp. 451–73.
Velleman, David J., "What Happens When Someone Acts," *Mind*, 101 (July 1992), 461–81.
Wittgenstein, L., *Philosophical Investigations*, secs. 609–55, trans. G. E. M. Anscombe. New York: Macmillan Publishing Company, 1953.

## Commentary

Nagel, Thomas, "What Is It Like to Be a Bat?" *The Philosophical Review* (October 1974), pp. 435–50. This essay can be found in numerous other places including *The Nature of Mind*, pp. 422–28, ed. David Rosenthal; and in *The Mind's I*, pp. 391–403, eds. Douglas Hofstadter and Daniel Dennett. For full bibliographical details of these books, see the bibliography at the end of this book.
Shoemaker, Sydney, "Qualia and Consciousness," *Mind*, C, no. 4 (October 1991), 507–22.

# Glossary

**Agent causation:** The occurrence of an event $E$ is an instance of agent causation if some agent $A$ wills that $E$ and brings it about that $E$. Agent causation contrasts with what is often referred to as event causation. In the latter case, but not in the former, the bringing about of event $E$ is explicable solely in terms of nonwilled events. *See also* Entailment view of causation, Regularity view of causation.[1]

**Anomalous monism:** The view that mental states supervene on brain states but that mental states are not physically reducible. Thus while materialism may be true, the mental resists description in a physical vocabulary. *See also* Reducible; Supervenience.

**Antecedent:** *See* Conditional.

**Begging the Question:** A form of reasoning in which the conclusion of the argument is merely a restatement of the premise. Such an argument is valid but nonetheless fallacious, because it assumes or takes for granted precisely what it is supposed to establish. A statement or claim that assumes precisely what is in dispute is also said to beg the question. Also referred to by its Latin name, *petitio principii,* or more commonly as a circular argument. *See* Valid argument.

**Biconditional:** A conjunction consisting of two conditional sentences of the form $\{$(If $p$ then $q$) and (if $q$ then $p$)$\}$. Expresses the same thing as (If and only if $p$ then $q$). May be symbolized as: $\{(p \supset q) \ (q \supset p)\}$, or more compactly as $(p \equiv q)$.

**Cartesian:** Of, or relating to, any of the theories of Descartes.

**Category mistake:** Conceiving of something as belonging to a category to which it does not belong. To suppose, for example, that horsepower is an item that may be listed in the inventory of parts stocked in an automobile shop is to commit a category mistake. Horsepower indicates the physical thrust or force which an engine is capable of and not some *thing* which constitutes a part of engines. Some theorists, notably Gilbert Ryle,[2] have made much of this mistake in their challenge to substance dualism.

***Ceteris paribus:*** (Latin) "Other things being equal." An expression typically employed as an epistemic hedge to protect some assertions, predictions, or questions as, for example, in: "In

---

[1] See John Lachs, "Epiphenomenalism and the Notion of Cause," The Journal of Philosophy, LX, no. 6 (March 14, 1963), 142–43.

[2] See Gilbert Ryle, *The Concept of Mind* (London: Hutchinson & Co., 1960), pp. 18–23.

these circumstances, *ceteris paribus*, organism *O* will engage in behavior *B*." *See* 'Epistemic hedge.'

**Claim:** Whatever we assert to be the case.

**Cognitive:** Having to do with knowing, perceiving, remembering, and so on.

**Conditional, Conditional statement:** A hypothetical proposition; a compound statement of the form "If *p*, then *q*." Its constituent statements, represented by *p* and *q*, are known respectively as the antecedent and consequent of the conditional. There are several different ways in which antecedents may be related to their consequents. Minimally, therefore, a conditional expressed as "If *p*, then *q*"—symbolically, $(p \supset q)$, or alternatively $(p \rightarrow q)$—is interpreted as asserting only that it is not the case that the antecedent is true and the consequent false; symbolically, $\sim(p\ \&\sim q)$. *See* Material implication.

**Consequent:** See Conditional above.

**Convention:** Common agreement.

**Entailment view of causation:** The view that the relationship between cause and effect is describable in terms of the logical model of entailment: a cause logically implies the effect. Following this model, if *A* is the cause of *B*, then the occurrence of *A* guarantees, or is sufficient for, the occurrence of *B*. The occurrence of *B* is entailed by the occurrence of *A*. On this view, it is impossible for *A* to occur and *B* not to occur. Further, since entailment is transitive, it stands to reason that *B*, too, as effect would have its own causal entailments; and so on, and on. *See also* Agent causation and Regularity view of causation.

**Epiphenomenalism:** The view that mental phenomena are the products of brain processes and cannot themselves be causes. By setting them off in this way from the brain processes which cause them, this view conflicts with the entailment view of causation. *See* "Entailment view of causation."

**Epistemic hedge:** An expression a speaker or writer uses to secure a knowledge claim against objections or counterattack; as in: "Provided that the senator from Illinois makes no serious campaign blunders, I know he will win re-election." The claim to know the outcome of the election is qualified by a "hedge"—the conditional clause which goes before it. *See Ceteris paribus*.

**Epistemology:** The area of philosophy concerned with such notions as knowledge, truth, and belief.

**Existential import:** *See* Particular proposition.

**Functionalism:** The view that identifies mental states with certain functional states of an organism.

**Identity of indiscernibles:** If *x* has every property *y* has, and *y* has every property *x* has, then *x* and *y* are identical. Symbolically: $(F)(Fx \equiv Fy) \supset (x = y)$. *See* Indiscernibility of identicals.

**Identity of reference:** A synonymous expression is "sameness of reference." An example is any circumstance in which two distinct terms or names identify one and the same object. "Evening Star" and "Morning Star" identify one and the same object, namely, Venus. Cicero and Tully are two different names for one and the same person.

**Indiscernibility of identicals:** If *x* and *y* are identical, then any property *x* has *y* has and, equivalently, any property *y* has *x* has—symbolically: $(x = y) \supset (F)(Fx \equiv Fy)$. Sometimes referred to as Leibniz's Law. *See* Identity of indiscernibles.

**Material implication:** A relation which exists between the propositions represented by the terms "*p*" and "*q*" when the conditional of the form $(p \supset q)$ is true. The antecedent, *p*, materially implies the consequent, *q*. *See* Conditional.

**Metaphysics:** The area of philosophy concerned with inquiring into the *nature* of what there is.

**Monism:** The ontological view that all phenomena are manifestations of just one ultimate reality or substance. For some, that ultimate reality is physical; for others—some idealists, for example—it is spiritual. This view contrasts with Cartesian substance dualism.

**Ontic:** Pertaining to matters ontological, relating to being.

**Ontology:** The area of philosophy concerned with the study of *what is* or exists. Usually considered by some a branch of metaphysics.

**Particular proposition:** A proposition of the form "Some *S* and *P*," or "Some *S* are not *P*." Particular, unlike universal, propositions are regarded as having *existential* import. This means that they are considered as affirming the *existence* of whatever is represented by their subject terms. Hence, for example, "Some ghosts are blue" is rendered as the conjunction consisting of two atomic propositions: (1) "At least one ghost exists" and (2) "That ghost has the property of being blue." *See* Universal proposition.

**Premise:** A proposition from which inference to one or more other propositions is drawn.

**Proposition:** Usually a synonym for "statement." It refers to what is expressed by any meaningful declarative utterance. A simple or atomic proposition (statement) contains no further propositions (statements). A proposition is either true or false.

*Quale* **(plural, qualia):** A supposedly unique, possibly irreducible quality possessed by some of our experiences. Sometimes expressed, thanks to Thomas Nagel, as the feeling of "what it is like to be" a so and so, or "to see" or "feel" such and such.

**Reducible:** Completely describable in the vocabulary of a lower-level, that is, more basic, science. If, for example, all that exists is physical, then presumably all phenomena are physically reducible, meaning that they can be completely described in some physical vocabulary.

**Regularity view of causation:** The relationship between two events or states such that the second regularly follows the first and is held to be brought about by it. Metals expand when heat is applied to them. This is an instance of constant conjunction of two phenomena where the first, in this case heat, is invariably followed by the second, expansion of whatever metal to which heat is applied. Of course not every pair of regularly conjoined phenomena indicates this causal relationship; on the contrary, the pair may jointly be the effect of some antecedent event or set of events. See Hume on causation.[3] *See also* Agent causation and Entailment view of causation.

**Semantic:** Concerned with the meaning—connotative, denotative—or reference of terms. *See* Syntactic.

**Sound argument:** A valid argument all of whose premises are true. *See* Valid argument.

**Substance dualism:** The view that holds that mind and body are two metaphysically distinct substances.

**Supervenience:** Within the context of mind body issues, describes a relation between the mental and brain states of an organism such that there occurs a change in the organism's mental states if and only if there is a corresponding change in the organism's brain states. In this way, mental states are said to supervene on brain or physical states.

**Syllogism:** An argument form consisting of two premises—a major and a minor—from which a third proposition, a conclusion, is derived by inference.

**Syntactic:** Pertaining to the rules of grammar which structure a language. Any language, natural or artificial, has structure and hence may be said to have a syntax. It is debatable whether representation in a language is inevitably syntactic.[4]

**Truth value:** The property of being true or false. Applies to individual propositions but not to arguments.

**Universal proposition:** A proposition of the form "All $S$ are $P$," or "No $S$ are $P$." Such propositions affirm or deny that the property or relation $P$ is true of each and every member of the class represented by the subject term $S$.

**Valid argument:** An argument such that it is impossible for its premise to be true and its conclusion false. *See* Sound argument.

---

[3]Hume, *On Human Nature and the Understanding,* ed. Antony Flew (New York: Collier Books, 1962), pp. 187–218.

[4]See the discussion of connectionism with regard to representation in Chapter Three.

# Bibliography

AUGUSTINE, *Later Works.* John Burnaby, trans. Philadelphia: Westminster Press, 1955. See *The Trinity,* bk. X, sec. 16.
———*Concerning the City of God.* trans. Henry Bettenson. London: Penguin Books, 1984.
———*The Concept of a Person.* New York: St. Martin's Press, 1963.
AYER, A. J., *Philosophy in the Twentieth Century.* New York: Vintage Books, 1982.
BELLAH, ROBERT N., *Beyond Belief.* Berkeley: University of California Press, 1991.
BLANSHARD, BRAND, "The Case for Determinism," in *Determinism and Freedom in the Age of Modern Science,* ed. Sidney Hook. New York: New York University Press, 1958.
BLOCK, NED, "Troubles with Functionalism," in *The Nature of Mind,* ed. David Rosenthal. New York: Oxford University Press, 1991.
BORST, C. V., ed., *The Mind/Brain Identity Theory.* New York: St. Martin's Press, 1970.
BRODY, BARUCH A., *Identity and Necessity.* Princeton, N.J.: Princeton University Press, 1980.
BUTLER, JOSEPH, "Of Personal Identity," in *Personal Identity,* ed. John Perry. Berkeley: University of California Press, 1975.
CALKINS, MARY WHITON, *The Metaphysical System of Hobbes,* pp. 85–87. La Salle, Ill: Open Court Publishing Company, 1963.
CAMPBELL, C. A., "Is 'Freewill' a Pseudo-Problem?" *Mind,* LX, no. 240, (October 1951).
CAMPBELL, KEITH, *Body and Mind.* Notre Dame, Indiana: University of Notre Dame Press, 1984.
CARE, NORMAN S., AND ROBERT H. GRIMM, eds., *Perception and Personal Identity.* Cleveland, Ohio: Case Western Reserve University, 1969.
CHISHOLM, RODERICK, "The Loose and Popular and the Strict and Philosophical Senses of Identity," in *Perception and Personal Identity,* eds. Norman S. Care and Robert H. Grimm. Cleveland, Ohio: Case Western Reserve University, 1969.
CHRISTENSEN, SCOTT M., AND DALE R. TURNER, eds., *Folk Psychology and the Philosophy of Mind.* Hillsdale, N.J.: Lawrence Erlbaum Associates, Publishers, 1993.
CHURCHLAND, PAUL M., "Eliminative Materialism and the Propositional Attitudes," *Journal of Philosophy,* LXXVIII, no. 2 (1981).
———, *Matter and Consciousness.* Cambridge, Mass. MIT Press, 1988.
CLARK, ANDY, "Systematicity, Structured Representations and Cognitive Architecture: A Reply to Fodor and Pylyshyn," in *Connectionism and the Philosophy of Mind,* eds. Terence Horgan and John Tienson. Dordrecht: Kluwer Academic Publishers, 1991.
COLE, DAVID J., JAMES H. FETZER, AND TERRY L. RANKIN, eds., *Philosophy, Mind, and Cognitive Inquiry.* Dordrecht: Kluwer Academic Publishers, 1990.

COPI, IRVING, *Introduction to Logic*. New York: Macmillan Publishing Company, 1986.

CRICK, FRANCIS, AND KRISTOF KOCH, "The Problem of Consciousness," *Scientific American*, 267, no. 3 (September 1992).

DAVIDSON, DONALD, "Mental Events," in *Experience and Theory*, eds. L. Foster and J. W. Swanson. Amherst: University of Massachusetts Press, 1970.

————, *Essays on Actions and Events*. Oxford, England: Clarendon Press, 1980.

DENNETT, DANIEL, *Brainstorms*. Montgomery, Vt.: Bradford Books, 1978.

————, "Artificial Intelligence as Philosophy and as Psychology," in *Philosophical Perspectives in Artificial Intelligence*, ed. Martin Ringle. Atlantic Highlands, N.J.: Humanities Press, 1979.

————, *The Intentional Stance*. Cambridge, Mass.: MIT Press, 1987.

————, *Consciousness Explained*. Boston: Little, Brown and Company, 1991.

————, "Three Kinds of Intentional Psychology," in *Folk Psychology and the Philosophy of Mind*, eds. Scott M. Christenson and Dale R. Turner. Riverside: University of California Press, 1993.

DESCARTES, RENÉ, *The Philosophical Works of Descartes*, trans. Elizabeth S. Haldane and G. R. T. Ross. Cambridge, England: Cambridge University Press, 1931.

————, *Discourse on Method* and *Meditations on First Philosophy*, trans. Donald A. Cress. Indianapolis, Ind.: Hackett Publishing Company, 1980.

————, *The Philosophical Writings of Descartes*, trans. John Cottingham, Robert Stoothoff, and Dugald Murdoch. Cambridge, England: Cambridge University Press, 1984.

DREYFUS, HUBERT, "Misrepresenting Human Intelligence," *Thought*, LXI (1986), 430–41.

FEIGL, HERBERT, "Mind-Body, *Not* a Pseudo-Problem," in *The Mind/Brain Identity Theory*, ed. C. V. Borst. New York: St. Martin's Press, 1970.

FODOR, JERRY, "The Mind-Body Problem," *Scientific American*, 244, no. 1 (January 1981).

————, "The Persistence of the Attitudes," *Psychosemantics*. Cambridge, Mass.: MIT Press, 1988.

————, "Propositional Attitudes," in *The Nature of Mind*, ed. David Rosenthal. New York: Oxford University Press, 1991.

FODOR, JERRY, AND BRIAN P. MCLAUGHLIN, "Connectionism and the Problem of Systematicity: Why Smolensky's Solution Doesn't Work," in *Connectionism and the Philosophy of Mind*, eds. Terence Horgan and John Tienson. Dordrecht: Kluwer Academic Publishers, 1991.

FOGELIN, ROBERT J., *Hume's Skepticism in the Treatise of Human Nature*. London: Routledge & Kegan Paul, 1985.

FOSTER, L., AND J. W. SWANSON, eds., *Experience and Theory*. Amherst: University of Massachusetts Press, 1970.

FRENCH, PETER, THEODORE E. UEHLING, AND HOWARD K. WETTSTEIN, eds., *Midwest Studies in Philosophy, Vol. IV: Studies in Metaphysics*. Minneapolis: University of Minnesota Press, 1979.

GARSON, JAMES W., "What Connectionists Cannot Do: The Threat to Classical AI," in *Connectionism and the Philosophy of Mind*, eds. Terence Horgan and John Tienson. Dordrecht: Kluwer Academic Publishers, 1991.

GRENE, MARJORIE, *The Aquinas Lecture, 1991: Descartes Among the Scholastics*. Milwaukee, Wis.: Marquette University Press, 1991.

HALDANE, JOHN, "Understanding Folk," in *Proceedings of the Aristotelian Society*, Supplementary Volume 62, 1988. Also reproduced in *Folk Psychology and the Philosophy of Mind*, eds. Scott M. Christensen and Dale R. Turner. Hillsdale N.J.: Lawrence Erlbaum Associates, Publishers, 1993.

HALL, HARRISON, AND NORMAN E. BOWIE, eds., *The Tradition of Philosophy*. Belmont, Calif.: Wadsworth Publishing Company, 1986.

HAMPSHIRE, STUART, *Thought and Action*. New York: Viking Press, 1959.

HIRSCH, ELI, *The Concept of Identity*. New York: Oxford University Press, 1982.

HOBBES, THOMAS, "Of Identity and Difference," *Concerning Body*, chap. XI, sec. 7, in *The Metaphysical System of Hobbes*, pp. 85–87, ed. Mary Whiton Calkins. La Salle, Ill.: Open Court Publishing Company, 1963.

HOFSTADTER, DOUGLAS, AND DANIEL DENNETT, *The Mind's I*. New York: Bantam Books, 1982.

HOOK, SIDNEY, ed., *Determinism and Freedom in the Age of Modern Science*. New York: New York University Press, 1958.

HORGAN, TERENCE, AND JOHN TIENSON, eds., *Connectionism and the Philosophy of Mind*. Dordrecht: Kluwer Academic Publishers, 1991.

HORGAN, TERENCE, AND JAMES WOODWARD, "Folk Psychology Is Here to Stay," *The Philosophical Review*, 94 (1985)

HOSPERS, JOHN, "Meaning and Free Will," *Philosophy and Phenomenological Research*, X, no. 3 (March 1950).

HUME, DAVID, *A Treatise of Human Nature*, ed. L. A. Selby-Bigge. Oxford, England: Clarendon Press, 1949.

———, *On Human Nature and the Understanding*, ed. Antony Flew. New York: Collier Books, 1962.

HUXLEY, THOMAS H., "Animal Automatism," in *Methods and Results: Essays*. New York: D. Appleton and Company, 1896.

JAMES, WILLIAM, "The Dilemma of Determinism," in *Essays on Faith and Morals*, selected by Ralph Barton Perry. New York: Longmans, Green and Co., 1947.

JONES, W. T., *A History of Western Philosophy: Hobbes to Hume*. New York: Harcourt Brace Jovanovich, Inc., 1969.

KANT, IMMANUEL, *Grounding for the Metaphysics of Morals*, trans. James W. Ellington. Indianapolis, Ind.: Hackett Publishing Company, 1981.

KIM, JAEGWON, "Causality, Identity, and Supervenience," in *Midwest Studies in Philosophy, Vol. IV: Studies in Metaphysics*, eds. Peter French, Theodore E. Uehling, and Howard K. Wettstein. Minneapolis: University of Minnesota Press, 1979.

KRIPKE, SAUL A., *Naming and Necessity*. Cambridge, Mass.: Harvard University Press, 1980.

LACHS, JOHN, "Epiphenomenalism and the Notion of Cause," *The Journal of Philosophy*, 60 (1963).

———, *George Santayana*. Boston: Twayne Publishers, 1988.

LAKATOS, IMRE, "Science and Pseudoscience," in *The Methodology of Scientific Research Programmes: Philosophical Papers, Vol. I.*, eds. John Worrall and Gregory Currie. Cambridge, England: Cambridge University Press, 1978.

LEWIS, DAVID, "Mad Pain and Martian Pain," in *Readings in Philosophical Psychology: Vol. I*, ed. Ned Block. Cambridge, Mass.: Harvard University Press, 1980.

LOCKE, JOHN, *An Essay Concerning Human Understanding*. ed. Peter Nidditch. Oxford, England: Clarendon Press, 1975.

LYCAN, WILLIAM G., ed., *Mind and Cognition*. Cambridge, Mass.: Basil Blackwell, Ltd., 1990.

McDERMOTT, DREW, "Artificial Intelligence Meets Natural Stupidity," in *Mind Design*, ed. John Haugland. Cambridge, Mass.: MIT Press, 1981.

McGINN, COLIN, *The Problem of Consciousness*. Oxford, England: Basil Blackwell, Inc., 1991.

MADELL, GEOFFREY, "Personal Identity and the Mind-Body Problem," in *The Case of Dualism*, eds. John R. Smythies and John Beloff. Charlottesville: University Press of Virginia, 1989.

MOODY, TODD C., *Philosophy and Artificial Intelligence*. Englewood Cliffs, N.J.: Prentice Hall, 1993.

MOORE, G. E., *Principia Ethica*. Cambridge, England: Cambridge University Press, 1929.

NAGEL, THOMAS, "What Is It Like to Be a Bat?" *The Philosophical Review* (October 1974).

———, *Mortal Questions*. Cambridge, England: Cambridge University Press. 1979.

———, *What Does It All Mean?* New York: Oxford University Press, 1987.

———, "The Mind Wins," *The New York Review of Books*, XL, no. 5, (March 4, 1993).

*The New York Times*, April 12, 1993, p. A7.

NISBETT, RICHARD E., AND D. D. WILSON, "Telling More Than We Can Know: Verbal Reports on Mental Processes," *Psychological Review*, 84 (1977).

NOONAN, HAROLD W., ed., *Personal Identity*. London: Routledge, & Kegan Paul, 1989.

PARFIT, DEREK, "Personal Identity," *Philosophical Review*, 80 (1971).

———, *Reasons and Persons*. Oxford, England: Oxford University Press, 1986.

PEARS, DAVID, *Hume's System*. Oxford, England: Oxford University Press, 1990.

PERRY, JOHN, ed., *Personal Identity*. Berkeley: University of California Press, 1975.

PHILLIPS, HOLLIBERT E., "On Appealing to the Evidence," *Philosophical Forum*, 22, no. 3 (Spring 1991).

POLLOCK, JOHN, *How to Build a Person*. Cambridge, Mass.: MIT Press, 1989.

POPKIN, RICHARD H., ed., *The Philosophy of the 16th and 17th Centuries*. New York: Free Press, 1966.

PYLYSHYN, ZENON, "Computation and Cognition: Issues in the Foundations of Cognitive Science" in *The Tradition of Philosophy*, eds. Harrison Hall and Norman E. Bowie. Belmont, Calif.: Wadsworth Publishing Company, 1986.

QUINE, W. V. O., *Methods of Logic* (3rd. ed.), New York: Holt, Rinehart & Winston, 1972.

REID, THOMAS, *Essays on the Intellectual Powers of Man*, ed. James Walker. Boston: Phillips, Sampson and Company, 1855.

RINGLE, MARTIN, ed., *Philosophical Perspectives of Artificial Intelligence*. Atlantic Highlands, N.J.: Humanities Press, 1979

RORTY, RICHARD, "Mind-Brain, Identity, Privacy and Categories," in *The Mind/Brain Identity Theory,* ed. C. V. Borst. New York: St. Martin's Press, 1970.

ROSENTHAL, DAVID, ed., *The Nature of Mind.* New York: Oxford University Press, 1991.

RYLE, GILBERT, *The Concept of Mind.* London: Hutchinson & Co., 1960.

SEARLE, JOHN R., "Minds, Brains, and Programs," *The Behavioral and Brain Sciences,* 3 (1980).

———, *Intentionality.* Cambridge, England: Cambridge University Press, 1983.

———, *The Rediscovery of Mind.* Cambridge, Mass: MIT Press, 1992.

SHAFFER, JEROME A., *Philosophy of Mind.* Englewood Cliffs, N.J.: Prentice Hall, Inc., 1968.

SHOEMAKER, SYDNEY, "Introspection and the Self," in *Midwest Studies in Philosophy, Vol. X: Studies in the Philosophy of Mind,* eds. Peter French, Theodore E. Uehling, and Howard K. Wettstein. Minneapolis: University of Minnesota Press, 1986.

———, "Qualia and Consciousness," *Mind,* C. no. 4 (October 1991).

SKINNER, B. F., *Science and Human Behavior.* New York: Macmillan Company, 1953.

SMART, J. J. C., "Sensation and Brain Process," *Philosophical Review,* 68 (1959).

SMITH, LOGAN P., *Little Essays Drawn from the Writings of George Santayana.* Freeport, N.Y.: Books for Libraries Press, 1967.

SMYTHIES, JOHN R., and John Beloff, eds., *The Case for Dualism.* Charlottesville: University Press of Virginia, 1989.

SPINOZA, BARUCH, *Ethics* in *The Philosophy of the 16th and 17th Centuries,* ed. Richard H. Popkin. New York: Free Press, 1966.

STICH, STEPHEN P., "The Future of Folk Psychology," *From Folk Psychology to Cognitive Science.* Cambridge, Mass: MIT Press, 1983a. Also reprinted in *Folk Psychology and the Philosophy of Mind,* eds. Scott M. Christensen and Dale Turner. Hillsdale, N.J.: Lawrence Erlbaum Associates, Publishers, 1993.

———, "Will the Concepts of Folk Psychology Find a Place in Cognitive Science?" *From Folk Psychology to Cognitive Science: The Case Against Belief.* Cambridge, Mass.: MIT Press, 1983b. Also reproduced in *Folk Psychology and the Philosophy of Mind,* eds. Scott M. Christensen and Dale Turner. Hinsdale, N.J.: Lawrence Erlbaum Associates, Publishers, 1993.

STORMS, MICHAEL, AND RICHARD E. NISBETT, "Insomnia and the Attribution Process," *Journal of Personality and Social Psychology,* 16, no. 2 (October 1970).

STRAWSON, PETER F., *Individuals.* London: Methuen & Co., Ltd., 1959.

TAYLOR, RICHARD, *Metaphysics* (4th ed.). Englewood Cliffs, N.J.: Prentice Hall, Inc., 1992.

TROUT, J. D., "Reductionism and the Unity of Science," in *The Philosophy of Science,* eds. Richard Boyd, Philip Casper, and J. D. Trout. Cambridge, Mass.: MIT Press, 1991.

VELLEMAN, J. DAVID, "What Happens When Someone Acts," *Mind,* 101 (July 1992), 461–81.

VENDLER, ZENO, *Res Cogitans.* Ithaca, N.Y.: Cornell University Press, 1972.

VERMAZEN, BRUCE, AND MERRILL B. HINTIKKA, *Essays on Davidson: Actions and Events.* Oxford, England: Clarendon Press, 1985.

VESEY, GODFREY, *Personal Identity: A Philosophical Analysis.* Ithaca, N.Y.: Cornell University Press, 1974.

WHITE, STEPHEN, *The Unity of the Self.* Cambridge, Mass.: MIT Press, 1991.

WILKES, KATHLEEN V., "The Relationship Between Scientific Psychology and Common Sense Psychology," *Synthese,* 89 (1991).

WITTGENSTEIN, LUDWIG, *Philosophical Investigations,* trans. G. E. M. Anscombe. New York: Macmillan Publishing Company, 1953.

ZIFF, PAUL, "About Behaviorism," *Analysis,* 17, no. 2 (October 1956).

# Index

Churchland, Paul, 124–25, 129, 131
  quotes by, 111, 116, 118–19
Circular argument. *See* Begging the
  question
Claims. *See also* Propositional attitudes
  acceptability of, 61–62
  identity, 67–69
  verifiability of, 63
CN. *See* Causal necessitation
*Cogito* argument, Descartes', 4, 11
Cognition
  and computation, 80–85, 85–89
  limits of human, 93, 94–95, 96
  and syntax, 86–88
  systematicity of, 86–87
Cognitive architecture
  connectionist, 85–87, 88
  serial, 82, 86, 88
  verbal and non-verbal, 121–23, 128
Cognitive closure, 94–95, 96
Cognitive science research, 122–24, 134–35
Commonsense ascription, 13–14, 106,
  117–18. *See also* Folk psychology (FP)
  of the obvious, 3, 17
Compatibilism, 148
Composita, continuity of, 37–38, 40
Computation
  and cognition, 80–85, 85–89
  reduction of mind to, 82–85
Connectionism, 85–89
Consciousness, 90–101
  definitions of, 98–101
  as essential, 90–91
  intentionality and, 99, 102–07, 140
  and memory, 48–55
  person and, 43–44
  physicalist view of, 18–19
  and qualia, 148–49
  reducibility of, 92–93, 93–94, 95–97
  and supervenience, 107–10
  understanding, 91–95
  views of, 95–98
Content of propositional attitudes, 115, 120
Continuity
  *See also* Memory; Persistence over time
  of composita, 37–39, 40
  of identity, 50–53, 57
Crick, Francis, 100

Davidson, Donald, 14, 132–33, 138, 143, 146
Decision making, 144–45
Decomposition, recursive, 82, 83
Deduction, Descartes on, 6–7
Demonstration, problems of, 3–4

Dennett, Daniel, 82, 83, 103, 105, 133
Derived intentionality, 104
Descartes, René
  challenges to, 8–12, 24
  dualism of, 5–16
  quotes by, 1, 5–10
Designators, identity, 32–33
Desire, 125
  the folk psychology of, 111–14, 121,
    130, 133
Digital computation, 82
Disappearance form, of identity theory, 67,
  68, 71–72, 92, 95
Dispositions, 63–65, 73
Dissonance and self-attribution, 121–23,
  128, 135
Doings and actions, 138–41, 146. *See also*
  Causation; Intentionality
Driving a car, 140
Drugs, mind-altering, 11
Dry river problem, 35, 38–39
Dual-aspect theories, 19–20, 23
Dualism, 98
  alternative forms of, 16–23, 24
  arguments against, 8–12
  arguments for, 13–15
  Cartesian, 5–16
  functionalism and, 73, 74, 77
  supervenient, 108–09
  as a theory, 23

Effects. *See* Actions; Causation
Ego. *See also* The *I*
  the Cartesian, 11
  indivisible identity and, 47–48, 52–55
Eliminativism, 67, 92, 95, 106–07, 143, 147
  critiques of, 124–32, 133, 136
  and folk psychology, 111, 116, 118–25,
    128–29
  and noneliminativists, 133–35
Empirical functionalism, 74–75
Entailment, causal, 18
Epiphenomenalism, 17–19, 24, 109, 144
  monist, 23
Epistemology
  mistakes in, 2–3
  and ontology, 55
Ethics, 107–08
Evaluation, scientific. *See* Scientific
  hypothesis
Event causation. *See also* Causation; Mental
  events
  minded or mindless, 104–05, 138–39
Event-tokens, 130, 132